# TOWARD THE HEALTHY CITY

# TOWARD THE HEALTHY CITY

## People, Places, and the Politics of Urban Planning

Jason Corburn

The MIT Press
Cambridge, Massachusetts
London, England

MIT Press books may be purchased at special quantity discounts for business or sales promotional use. For information, please email special_sales@mitpress.mit.edu or write to Special Sales Department, The MIT Press, 55 Hayward Street, Cambridge, MA 02142.

This book was set in Scala serif and Scala sans by SNP Best-set Typesetter Ltd., Hong Kong and was printed and bound in the United States of America.

Library of Congress Cataloging-in-Publication Data

Corburn, Jason.
Toward the healthy city : people, places, and the politics of urban planning / Jason Corburn.
     p.   ;   cm.—(Urban and industrial environments)
Includes bibliographical references and index.
ISBN 978-0-262-01331-4 (hbk. : alk. paper)—ISBN 978-0-262-51307-4 (pbk. : alk. paper)  1. Urban health. 2. Urban health—California—San Francisco. 3. City planning. 4. City planning—California—San Francisco. I. Title. II. Series: Urban and industrial environments.
[DNLM: 1. City Planning 2009003193 organization and administration—San Francisco. 2. Urban Health 2009003193—San Francisco. 3. Health Planning—organization and administration—San Francisco. 4. Minority Health—San Francisco. 5. Urban Renewal—organization and administration—San Francisco. WA 380 C792t  2009]
RA566.7.C673  2009
362.1′042—dc22                                                    2009003193

10 9 8 7 6 5 4 3 2

for Azure Sky and Satya Rain

# Contents

# Acknowledgments

This book would not have been possible with the support and insights of Rajiv Bhatia and Lili Farhang at the San Francisco Department of Public Health. Rajiv invited me to explore the intricacies of his work and to participate in meetings and discussions at the DPH. He welcomed me into his home during my many trips from New York to San Francisco. Lili invited me to numerous internal and external meetings of the SFDPH, shared wonderful insights about their emerging practice, and helped ensure that recordings of the ENCHIA process went smoothly. Other former and current SFDPH staff, including Carolina Guzman, Fernando Ona, Cyndy Comerford Scully, Megan Gaydos, Shireen Malekafzali, and Mitch Katz, were also especially helpful and generous with their time. Oscar Grande of PODER and April Veneracion of SOMCAN offered insights about community dynamics, and April allowed me to interview her staff at length to understand SOMCAN's role in the Trinity Plaza and Rincon Hill cases. Staff at the San Francisco planning department provided data and insights about the challenges of planning practice in their city and the developing partnerships with the DPH. Juliet Ellis of Urban Habitat, Margaret Gordon of West Oakland, Victor Rubin of PolicyLink, Bob Prentice of the Public Health Institute, Tony Iton of the Alameda County Public Health Department, and Diane Aranda of The California Endowment all offered insights from their practice on healthy planning activities across the Bay Area.

The research that led to this book was made possible by the support of a Robert Wood Johnson Foundation Investigator Award in Health Policy Research. I am also indebted to Bruce Link and Peter Bearman at Columbia University for providing initial seed money for the research and offering intellectual guidance and mentorship.

Most important, Judea offered moral support and understanding throughout this process and inspired me to always try and just "tell it like it is."

# 1 Some Challenges for Healthy City Planning

Urban places and the city planning processes that shape them—particularly those processes governing land use, housing, transportation, job opportunities, social services, the quality of the urban environment and opportunities for public participation in local government—are increasingly understood as powerful determinants of population health. Premature death, and unnecessary burdens of disease and suffering, are disproportionately concentrated in city neighborhoods of the poor and people of color, where residential segregation concentrates poverty, liquor stores outnumber supermarkets, toxic sites are adjacent to playgrounds, and public resources go to incarceration rather than education. While urban divestment, redlining and racist neglect were largely to blame for many urban ills and inequities of the twentieth century, city planners in the twenty-first century are increasingly faced with the added challenge of revitalizing neglected urban neighborhoods in ways that improve health and promote greater equity.

How can modern city planning, a profession that emerged in the late nineteenth century with a goal of improving the health of the least-well-off urban residents but lost this focus throughout the twentieth century, return to its health and social justice roots? What are the connections among contemporary city planning processes, not just physical outcomes, and health equity? What new political processes can help reconnect planning and public health with a focus on addressing the social determinants of health inequities in cities?

This book answers these and other questions by highlighting how public health and planning agencies along with community-based coalitions are redefining environmental health politics in cities to improve the health of people and places. Twenty-first century efforts to reconnect the fields in the United States have, to date, focused on a very limited conception of healthy planning, such as how physical design changes in cities might increase physical activity and thereby improve health. This book highlights that physical changes to places without accompanying political and institutional change will ultimately fail to improve the health of disadvantaged urban populations and move urban politics toward planning more healthy and equitable cities. Further, while much contemporary research documents what's wrong with cities, particularly in poor communities of color, much less work aims to explore what political and administrative changes in municipal government can improve the well-being of people and places. *Toward the Healthy City* explores how government agencies and community coalitions in the San Francisco Bay Area are reconnecting city planning by working to change the social, scientific, and political institutions that make places and populations healthy. The book offers a new decision making framework—called healthy city planning—that address the political conditions and institutional changes that must occur in order for urban planning and public health to reconnect to promote greater health equity. Healthy city planning will require new issue and problem framings, investigative and analytic techniques, and inclusive and deliberative public processes that together can generate new norms, discourses, and practice for greater health equity. As *Toward the Healthy City* argues, healthy city planning must be viewed as healthy urban governance, where both the *substantive content* of what contributes to human well-being—the physical and social qualities that promote urban health—and the decision-making *processes and institutions* that shape the distributions of these qualities across places and populations are improved.

## Unhealthy and Inequitable Cities

American cities—or more precisely certain neighborhoods in these cities—are facing a health crisis. While not a new phenomenon, the urban poor, immigrants and people of color die earlier and suffer more, by almost every measure of disease, than any population group in the United States. A sampling of evidence is as staggering as they are disturbing:

• In the New York City area, the predominantly poor, minority neighborhoods of the South Bronx, Harlem, and Central Brooklyn have rates of diabetes, asthma, mental illness, and HIV/AIDS that are nearly double that of the rest of the city (Karparti et al. 2004).

- In Boston's predominantly African-American and Latino Roxbury neighborhood, asthma rates between 2003 and 2005 for children under 5 were the highest in the city and more than double the citywide average (The Health of Boston 2007:35).
- The death rates from diabetes among Puerto Ricans in Humboldt Park and West Town neighborhoods of Chicago are more than twice the citywide average and 34 percent of Puerto Rican children in these neighborhoods have asthma, one of the highest rates recorded anywhere in the country (Whitman et al. 2006).
- Infant mortality for African-Americans living in the City of Compton, Los Angeles County, California, in 2004 was 17.3 deaths per 1,000 live births, the highest in the state of California and nearly two-and-a-half times greater than the rate for the United States (McCormick and Holding 2004).
- Deaths from cardiovascular disease in the predominantly African-American east side of Detroit are the highest in the city and over twice the national average (Schulz et al. 2005).
- The Bayview–Hunters Point neighborhood in San Francisco, where Latinos and African-Americans are a majority, has the highest rates of adult and pediatric asthma, adult diabetes, and congestive heart failure in the entire city (BHSF 2007).

What explains these disturbing and, as I will show in subsequent chapters, persistent but avoidable patterns of death and disease? Public health has a history of searching for the one "big cause" or explanation for differences in health outcomes across populations, from nineteenth-century theories of miasma and contagion to medical care and genetic explanations of the twenty-first century. Yet urban health researchers and professionals are increasingly exploring how a combination of place-based physical, economic and social characteristics and the public policies and institutions that shape them—not genetics, lifestyles or health care—are the cause of inequitable distributions of well-being in cities. For example, Adam Karpati, assistant commissioner of the New York City Department of Health and Mental Hygiene, noted in testimony to the New York City Council that the concentration of health disparities in poor, African-American and Latino neighborhoods are not likely due to disparities in access to health care, risky individual lifestyles, or genetic differences, but that:

They are due primarily to differences in the social, economic, and physical conditions in which people live and the health behavior patterns that arise in these settings. "Health disparities" are more than "health-care disparities" . . . one lesson from the health data is that disparities exist for almost every condition. This observation suggests that, regardless of the specific issue, poor health shares common root causes. It is important to remember, then, that strategies aimed at particular issues need to be complemented by attention to those root causes of poor health: poverty, discrimination, poor housing, and other social inequities. Fundamentally, *eliminating health disparities is about social justice*, which is the underlying philosophy of public health. (Emphasis added; Karpati 2004)

*Toward the Healthy City* explores how city planning processes can address the "root causes" of health inequities.[1] I reveal how urban governance practices can alter the social determinants of health (SDOH), including the quality of employment and educational opportunities, affordable housing, access to healthy food, transit that serves a range a users, safe spaces for social interaction, and toxic-free environments, all fundamental drivers of health inequities according to the World Health Organization (WHO 2008). This book explores a new political framework that could improve upon and extend in new ways current efforts to address urban health inequities (Barton and Tsourou 2000; Diez-Roux 2001; Duhl and Sanchez 1999; Fitzpatrick and LaGory 2000; Freudenberg et al. 2006; Frumkin et al. 2004; Geronimus 2000; Kawachi and Berkman 2003).

## City Planning as Urban Governance

Planning practice as conceived in this book is about the processes, institutions, and discourses that generate the physical plans and interventions that shape cities. While the everyday practice of city planning has some formal rules, such as drafting land use plans and including the public in environmental review processes, planners regularly have to make discretionary decisions that shape the content and direction of these processes. These discretionary decisions include such subjective judgments as how much information to release to the public, the selection of the consultant team that often performs analyses, the standards of acceptable evidence and norms of inquiry in review processes, which interest groups to invite to public processes, and how participatory processes will adjudicate disputes and reach agreement (Friedman 1987; Forester 1999). These decisions have a significant influence over the content and outcomes of planning processes, such as whether they do or do not respond to claims of bias, discrimination and inequality. Importantly, the politics of planning in America is also shaped by "planners"—from the private sector to community members—that sit outside of governmental planning agencies. Public–private planning partnerships, autonomous public authorities managing ports and airports, quasi-public redevelopment corporations, nonprofit community development corporations, and the privatized traditional public services in cities have all blurred the boundaries between public, private, and community planning and the political alliances and interests of "planners" (Fishman 2000; Graham and Marvin 2001; Harvey 1989). Thus I view urban planning as simultaneously about the micro-politics of cities—or the day-to-day negotiations over development and management decisions (Majone 1989)—and the macro-politics of cities—or conflicts about how different political ideologies ought to shape the place-based goals and outcomes of planning processes (Hajer 2001).

This micro and macro conception of the politics of planning remains controversial among theorists but suggests that planning practice ought to be considered an essential part of urban governance (Fainstein 2000; Yiftachel and Huxley 2000). Just as the spheres of political, economic, and social life overlap in the activities of everyday lives, the term governance as used here emphasizes the interactions, relations, and meaning-making that occurs as organizations attempt to influence collective action (Cars et al. 2002; Young 1996). Governance is not just about government, it is also about the struggles and conflicts between formal institutions and organizations and informal norms and practices, and how actors use both formal and informal processes to shape public decisions.[2] Urban governance includes a complex mix of different contexts, actors, arenas, and issues, where struggles over power are exposed in public discourses or embedded in tacit day-to-day routines. While I expand on the idea of planning as urban governance in later chapters, I use the term here to make explicit the political conditions that can lead planners to use or abuse power, respond to or even resist market forces, work to empower some groups and dis-empower others, promote multi-party consensual decision making or simply rationalize decisions already made (Forester 1999).

## Public Health Promotion in the City

By public health I refer to the public policies, practices, and processes that influence the distribution of disease, death, and well-being for populations, or what the field generally calls health promotion. Similar to my view of planning, the work of public health is often framed as occurring in both formal governmental institutions and informal governance processes. For example, the US Institute of Medicine's (1988:7) definition of public health states that the profession aims to fulfill:

society's interest in assuring the conditions in which people can be healthy ... It links many disciplines and rests upon the scientific core of epidemiology. ... [T]he committee defines the organizational framework of public health to encompass both activities undertaken within the formal structure of government and the associated efforts of private and voluntary organizations and individuals.

Also similar to my view of city planning, public health should be viewed as an ongoing practice, not "merely the absence of disease or infirmity," as the World Health Organization so articulately stated over half a century ago (WHO 1948). The 1986 Ottawa Charter for health promotion further clarified that health is a "resource for everyday life, not the objective of living" and "is a positive concept emphasizing social and personal resources, as well as physical capacities" (WHO 1986). Health promotion, the WHO has repeatedly emphasized, cannot be achieved by the health sector alone but also demands coordinated action across non–health policy areas of government, such as social, economic, service, and environmental sectors, along with participation by nongovernmental organizations, industry, and the media (WHO 2008).

**Building on the International Healthy City Movement**

This book builds on and explores ways to extend the work of the international healthy cities movement that originated in the European offices of the World Health Organization (WHO 1988). Early leaders of the international healthy city movement were Trevor Hancock and Leonard Duhl (1988), who suggested that the healthy city is a place that is continually creating and improving the physical, social, and political environments and expanding the community resources that enable individuals and groups to support each other in performing all the functions of life and in developing themselves to their maximum potential. Hancock and Duhl (1988:23) go on to note:

[W]e must develop and incorporate into our assessment of the health of a city a variety of unconventional, intuitive and holistic measures to supplement the hard data. Indeed, unless data are turned into stories that can be understood by all, they are not effective in any process of change, either political or administrative.

I will highlight how "planners" in the United States are employing new norms, analytic tools, and decision-making processes to capture some of these qualities of the healthy city. Drawing from the analytic criteria of the WHO for healthy cities, I show how contemporary healthy planning work in the United States is extending these international ideas. Despite barriers of earlier practices, opportunities exist for implementing healthy urban environments whose characteristics can exceed the ideal principles outlined by the WHO (as shown in the sidebars below and next page).

This book differs from and extends the work of the international healthy cities movement in some important ways. First, the WHO healthy cities program has not emphasized the combination of policy processes, science norms, and organizational network building that might contribute to healthy urban development and city planning more generally (Tankano 2003:5). Second, after two decades, the World Health Organization's healthy cities program in Europe has only had limited success integrating analyses of problems that might be driving health inequities in cities with developing healthy urban plans and implementing these plans (De Leeuw and Skovgaard 2005). Third, evaluations of the European healthy cities

---

**WHO Characteristics of a Healthy City**

- A clean, safe physical environment of a high quality (including housing quality)
- An ecosystem that is stable now and sustainable in the long term
- A strong mutually supportive and nonexploitative community
- A high degree of participation, and control, by the citizens over the decisions affecting their lives, health, and well-being
- The meeting of basic needs (food, water, shelter, income, safety, and work) for all the city's people
- Access by the people to a wide variety of experiences and resources, with the chance for a wide variety of contact, interaction, and communication
- A diverse, vital, and innovative economy
- The encouragement of connectedness with the past, with the cultural and biological heritage of city dwellers, and with other groups and individuals
- A form that is compatible with and enhances the preceding characteristics
- An optimum level of appropriate public health and sickness care services, accessible to all
- High health status (high levels of positive health and low levels of disease)

Source: World Health Organization (1995).

---

### WHO Principles for Developing a Healthy Cities Project

- **Equity**   All people must have the right and the opportunity to realize their full potential in health.
- **Health promotion**   A city health plan should aim to promote health by using the principles outlined in the Ottawa Charter for Health Promotion (Annex 1): build healthy public policy; create supportive environments; strengthen community action and develop personal skills; and reorient health services.
- **Intersectoral action**   Health is created in the setting of everyday life and is influenced by the actions and decisions of most sectors of a community.
- **Community participation**   Informed, motivated and actively participating communities are key elements for setting priorities and making and implementing decisions.
- **Supportive environments**   A city health plan should address the creation of supportive physical and social environments. This includes issues of ecology and sustainability as well as social networks, transportation, housing and other environmental concerns.
- **Accountability**   Decisions of politicians, senior executives and managers in all sectors have an impact on the conditions that influence health, and responsibility for such decisions should be made explicit in a clear and understandable manner and in a form that can be measured and assessed after time.
- **Right to peace**   Peace is a fundamental prerequisite for health and the attainment of peace is a justifiable aim for those who are seeking to achieve the maximum state of health for their community and citizens.

Source: World Health Organization (1997).

program have not suggested if the growth of cities participating in the movement—from a handful to over 1,500—has altered regional urban management, development, and planning decisions.

Yet, important for the analytic framework offered in this book, the WHO healthy cities program in Europe has developed a set of evaluative categories that recognize the need for political and institutional change in order to move toward the healthy city. The WHO framework, called "Monitoring, Accountability, Reporting, and Impact assessment" or MARI, recognizes that healthy cities must be simultaneously attentive to changes in the underlying principles behind a healthy city, involve new actors, draft new policies, and identify and implement new methods of monitoring and evaluating procedural and health outcome changes (De Leeuw 2001).

A selection of criteria from the MARI framework used by the WHO to designate healthy cities suggest that the healthy city is not a static condition nor a limited set of health outcome measures but rather a commitment to continually improving the well-being of populations, places, and policy-making processes with an explicit emphasis on reducing health inequities (see the sidebar above).

## Science and the Healthy City

A crucial aspect of healthy city planning, and one often overlooked or viewed uncritically by both urban planning and public health scholars, is the appropriate role for science and technology. As my historical review in chapter 2 considers in more detail, science and technology were often viewed by urban developers, governments, and researchers as tools to simultaneously improve the qualities of places and change the unhealthy behaviors of individuals. I show how this view of science, often labeled "moral environmentalism," has not only regularly failed to improve the health of the least well off places and population groups in cities but also acted to further alienate disadvantaged groups from processes of science and how they can influence urban governance.

*Toward the Healthy City* argues that science has encoded ways of knowing and acting in both urban planning and public health and that these embedded practices are some of the most significant barriers for moving toward more healthy and equitable cities. For example, I will trace the connections between city planners and public health professionals when the city was viewed as a *field site*—where a preexisting reality was discovered by surveyors, ethnographers, and residents who developed a keen personal sensitivity to the uniquely revealing features of their particular place. This was the dominant "science of the city" during the American Sanitary and Progressive eras, and local institutions such as Settlement Houses and neighborhood health centers helped craft policy responses. However, as germ theory, bacteriology, and the biomedical model set in, a new urban health science emerged—*the city as a laboratory.* The laboratory view of the city realigned urban policies to reflect legitimacy in laboratory settings, where findings and interventions could be applied anywhere and to all population groups because they reflected the placeless, standardized, and controlled environment of the ideal laboratory. The context-specific polices during the city as field site era were largely replaced by universal, nonspecific interventions, such as chemical treatment of drinking water and childhood immunizations administered by centralized and specialized bureaucracies. *Toward the Healthy City* offers a critical examination of how scientific views of the city have not only separated planning and public health but have shaped the analytic and political processes that underwrite city governance today. I argue that new orientations toward science are needed to help bridge the "two cultures" of the laboratory and field site views in order to promote greater health equity in cities (Snow 1962).

Moving toward healthy city planning will require a recasting of science and expertise, similar to calls for a new science in order to address the urgent issues of climate change and sustainability (Cash et al. 2003; Lubchenco 1998). This new "paradigm" calls for a shift away from experimental science driven from inside existing disciplines by scientists working alone to a view of scientific practice that is more dispersed, context-dependent, and problem-oriented (Nowotny et al. 2001). I will show that the science underwriting the healthy city is inherently political; its facts are uncertain, values in dispute, stakes high, and decisions urgent—all contributing to what Funtowicz and Ravetz (1993) have called postnormal science.[3] In postnormal conditions science crosses disciplinary lines, enters into previously unknown investigative territories, requires the deployment of new methods, instruments, protocols, and experimental systems, and involves politically sensitive processes and results. This book highlights that legitimate science for healthy city planning must be co-produced, where researchers, government agencies, and lay publics engage in polycentric, interactive, and multipartite public sharing of information (Jasanoff 2004). *Toward the Healthy City* explores how this view of science might be applied in governance practices, from new research partnerships that redefine environmental health to the development of healthy city indicators for assessing and monitoring urban planning decisions.

## Toward a Politics of Healthy Planning: Populations, Places, Processes, and Power

*Toward the Healthy City* begins by examining the historical connections and disconnects between city planning and public health in order to highlight some of the unaddressed political challenges facing contemporary efforts to reconnect the fields. Addressing the disconnects between the fields of planning and public health is essential not only for improving local governance but also for understanding and addressing global political change. For example, in 2001 the UN Centre on Human Settlements (Habitat) (UNCHS 2001:1) stated in their *State of Cities* report that cities are where they expect the solutions to society's most pressing problems to emerge:

For better or worse, the development of contemporary societies will depend largely on understanding and managing the growth of cities. The city will increasingly become the test bed for the adequacy of political institutions, for the performance of government agencies, and for the effectiveness of programmes to combat social exclusion, to protect and repair the environment and to promote human development.

Once viewed as sites of parochial and even xenophobic policy making, local governments are increasingly being recognized as sites of progressive reform and innovation (Appadurai 2001; Fung 2006).

**Table 1.1**
Political frames for healthy city planning

| | |
|---|---|
| Population health | • Emphasizes distribution of health inequities across groups<br>• Targets social determinants of health, not individual behaviors, genetics or health care |
| Places | • Defined as the combination of physical, social, and material characteristics, the institutions and policies that shape them, and the attributions of meaning to these qualities<br>• A relational view investigates the interactions among the multiple characteristics and the contestations over assigned meaning and their interpretations |
| Processes | • Governance as the formal and informal organizations and practices that shape collective action<br>• Exploring the mechanisms for how social inequities get "embodied" |
| Power | • Fundamental to shaping and reshaping of cities<br>• Power over and with are possible, and often expressed in norms of expertise, structural racism, and condoning of white privilege |

A new set of political frames are necessary for moving toward a new practice of healthy city planning. As Shon and Rein (1994) note, *how* policy issues are framed from the outset affects the quality of solutions; defined too narrowly or too broadly, public policy solutions will suffer from the same defects. The frames for moving toward healthy city planning include considerations of population health, a relational view of place, processes of governance, and relations of power (see table 1.1).

## Population Health

While the term "population" can imply something different in the fields of demography, geography, and urban studies, population health is concerned with assessing and addressing why some social groups are healthier than others while paying attention to how social inequalities determine health inequities (Evans and Stoddart 1990). Two central questions in population health are "what explains the *distribution* of disease and well-being across populations" and "what drives current and changing patterns of inequalities in well-being across population groups?" By emphasizing *distribution* as distinct from *causation*, population health investigates how social, political, and economic forces—from racism, to economic policies, to neighborhood environments—shape which groups get sick, die earlier, and suffer unnecessarily.

Population health focuses on changing the *social determinants of health* (SDOH) defined by the World Health Organization (Wilkinson and Marmot 2003) as "the causes of the causes." The SDOH include the positive and negative influences that explain population well-being, including the social gradient (or the idea that the further down one sits in the social ladder, the shorter is life expectancy and the greater is incidence of disease); stress; early-life support; educational status; employment, working conditions and unemployment; and access to food, housing transportation, and health services; income; social exclusion and social support (Raphael 2006; WHO 2008). A population health approach is thus not limited to so-called proximal or "downstream" (i.e., closer to the individual and assumed greater causal strength for explaining disease) risk factors such as smoking or physical activity. Nor does a population health approach, as used in this book, focus exclusively on the distal or "upstream" (i.e., father from the body and assumed to be a less potent causal explanation) social structures, processes, and distributions of power that are blamed for perpetuating inequality and health disparities (Yen and Syme 1999).[4] Healthy city planning must embrace a view of population health that treats the proximate/ downstream and distal/upstream dichotomy as problematic and instead seeks to identify what combination of forces—political, social, economic, biologic, and so forth—in certain places are likely driving population distributions of death and disease and what policy interventions might alter these forces (Krieger 2008).

### Place, in a Relational View

A central feature of population health, and one that differentiates it from other models of public health, is that context and features of the built and social environments are understood as key drivers of well-being, not merely the background for other mechanisms driving morbidity and mortality to take place. The influence of place, neighborhood, or context is increasingly recognized as major, if not the most important, determinant of human well-being (Cummins et al. 2005; Diez-Roux 2001, 2002; Frumkin 2005; Geronimus 2000; Hood 2005; Macintyre et al. 2002). Urban place characteristics, such as affordable housing, access to healthy food, employment opportunities, quality education, public transportation, social networks, and cultural expression, are social determinants of health and so fall within the domain of many urban governance processes (Burris et al. 2007). Yet the role of place in urban planning and policy remains controversial, particularly in debates over whether place-based policies can address urban and regional inequality (Dreier et al. 2004; Hayden 1997; Harloe et al. 1990; Logan and Molotch 1987; Orfield 1997).

The second policy frame for healthy city planning demands not only taking place seriously, but viewing place characteristics *relationally*. A relational view of place emphasizes that the physical and social characteristics in spaces matter for well-being, but these features cannot be separated from the meanings that people in different places assign to these characteristics. In other words, the interactive processes of assigning meaning to a place, and these meanings themselves, are crucial aspects of thinking and acting relationally about how places engender health or distribute premature morbidity and mortality (Gieryn 2000; Graham and Healey 1999; Jackson 1994; Whyte 1980).

Therefore, as I argue in this book, healthy places ought to be understood as being doubly constructed; physically (the buildings, streets, parks, etc., often termed the "built environment") and socially (through the assigning of meanings, interpretations, and narratives as well as the construction of networks, institutions and process to shape these meanings and outcomes). This relational view highlights the processes that simultaneously connect the material, social, and political and ultimately turn a physical spot in the universe into *a place*. Yet the social and political processes behind the construction of place-based meanings are often contested and almost always contingent. A crucial aspect of healthy place-making is creating forums for ongoing public discourse that allows for debate over existing meanings and the construction of new meanings, particularly as demographics change. By taking a relational view of places, healthy city planning processes can help reveal the often hidden relations of power and inequality that are manifested in the physical, material, and social characteristics of places (Emirbayer 1997; Escobar 2001).[5]

Importantly the relational view of places aims to shift research and practice away from a conceptualization of places as a set of quantitative variables that act as static covariates in regression models (Diez Roux 1998, 2001; Duncan and Jones 1993; Ewing et al. 2003; Frank et al. 2006; Handy et al. 2002). Defining place characteristics as only static variables obscures the subjective meanings people assign to the features in the places where they live, work, pray and play—such as a "relaxing park," "safe street," and "good school." One dangerous result of research that limits analyses of place and health to quantitative methods alone is that the selected variables must show a statistically significant "place effect" on well-being (usually health outcomes), or the study may wrongly conclude that individual biology, behaviors or genes—not some aspect of place—are to blame for health status. A similar weakness of variable-centered studies of place and health is that a positive finding, such as a statistical correlation between physical characteristics of neighborhoods and health outcomes, may lead to overly physically deterministic conclusions, such as the idea that the presence or absence of a park, bicycle lane, or grocery store is the primary determinant for why nearby populations are or are not physically active or eat healthy foods. A relational view aims to act as an alternative to these framings of place by emphasizing the mutually reinforcing relationships between places, people, and meaning-making, on the one hand, and the political institutions and processes that shape these relationships, on the other (Cummins et al. 2007).

## Processes for the Healthy City

A third policy frame for healthy city planning aims to move practice beyond a focus on people and places by emphasizing the processes, here called urban governance, that shape health promoting opportunities for people and place-based characteristics. Urban policy making has long debated whether to focus *either* on improving opportunities for individuals or the qualities of places (Bolton 1992). Implicit within the people-based versus place-based policy debate is the idea that a conflict exists between two possible goals of policy: improving the welfare of people as individuals, *regardless of where they live*, and improving the welfare of groups by improving qualities of their place. Education, job and family assistance, Section 8 housing subsidies, family relocation programs, and certain types of health care assistance form the core of people-based policy approaches, while strategies aimed at improving infrastructure, building affordable housing, and issuing neighborhood block grants are examples of place-based policies. In a world of limited resources, people-based and place-based policies are often pitted against one another.

*Toward the Healthy City* extends this discourse by emphasizing that not only are policies focused on people and place important for healthy cities, but that greater attention needs to be paid to the institutional processes that shape these policies. Institutions are not just the formal structures or procedures of government but rather an established way of addressing certain social issues, such as norms of practice, that become "taken for granted" and accepted over time (Healey 1999). One process dimension for healthy city planning is the meaning-making described above. A second process, also mentioned earlier, is that of science. As I will show throughout this book, reconnecting planning and public health will require processes of analysis that are "trans-disciplinary," or a science that opens up the boundaries of existing fields and disciplines, notions of expertise, and the legitimate participants for shaping science policy. The institutionalist view examines when established processes, such environmental impact assessment, or new processes, such as health impact assessment, might best promote the goals of healthy city planning.

A third process aspect of healthy city planning is for practitioners to more clearly articulate the processes through which they think the characteristics of places get "embodied" (Krieger and Davey Smith 2004). The notion of the bodily imprint of social conditions was powerfully expressed in 1844 by Friedrich Engels in *The Condition of the Working Class in England*, where he observed how the sufferings of children working in wretched conditions were "indelibly stamped" on adults. Geronimus (2000) argues that chronic discrimination, stress, and exposure to home, neighborhood, and workplace hazards results in a persistent "weathering" on the bodies of the poor and people of color that denigrates the immune, metabolic, and cardiovascular systems and fuels infectious and chronic disease. Nancy Krieger (2005:350) claims that our "bodies tell stories about—and cannot be studied divorced from—the conditions of our existence." The implication for healthy and equitable city planning is that practitioners will need to critically engage with how history leaves a biologic imprint on populations through processes of embodiment; investigating these mechanisms is crucial, since our bodies can often "tell stories that people cannot or will not tell, either because they are unable, forbidden, or choose not to tell" (Krieger 2005: 350).

### Power and Health Equity

The fourth policy frame for moving *Toward the Healthy City* is to address power inequalities in cities and across metropolitan regions more generally. Questions of who has power, where it derives from, how it is deployed, and to what ends are seminal in urban politics (Banfield 1961; Dahl 1961; Domhoff 1986; Dreier et al 2004; Mollenkopf 1983; Stone 2004). Power in healthy city planning includes the ability to affect institutional, disciplinary, and bureaucratic changes. While the elite, pro-growth coalition articulated by Logan and Molotch (1987) has tended to dominate analyses of urban political power, De Leon (1992) and others have highlighted how organized coalitions have resisted "growth machines" to promote a more progressive urban politics. Power relationships can enable or place constraints on group and individual abilities to resist exposures to material and social health hazards.

Power also operates in urban politics to keep certain issues and interests off the political agenda (Lukes 2005). For instance, scientific knowledge often acts as a powerful discourse of exclusion and to mask the political and social dimensions of policy issues (Hacking 1999; Jasanoff 2004). Claims of expertise act as a form of power, such as when scientists prematurely minimize potential uncertainties surrounding an issue in order to help shape and legitimize political decisions (Wynne 2003). While experts are expected to play an increasing role in shaping science-based policy decisions—including those of healthy city planning—the rules for demarcating who is "expert enough" to participate in these processes are almost entirely unwritten, open to wide bureaucratic judgment, and, as I will show, reveal entrenched power struggles over urban governance.

Any effort to improve the quality of life in American cities must also address the power inequities perpetuated by structural racism and white privilege (Massey and Denton 1993; Greenberg and Schneider 1994; Wacquant 1993). The origins of urban inequality cannot be divorced from structural racism, such as federal housing policies that not only denied home ownership to urban African-Americans but physically destroyed many predominantly black neighborhoods under the guise of urban renewal (Ford 1994; Sugrue 1996; Wallace and Wallace 1998; Williams and Collins 2001). Moving *Toward the Healthy City* requires that practitioners address the combinations of policies, institutional practices, cultural representations, and other norms that perpetuate racial group inequity and allow for privileges associated with "whiteness" (Aspen Institute 2004; Bonilla-Silva 1997; Ford 1994).[6]

## Healthy City Planning in the San Francisco Bay Area

*Toward the Healthy City* explores how these political frames can shape a new practice of healthy city planning through a series of case studies from the San Francisco Bay Area[7], where governmental agencies, community organizations, researchers, and others have experimented with new city and regional land use policies aimed at promoting health equity. The city and county of San Francisco and the entire Bay Area is an ideal site to investigate the politics of healthy city planning because the region is struggling to address the forces that contribute to social and health inequities in many postindustrial urban areas, including a decline of affordable housing, hyperresidential segregation, loss of low-skilled well-paying jobs, regional land use sprawl, and neighborhood-scale inequalities of access to transit, supermarkets, open space, and other health-promoting amenities. Yet, at the same time, local governments and civic organizations across the region often innovate with environmental health and social policies that act as models for future state, national, and in some cases, international policy action. For example, the cities in the Bay Area spurred the banning of lead in gasoline and legislated the nation's first Sustainability Plan and Precautionary Principle ordinance. The city of San Francisco has banned the sale of cigarettes in retail pharmacies, has the nation's most ambitious urban recycling, composting and "zero–solid waste" programs, and was the first to attempt to provide universal health care to its residents (Knight 2008).

Studying population health in the Bay Area is also important because, perhaps surprisingly, the region is one of the least healthy metropolitan areas in the United States. For example, a study tracking the progress of the 100 largest US cities toward achieving the goals of *Healthy People 2010*, San Francisco, Oakland, and San Jose (three of the Bay Area's largest cities) ranked in the bottom quintile—below New York, Los Angeles, Chicago, Miami, and Atlanta (Duchon, Andruis, and Reid 2004). Health inequities also plague San Francisco's neighborhoods. For example, African-Americans in San Francisco lose more years of life to just about every possible cause of death than city residents of other racial backgrounds (Aragón et al. 2007). The infant mortality rate for African-American San Franciscans is 11.6 per 1,000 live births, compared to 2.8 for whites and 4.1 for the city as a whole (BHSF 2004). Over 16 percent of African-American babies born in San Francisco have low birth weights, compared to 6.2 percent for whites and 7.4 percent for the city as a whole. Nearly 17 percent of the population in the largely African-American and Latino community of Bayview–Hunters Point has been hospitalized for adult diabetes and the Tenderloin neighborhood, where two-thirds of the population are people of color, ranks second behind Bayview for incidence of chronic disease (BHSF 2007). The South of Market area (SoMa), where over half the population is Latino and Asian, has the highest rates of mental illness in the city of San Francisco (BHSF 2007).

Another objective for looking in-depth at urban governance in one region is to provide the "thick description" that can highlight the distinctive needs and place qualities that can help planning practices promote health equity. While many studies of the connections between land use planning and heath aim to identify "best practices," or the possibility of melioration through imitation, the cases in this book emphasize that practitioners should engage with the cultural specificities of places and not aim for one-size-fits-all interventions. By exploring the political and cultural challenges for healthy city planning in the San Francisco Bay Area, the cases presented in this book offer analysis and comparison within and across a complex metropolitan region, noting the forces that may be unique to the area and those that can contribute to healthy planning in cities everywhere.

**The Cases**

*Toward the Healthy City* is structured around three cases detailing how government agencies, community activists, researchers, and others in San Francisco and across the Bay Area have attempted to practice healthy city planning. Each case describes how traditional planning issues, such as housing development, a neighborhood rezoning plan, the environmental impact assessment process, and drafting a general plan, were reframed as health and justice issues, the influence this reframing had on institutional practices, and how the process outcomes are expected to promote health equity. The cases were selected because they each highlight one or more crucial aspects of the politics of healthy city planning, from how urban issues and problems get redefined as health equity issues, to how new institutional practices across disciplines and agencies are organized, to the gathering and public justification of the new evidence base used to support healthy city planning practices. The cases also highlight that healthy city planning is not one but a set of diverse practices that are more likely to emerge from the work of community-based organizations and public health departments than planning agencies. Each case explores why this might be so and highlights the barriers and opportunities for reconnecting city planning and public health in the San Francisco Bay Area. The cases include the reframing of environmental health practice, healthy urban development, and using health impact assessment for urban and regional planning.

**Reframing Environmental Health**
In the Bayview–Hunters Point neighborhood of San Francisco, where environmental justice activists have worked for decades to get government

agencies to address toxic exposures and health issues in their community, activists were instrumental in helping to reframe environmental health practice in the city. Local activists partnered with the San Francisco Department of Public Health (SFDPH), Environmental Health Section, to explore the relationships between disease and pollution. The partnership conducted a community health survey, and to the surprise of the agency, the survey revealed that the most important environmental health issues for community members were violence, access to healthy food, and affordable housing—not pollution. The partnership lead to new projects and programs within the SFDPH to address community concerns, including a project focused on addressing the multiple determinants of food insecurity in Bayview. This chapter explores why and how this shift occurred within the SFDPH, and investigates how local and international social movements came together to alter health promotion strategies across the entire agency. I detail both the forces that gave rise to the reframing of environmental health and the new practices that embody the new definition. The case also highlights the political conditions that enabled the new definition of environmental health to spread to non–health focused organizations, particularly the city planning department and community-based activist groups.

## Healthy Urban Development

The second case explores how the new environmental health orientation of the San Francisco Department of Public Health was applied to urban development projects. In one project, the Trinity Plaza redevelopment, the developer planned to demolish the rent-controlled building and build a market-rate condominium in its place. At the urging of a coalition of community-based organizations called the Mission Anti-displacement Coalition, that had worked for years to stop rapid gentrification and rising property values during the 1990s dotcom boom, the SFDPH analyzed the likely human health impacts of the residential displacement and unaffordable housing from the Trinity Plaza project. The analysis was submitted as part of the project's environmental impact report, and the case follows the debates between the planning and health agencies over whether the health impacts of housing and related social determinants of health fall within the purview of environmental assessment. In a second development project, the Rincon Hill Area Plan, new high-rise condominiums and high-end retail stores were planned in the low-income South of Market area (SoMa) of San Francisco. Activists and the city's Planning Department again asked the health agency to analyze the "environmental impacts" from the project. The health agency noted the positive and negative social determinants of health that would likely result from the project, including creating new jobs, concentrating residential segregation by building affordable units off-site and straining existing capacity of local schools, transit and parks. While both projects were approved, each included alterations to mitigate likely health impacts, such as guaranteeing that all affordable units in the Trinity Plaza case would be preserved and, in the Rincon Hill project, the developer agreed to pay an impact fee to support a community benefit fund controlled by local organizations. The case study examines how a health agency participated in the planning process for the first time, made the case for the direct and indirect health impacts of urban development and altered the environmental review process to include health analyses. The chapter highlights key political questions for healthy city planning, such as when and how to use existing planning processes to promote health equity, the role for community planning in promoting healthy development, and the institutional challenges for reconnecting the municipal bureaucracies of public health and planning?

## Health Impact Assessment for Urban and Regional Planning

The third case explores the first participatory health assessment of a land use planning issue in San Francisco, called the Eastern Neighborhoods Community Health Impact Assessment (ENCHIA), and how this process helped stimulate the institutionalization of health impact assessment in planning practices across the entire San Francisco Bay Area. The ENCHIA involved over twenty-five different public agencies and nongovernmental organizations and was organized by the SFDPH to allow these groups to collaboratively evaluate the positive and negative impacts of a rezoning plan. The process developed a collective vision of the healthy city, selected indicators to attach to the vision, gathered and spatially analyzed new data to measure the indicators, and combined these data into a land use and health screening tool called the Healthy Development Measurement Tool (HDMT). The case study explores the inner workings of the ENCHIA, including how the process was designed and managed, the products it produced, and how conflicts over the content and direction of the process were handled? I also examine how the ENCHIA has influenced healthy planning practices across the Bay Area metropolitan region. The chapter examines the forces that enable healthy city planning to become healthy regional governance, such as new coalitions involving governmental and nongovernmental organizations and the construction of new networks for monitoring healthy planning activities that can hold governments and the private sector accountable.

## Research Methods

The cases offered here draw from four years of research from 2004 to 2008, including interviews, participant observation in public meetings and within city agencies, and reviews of original documents. The San Francisco Department of Public Health, Environmental Health Section, gave me access to scores of documents for each case, including written reports, original data, and confidential emails and meeting notes. The health agency also provided me with the opportunity to follow the work of the ENCHIA from its inception to conclusion, where I attended tens of meetings, regularly interviewed participants, and observed internal agency meetings within the San Francisco Department of Public Health. I also performed three evaluations of the ENCHIA, two during the process and one at its conclusion. These evaluations included confidential face-to-face and telephone interviews with over forty participants and in one case, a written survey instrument. I also audio recorded each ENCHIA meeting and generated transcripts of the dialogues. All these data—the interviews, surveys and meeting transcripts—aided in my reconstruction of all the cases, since many of the ENCHIA participants were also involved in the other cases presented here. The cases also reflect in-depth interviews with staff from many of the community-based organizations involved in each of the cases presented here and staff in the San Francisco Planning Department. Finally, I performed content analyses of media coverage for each of the cases in an effort to understand how outside observers were characterizing the events behind each case.

## Outline of the Book

In the next chapter, I offer a critical review of the histories of modern American city planning and public health from the late nineteenth century through the dawn of the twenty-first century. I observe that both fields emerged with similar concerns of improving the health of the least-well-off urban populations, and this helped connect their work as each field aimed to address infectious disease through new sanitary, housing, and social programs. However, work in the fields diverges by the turn of the twentieth century, and with a few exceptions the professions of city planning and public health continue to move further apart for the next one hundred years. I trace the policies, programs and science behind this disconnect through five eras: (1) 1850s to 1900s, miasma and the sanitary city; (2) 1910s to 1920s, germ theory and the rational city; (3) 1930s to 1950s, the biomedical model and the pathogenic city; (4) 1960s to 1980s, crisis and the activist city; and (5) 1990s to 2000s, social epidemiology and the resilient city. The chapter emphasizes that five interrelated themes acted to separate the fields and move each away from their social justice roots: (1) reaction to health and urban crises by removing and displacing people and physical blight; (2) reliance on technical rationality and biomedical science; (3) moral environmentalism or the belief that rational physical designs could change social conditions for the poor; (4) scientific representations of the city as laboratory rather than a field site; and (5) increased professionalization, bureaucratic fragmentation, and specialized expertise. The chapter concludes by suggesting that these themes remain encoded in the institutions of planning and public health and that contemporary efforts aimed at healthy city planning must find ways to overcome these challenges and reconnect with the social justice roots of the fields.

In chapter 3, I show how contemporary city planning processes typically fail to address the social determinants of health and thus help perpetuate health inequities in cities. Using the example of the environmental impact assessment process, I suggest how planning processes might engage with the social determinants of health and review the range of ways human health is positively and negatively influenced by planning practices. I go beyond the usual focus on the outcomes of planning practice, such as transportation systems, housing, and different land uses, to consider how planning processes contribute to human health outcomes.

In chapter 4, I offer a framework for responding to the political and institutional challenges outlined in chapter 2 and the adverse health outcomes described in chapter 3. I consider a set of alternative issue framings that build on the political conditions for healthy city planning outlined in the introduction—namely population health, the relational view of place, governance processes, and an attention to power. The issue frames include moving from (1) reaction to crises with strategies of removal to promoting health through precaution and prevention; (2) a reliance on scientific rationality to the co-production of scientific and political knowledge; (3) physical determinism to a relational view of places, where physical and social characteristics, along with the meanings assigned to places are the focus of analysis and policy; (4) views of the city as laboratory to embracing the field site and population health view of cities; and (5) professionalization, bureaucratic fragmentation, and specialization to building new regional policy and health equity monitoring networks. I use these new issue frames to help analyze the case studies of healthy city planning experiments in the San Francisco Bay Area.

In chapter 5, I present the first case study and reveal how environmental health was reframed to embrace the social determinants of health equity. In chapters 6 and 7, I analyze the political conditions that enable or stymie implementation of the healthy city planning framework from the neighborhood to the regional scale.

In the concluding chapter 8, I draw the key lessons for planning and urban policy making from the case studies. I return to the analytic framework outlined in chapter 4 and evaluate the extent to which the cases pursued these political conditions, what additional factors beyond the framework are necessary to promote healthy and equitable planning, and the general policy lessons suggested by the framework and the case studies. I emphasize that the politics of healthy city planning is an ongoing practice that must engage with the emerging science of the social determinants of health while also learning by doing in collaborations among government agencies, community groups, scientists, and others. I end the book with recommendations for urban planners, public health professionals, and community members seeking to plan more healthy and equitable cities.

## 2    Retracing the Roots of City Planning and Public Health

"To open the door of opportunity for health, we must close the door for exploitation of land. Charity in congested districts is exploitation's most powerful ally. A government must prevent what charity can only mitigate. . . . Taxation is Democracy's most effective method of achieving social justice—including city planning. . . . A city without a plan is like a ship without a rudder." These statements opened Benjamin Clarke Marsh's book, *An Introduction to City Planning: Democracy's Challenge to the American City*, published in 1909 only weeks before the first National Conference on City Planning and the Problems of Congestion. The book accompanied an exhibition put on by the Committee on the Congestion of Population (CCP) in New York, a group led by Marsh and other progressives including Florence Kelley and Mary Simkhovitch. Both the book and exhibition were timed to shape public debate over an emerging profession—city planning—and to ensure that concerns for human health and social justice became the primary mission of the new field.

The architects and engineers that dominated city planning at the turn of the twentieth century responded with disdain to Marsh's comments and his social welfare agenda. The most pointed and public response came from Frederick Law Olmsted Jr., son of the renowned landscape architect and first general secretary of the United States Sanitary Commission. The younger Olmsted was outraged that Marsh would mock his metaphor that compared planners to pilots of a ship, "always holding fast to the direction that his foresight dictates, regardless of the clamor from shortsighted shipmates who urge him to turn aside into smoother water close at hand" (Olmsted Jr. 1908:6). However, instead of responding directly to Marsh, Olmsted Jr. used his keynote address to the second National Conference on City Planning and the Problems of Congestion to argue for a radically different agenda for the planning profession. He proclaimed:

The complex unity, the appalling breadth and ramification, of real city planning is being borne in upon us as never before, and one of the main purposes of such a conference as this, I take it, is to assist the workers in all the different parts of this complex field to understand these interrelationships more clearly. The ideal of city planning is one in which all these activities—all the plannings that shape each one of the fragments that go to make up the physical city—shall be so harmonized as to reduce the conflict of purposes and the waste of constructive effort to a minimum, and thus secure for the people of the city conditions adapted to their attaining the maximum of productive efficiency, of health and of enjoyment of life (Olmsted Jr. 1910: 3).

Capitalizing on his famous lineage and prominent position on the national stage, Olmsted Jr. advanced a vision of planning rooted in the City Beautiful ideal, where aesthetics, efficiency, and comprehensive physical plans were the goals of city planning, not social justice. He concluded his keynote address by outlining the three issues that uniquely defined city planning; circulation of transportation, the design of public spaces, and the development of private land. Strategies for improving the health and well-being of the urban poor were conspicuously absent.

According to Jon A. Petersen, author of *The Birth of City Planning in the United States, 1840–1917* (2003), the debate between Marsh and Olmsted Jr. "ranks with the McMillan Plan for Washington as a definitive episode in the birth of city planning in the United States" (p. 245) and is crucial for understanding how and why city planning emerged as a novel discipline distinct from those concerned with social welfare in cities (p. 248). While Marsh and Olmsted Jr. shared a faith in planning as a tool for change, Marsh wanted the field to tackle the inequities from "population congestion" through new urban taxes, limits on private property rights, and increasing government regulations; Olmsted Jr. viewed the field as a new, technical extension of architecture and engineering. Olmsted Jr. and his supporters would eventually prevail, and by the third national city planning conference in 1911, "population congestion" had been dropped from the meeting's title.

Yet, what additional social, political, and scientific forces—beyond the Olmsted Jr. and Marsh debate—helped define early city planning as a technocratic and design-oriented field? What role did public health have in shaping city planning, and what influence did city planners have on the field of environmental health? What lessons can the historical trajectories of city planning and urban public health have for contemporary efforts aimed at reconnecting the fields for healthy and just city planning? This chapter answers these and other questions through a critical historic review of modern city planning and public health.

## Toward a Critical History of City Planning and Public Health

While the field of urban planning is as old as cities themselves, the modern profession that today is comprised of the political, social, and physical governance of cities was born out of debates such as the one between Marsh and Olmsted Jr. Modern public health emerged to address some of the same concerns of city planners, including urban outbreaks of infectious disease and desires to make disorderly cities more disciplined. However, today the two fields are largely disconnected. This chapter explores some reasons behind the separation of public health from city planning and the impact the split has had on institutions of environmental health science and urban governance. The historical review is offered in order to reveal some of the challenges faced in contemporary efforts to reconnect the fields, as will be explored in subsequent chapters. While a comprehensive history of two vast and complex fields—from the late nineteenth through the twentieth century—is beyond the scope and intent of this chapter, I will highlight persistent tendencies and institutions of power that emerge by examining critical events and popular movements within each field. To accomplish this review, I orient the histories of city planning and public health through a set of overlapping themes: hazard removal, scientific rationality, moral environmentalism, and professionalization, all characterizing the city as a "truth spot."[8]

As this chapter will show, in responding to real or perceived urban crises, city planning and urban public health emerge with technologies of *physical removal and displacement*—of wastes, infrastructure, and "pathogenic" people. This is evident from the waste removal programs of the Sanitary Era through the discriminatory housing and urban renewal policies of the post–World War II period. Second, *scientific rationality* arguments offer justification for both physical interventions and the creation of new political and social institutions, from the construction of sewage systems to the creation of new bureaucracies for urban management. A third theme that shapes both fields is a belief in *moral environmentalism*, or the idea that rational physical and urban designs can change social conditions, particularly for the poor. This chapter also discusses how science helped *professionalize* a new class of technical experts and public administrators in each field, disconnecting their once common knowledge base and creating specialized bureaucracies, disciplinary boundaries, and an elite corps of technocrats. Finally, I explore how "the city" was treated as the locus of scientific truths in each field—as both the empirical referent of analysis and physical venue where legitimate investigation took place—but as this waned in the last two decades of the twentieth century the fields grew apart. Throughout the historical review, I emphasize the central role of science in legitimizing urban policies by characterizing the city as either a laboratory—a restricting and controlling environment whose placelessness enables generalizations to anywhere—or a field site, where a preexisting reality is discovered by surveyors, ethnographers, and others who develop keen personal sensitivities to the uniquely revealing features of their place.

## 1850s to 1900s: Miasma and the Sanitary City

On the eve of the Civil War, American cities were rapidly industrializing and trying to cope with overcrowded housing, noxious industrial, human and animal wastes, and devastating outbreaks of infectious diseases such as typhoid, cholera, and yellow fever (Reps 1965; Riis 1890). Characterized as dark and dirty slums (Woods 1898), urban neighborhoods were blamed for the social "pathologies" of urban life, including violence, crime, "loose morals, bad habits, intemperance, and idleness" (Boyer 1983:17). Newly established municipal sanitary commissions in America looked to their European counterparts for solutions, where researchers hypothesized that *miasma*—filth and foul air—indicated pathogens and was to blame for disease outbreaks.

One influential European report, Edwin Chadwick's 1842 *Report on the Sanitary Conditions of the Labouring Population in Great Britain*, documented that the "gentry and professional" classes lived longer than "laborers and artisans," and claimed that mortality was distributed according to the social and physical composition of different residential districts (Chadwick 1842). Chadwick's work and research methodology was influenced by French epidemiologist Louis René Villermé, who demonstrated thirteen years earlier that the wealthier the Parisian neighborhood, or *arrondisement*, the healthier the population (table 2.1). These reports were among the first to explicitly show that health, far from being fixed, bore

**Table 2.1**
Villermé's data on health gradients in 1817 Paris, France, by a neighborhood measure of wealth that is a percentage of untaxed rents, with taxed rents being paid only by the wealthy

| Arrondisement (neighborhood) | Population in 1817 | Percentage of untaxed rents | Average annual mortality in the total population |
|---|---|---|---|
| 2 (wealthiest) | 65,623 | 7 | 1 in 62 |
| 3 | 44,932 | 11 | 1 in 60 |
| 1 | 52,421 | 15 | 1 in 60 |
| 4 | 46,624 | 15 | 1 in 58 |
| 11 | 51,766 | 19 | 1 in 51 |
| 6 | 72,682 | 21 | 1 in 54 |
| 5 | 56,871 | 22 | 1 in 53 |
| 7 | 56,245 | 22 | 1 in 52 |
| 10 | 81,133 | 23 | 1 in 50 |
| 9 | 42,932 | 31 | 1 in 44 |
| 8 | 62,758 | 32 | 1 in 43 |
| 12 (poorest) | 80,079 | 38 | 1 in 43 |

Source: Adapted from Krieger and Davey-Smith (2004:93).

the imprint of place-based economic inequalities and could be affected by government policies.

Two years after Chadwick's landmark report, Friedrich Engels published *The Conditions of the Working Class in England in 1844*, documenting that mortality rates around Manchester, England, were stratified by three classes of streets and houses based on physical condition (Engels 1968). He also observed "how the sufferings of childhood are indelibly stamped on the adults" (1844:115) resulting in a cumulative bodily impact from harsh working conditions, poor food, inadequate housing, and lack of medical care. Engels (1844:118–19) noted:

All of these adverse factors combine to undermine the health of the workers. Very few strong, well-built, healthy people are to be found among them . . . They are for the most part, weak, thin and pale. . . . Their weakened bodies are in no condition to withstand illness and whenever infection is abroad, they fall victims to it. Consequently they age prematurely and die young. This is proved by the available statistics of death rates.

While Chadwick's report recommended building new public housing along with specific neighborhood improvements without placing blame,

Engels blamed locally polluting industries for creating unhealthy work-places and neighborhoods and argued that the antagonistic class relations of capitalism must be resolved in order to improve the public's health. American cities also faced increasing health inequalities and the sanitary debate would surface after the publication of two similar reports.

John H. Griscom, New York City's chief sanitary inspector, published *The Sanitary Conditions of the Laboring Population of New York* in 1845, using research methods and advancing recommendations derived from Chadwick's report. Five years later, Lemuel Shattuck, sanitary commissioner in Massachusetts, published the *Report of the Sanitary Commission of Massachusetts* in 1850. The reforms advocated by both of these early sanitarians included housing improvements, construction of drinking and waste water systems, and regular street cleaning and refuse removal. American sanitarians rejected both Chadwick's recommendation of building public housing for the poor and Engels's demand for a restructuring of the capitalist system. The American sanitarians opted for a utilitarian approach to reform. As Burrows and Wallace (1999:785) note:

Among Griscom's many striking departures from conventional bourgeois wisdom was his refusal to blame the poor for their wretched housing. He knew that lack of freshwater and adequate sanitation made it impossible for residents to keep clean and pious homes. . . . On the other hand, he didn't blame the rich, as the reformers did. Rather he appealed to them to provide decent housing, not just as "a measure of humanity, of justice to the poor," but as a matter of self interest. Bad housing meant sick workers, and sick workers meant lower profits, higher relief outlays, and higher taxes.

Despite calls for pragmatic action and the view that unsanitary environmental conditions were a danger for everyone, the urban sanitary reforms suggested in these reports were largely ignored at the time of their release.[9]

Reconstruction dominated the political agenda of the day and widespread mistrust of centralized government led most Americans to turn to local ward politicians or private groups for such vital urban services as water supply, street sanitation, and even fire protection. Urban pollution was also seen as a sign of progress, not a potential hazard. Private industry was revered for its potential to raise living standards and increase consumption. As soldiers, newly freed slaves, and European immigrants flooded into urban areas, sanitarians argued that their proposed reforms could confine the undisciplined and undesirable traits of slum dwellers and allow the "socially responsible man" to "appear from beneath the vice of depravity" (Boyer 1983:18). Combining economic efficiency, public health, and morality arguments, sanitarians began to gain the political support they needed to implement their reforms and link the professions of city planning and public health (Duffy 1990).

### Racism, Sanitary Engineering, and Waste Removal
Sanitarians advanced the idea that physical evils were productive of moral evils (Rosen 1993). This was partly out of necessity, as the wealthy and elites commonly believed that poverty bred "sinful" behaviors that caused disease, but it was also rooted in racism. Many elite, including scientists and physicians, perpetuated ideas that the poor, immigrants, and especially African-Americans had genetic defects that led to their immoral behavior and explained the origins of infectious diseases. This racist science advanced such dubious ideas of the time that race was a valid biologic category, that the genes that determine race were linked to those that determine health, and that the health of a population is largely determined by the biological constitution of the population (DuBois 1906; Kevles 1985). While these eugenic ideas lacked scientific merit, they helped perpetuate public health practices grounded in the belief that race was a biologic category and health behaviors could be changed through physical environmental interventions (Cooper and David 1986).

The groundbreaking work of W. E. B. DuBois, among others, challenged the dominant medical and scientific view at the time that inherent racial inferiority was to blame for health disparities between whites and blacks. In his 1906 edited publication, *The Health and Physique of the Negro American*, DuBois used statistics from northern and southern cities to argue that health inequities facing African-Americans were a consequence of their poorer economic, social, and sanitary conditions, as compared to whites. DuBois (1906 [AJPH 2003: 276]) noted in a study of African-American infant mortality in Philadelphia:

The high infantile mortality of Philadelphia today in not a Negro affair, but an index of a social condition. Today the white infants furnish two-thirds as many deaths as the Negros, but as late as twenty years ago the white rate was constantly higher than the Negro rate of today—and only in the past sixteen years has it been lower than the Negro death rate of today. The matter of sickness is an indication of social and economic position.

Sanitary engineers began to justify the construction of new urban infrastructure in response to health crises, and these interventions, such as freshwater delivery systems, seemed to improve population health. However, before the 1890s urban sanitary interventions were often financed and operated by private firms that delivered services only to those that could pay. As Joel Tarr notes in *The Search for the Ultimate Sink: Urban Pollution in Historical Perspective* (1996), it was not until the last decades of the nineteenth and early twentieth centuries that most cities acknowledged that large-scale infrastructure improvements, such as sanitary sewers and drinking water systems, would improve living conditions for all residents and prevent the spread of disease only if everyone was served. By 1910 more than 70 percent of cities with populations over 30,000 owned their own waterworks (Schultz and McShane 1978:393). This new public infrastructure required new urban and sometimes regional bureaucracies to provide long-term financing plans and ongoing management and maintenance. Efforts to engineer more healthy cities gave rise to multiple, and often fragmented, urban bureaucracies, including those concerned with waste collection, freshwater, sewerage, and housing (Peterson 1979).

Yet clean water for drinking and bathing did not end environmental pollution or disease. Cities were now faced with disposing vast quantities of dirty water. Physical and technical solutions dominated, as street-beds were paved to improve surface drainage and sewer pipes brought wastewater away from populated areas to marsh and coastal wetlands (Melosi 2000). Diseases such as typhoid continued to ravage cities, and it wasn't until filtration technology was widely instituted in both water and sewage systems that urban areas saw dramatic declines in deaths from infectious diseases (Meeker 1972).

An idea that emerged during this era that linked physical and social planning with public health goals was the sanitary survey. After a devastating yellow fever outbreak in and around Memphis in 1878, a sanitary survey was launched to describe every street, structure, and individual lot within the city to determine the location of diseases and environmental conditions that might "breed" diseases (Peterson 1979:90). The Memphis sanitary survey followed a similar New York City study in 1864 supported by wealthy merchants who recognized that a reputation for an unhealthy environment hindered economic growth (Duffy 1990:134). Employing physicians, chemists, engineers, and others, the Memphis survey canvassed neighborhoods house by house and block by block, eventually recommending a comprehensive, citywide approach for guiding city planning, including building a new water supply and sewer system, destroying shanties, damming bayous, developing a park along the shoreline, and repaving streets (Peterson 1979:90). The Memphis survey rejected the piecemeal interventions of many sanitary reforms and instead offered a citywide sanitary plan.[10]

### Contagion: People Removal

When removing the miasma didn't seem to reduce disease, the sick were removed from society. *Contagion*, the belief in the direct passage of poison from one person to another led to large quarantines, often of immigrants, and justified state-sponsored interventions in the economy, such as controlling shipping (Markel 1997). By 1893 the National Quarantine Act was passed mandating that the Marine Hospital Service (latter renamed the United States Public Health Service) screen foreigners at state quarantine stations and prevent the admission of "idiots, insane persons, . . . persons likely to become a public charge [and] persons suffering from a loathsome or dangerous contagious disease" (Mullan 1989:41). However, rates of immigrant rejection due to medical conditions varied across regions and reflected racial and ethnic segregation that characterized this era. Between 1894 and 1924, an average of 1 percent of European immigrants arriving at Ellis Island were turned back for medical reasons while about 17 percent of the Chinese, Japanese, and Korean immigrants arriving at Angel Island, in San Francisco Bay, were rejected (Daniels 1997:17).

Quarantines were also used within cities. After discovering the body of a Chinese immigrant that appeared to have died of bubonic plague in March 1900, San Francisco public health officials roped off the fifteen-block Chinatown neighborhood. Approximately 25,000 Chinese were quarantined and non–white-owned businesses in the area were forced to close. In June of the same year, a court ruled that the quarantine was racist and ended it, declaring that health officials acted with an "evil eye and an unequal hand" (Shah 2001:43). In New York City the Department of Health began forcibly separating children from their parents and placing them in quarantine during an epidemic of poliomyletis in 1916. However, wealthy parents were allowed to keep their stricken children at home if they could provide them with a separate room and pay for medical care (Garrett 2000:302).

The field of public health played a key role in promoting quarantines by creating new categories of disease. While less than 3 percent of newly arrived immigrants were diagnosed with an infectious disease in any year between 1891 and 1924, many more were quarantined for chronic mental or moral conditions, such as "feeblemindedness" and "constitutional psychopathic inferiority" (Markel and Stern 2002:764). Contagion policies often used the veil of science to justify policies of social exclusion (Brandt 1987).

## Parks and Playgrounds

The fate of immigrants also influenced land use planning activities during this time. Reformers argued that parks and outdoor recreation areas were needed to alleviate crowded urban living conditions and offer green "breathing spaces." While providing some relief from crowded living conditions, the creation of urban parks also displaced the populations already living in the newly planned areas. For instance, the establishment of New York's Central Park displaced over 1,600 people using the power of eminent domain, including an African-American community of property owners, churches, and cemeteries called Seneca Village (Rosenweig and Blackmar 1992). Most urban parks also reflected Jim Crow segregation, with separate places for African-Americans and whites.

The playground movement advocated for recreation spaces and challenged the idea that urban parks should only be places of leisure and contemplation. The movement was organized largely by women who sought to build urban recreation spaces to keep children off the streets and provide structured play time. Many playgrounds were located next to schools so that gymnasiums, reading rooms, and baths could all be used for children's recreation, literacy, and hygiene. However, the playground movement often perpetuated gender roles by targeting outdoor recreation for boys while girls were taught domestic roles (Gagen 2000). The movement was also known for teaching immigrant children "cooperative play and obedience to authority" (Boyer 1983). Public baths were often built inside or adjacent to new playgrounds. A private charity, the New York Association for Improving the Condition of the Poor (AICP), built one of the first public baths for the poor, driven largely by the belief that slum dwellers needed to be cleansed of moral failures and physical dirt (Williams 1991:24).

## The Settlement House Movement

Reformers in the Settlement House Movement also connected the work of planning and public health (Lubove 1974). The settlement houses were started by progressive whites that volunteered to live with the poor, share their culture, and become part of their neighborhood. Settlement houses organized and educated new immigrants in white, middle-class "American" language, work habits, and child-rearing (Carson 1990). They also provided impoverished neighborhood residents with food, day care, bathing facilities, libraries, art, and social events. Hull House in Chicago, founded by Jane Addams in 1889, was one of the most known settlements and housed many of the era's progressive reformers such as Alice Hamilton and Florence Kelley (Hamilton 1943). These women, influenced by the burgeoning Chicago School of Sociology that initiated the study of the neighborhood effects on well-being, worked with residents to document unsanitary neighborhood and workplace conditions and advocated on behalf of residents for new social policies (Deegan 2002; Hull House Maps and Papers 1970).[11]

An important contribution to the science of the city made by Hull House came through their involvement in a US Congress sponsored study in 1893 called, *A Special Investigation of the Slums of Great Cities.* Hull House resident Florence Kelley was selected to lead the survey of poverty in Chicago, and she enlisted other residents to design a social and physical survey of neighborhood conditions and residents (figure 2.1). Drawing inspiration from Charles Booth's maps of poverty in London (Booth 1902), Hull House residents also mapped their findings on the nationality, wages, and employment history of each resident on every street, often using color to show differences across households. The nationalities map was particularly significant for highlighting the "intermingling" of eighteen different nationalities in one small section of Chicago and the neighborhood's social hierarchy; blacks were clustered onto the least desirable blocks and Italians and Jews relegated to rear apartments in large tenements (O'Conner 2002:29). The survey results and maps were published in 1895 as *Hull-House Maps and Papers,* and while the book offered no explanation for the causes of poverty and social disorder, it was one of the first efforts in America to reveal the spatial patterns of social phenomenon and use maps as a tool for urban social justice activism (Philpott 1991).

### The Sanitary Era and an Emerging Science of the City
By the end of the nineteenth century modern American urban environmental health planning emerged as a field that used physical interventions to respond to urban public health crises. While planning and public health both addressed sanitation and housing reforms during this time, the

(D. L. – 268.)

UNITED STATES
DEPARTMENT OF LABOR,
1898.

Special Agent Expert.

# SOCIAL STATISTICS OF CITIES.

*City of*

## TENEMENT SCHEDULE.

| 1. Enumeration district. | 2. Ward. | 3. Number of dwelling-house in order of visitation. | 4. Number of tenement in order of visitation. | 5. House number and street. |
|---|---|---|---|---|
| | | | | |

6. Stories in house?

7. Tenements in house?

8. In which story is this tenement?

9. Number of rooms in this tenement?

10. Number of families in this tenement?

11. Number of persons in this tenement?

12. Weekly rent of this tenement?

13. Bath-room in this tenement?

14. Water-closet in this tenement?

15. Privy with this tenement?

16. Yard with this tenement?

17. Size of yard?

18. Where is washing hung to dry?

19. Light and air?

20. Ventilation?

21. Cleanliness?

22. Outside sanitary condition?

### THE HOME.

| INQUIRIES. | ROOM No. 1. | ROOM No. 2. | ROOM No. 3. | ROOM No. 4. | ROOM No. 5. | ROOM No. 6. |
|---|---|---|---|---|---|---|
| 23. Use | | | | | | |
| 24. Dimensions | | | | | | |
| 25. Outside windows | | | | | | |
| 26. Occupants, at night | | | | | | |

A1 22-08 — 10000

**Figure 2.1**
Hull House Survey of 1893
Source: Hull House Maps and Papers (1895)

driving ideology was physical removal, of both "environmental miasmas"—garbage, waste water, slum housing, "swamp" land, and so forth—and "undesirable and sick" people. These strategies tended to be piecemeal, with the exception of the sanitary survey, and rarely addressed industrial or consumption practices that led to environmental wastes. For sanitarians, the local solution to pollution was removal and dilution, but the downstream environmental health impacts were often ignored and unseen. In 1908 American President Theodore Roosevelt commented that "at the same time that there comes that increase in what the average man demands from the resources, he is apt to grow to lose the sense of his dependence on nature. He lives in big cities. He deals in industries that do not bring him in close touch with nature. He does not realize the demands he is making upon nature" (quoted from Merchant 1993:350). While specific housing reforms, such as bathrooms, ventilation, and fire escapes improved health, they were rarely accompanied by demands for the construction of new public housing for the poor (Marcuse 1980). Most reforms were grounded in the belief that advancements in science and technology could provide physical improvements that would make "pathogenic" urban environments and the "immoral" slum dwellers more orderly and healthy (Fairfield 1994). Professional white elites, from sanitary engineers to settlement house workers, rarely sought to organize a grassroots multiracial "urban environmental health" social movement or merge their work with concurrent movements for occupational health and safety and environmental conservation (Gottlieb 1993; Holton 2001; Merchant 1985; Rosner and Markowitz 1985).[12]

Environmental health science and political governance practices were also linked during this era. The widespread use of sanitary technologies facilitated a cultural and political shift in norms of responsibility for health and welfare. Municipal services, particularly water and sewerage, shifted from the domain of private individuals and industries to the state (Tarr 1996). Sanitarians convincingly argued that successfully constructing and operating drinking water and sewerage systems required a long-range and comprehensive vision—including the fiscal resources, land condemnation powers, centralized administration, and policing power justified by health crises—that only government could provide (Rosenkrantz 1972). New technologies of the city required new permanent bureaucracies within cities and regions, leading to the establishment of metropolitan water and sewer districts, with Boston's Metropolitan Sewage Commission, in 1889, being one of the first.

The rise of centralized sanitary bureaucracies also contributed to the development of a new common set of expert techniques that, engineers argued, could be applied universally. Models for determining the costs of major infrastructure projects emerged in the 1890s, aided by standard design and material assumptions, giving rise to new managerial expertise (Duffy 1990). Sanitary engineers also acquired a social status once only granted to scientists and physicians—virtuous, humble, loyal to the truth, and emotionally neutral—enabling these professionals to be viewed as nonpartisan professional problem-solvers working with military-like discipline and efficiency for the good of the city, and not a political interest (Melosi 2000). The *Journal of the Association of Engineering Societies* proclaimed in 1894 that "the city engineer is to the city very much what the family physician is to the family. He is constantly called upon to advise and direct in all matters pertaining to his profession" (Schultz and McShane 1978:403). However, the social authority and legitimacy of sanitarians as urban health experts was neither automatically granted nor readily accepted. Expert credibility was often gained through both active claims making and political coalition building, as in the case of settlement house workers who acted as organizers, researchers, and advocates (Rosenkrantz 1972). Yet emerging from this era was a new "science of the city" that included mutually constitutive relationships between science and technology, on the one hand, and political and administrative organization of the city, on the other.

## 1900 to 1920s: Germ Theory and the "City Scientific"

By the turn of the new century it was well-known in public health that both miasma and contagion failed to explain certain aspects of urban health, such as why, with ubiquitous filth, epidemics only occurred sometimes and in some places. Contagion offered a theory of how disease traveled but not where disease came from. By this time the driving ideology in public health shifted to *germ theory*, which stated that microbes were the specific agents that caused infectious disease (Susser and Susser 1996). Medical treatment and disease management began to supersede strategies of physically removing harms, and public health shifted toward interventions aimed at eliminating bacteria.

Bacteriology stimulated laboratory research aimed at developing vaccines to immunize the poor, rather than clean up their neighborhoods and workplaces. Laboratory public health research also tested drinking water, milk, and food for disease-carrying microbes. This research led to compulsory vaccinations for school-age children and the chlorination of municipal drinking water supplies (Leavitt 1992). Public concern over the health impact of contaminated food was stimulated by "muckrakers" such as Upton Sinclair, who published his exposé of working conditions in Chicago's meat-packing district, *The Jungle*, in 1906. Sinclair's work also energized labor unions, who would achieve significant reforms in the workplace after the devastating fire in 1911 at the Triangle Shirtwaist Company in New York City. Organized labor would improve living conditions for urban populations through such achievements as worker compensation laws, rules on child labor, eight-hour workdays, and other social safety-net guarantees (Rosner and Markowitz 1985).

By the post-WWI period, separate municipal departments for garbage collection, water supply and sewerage, nuisance removal, school health, housing, and occupational safety were established (Duffy 1990). As new agencies were established and separate disciplinary "silos" emerged for urban issues, professional specialization increased and collaborative work between the fields decreased, further separating public health from urban planning. The physicians that were now running public health agencies viewed the housing, playground, and other environmental reforms of the early Progressive Era as expensive "social experiments" (Kraut 1988). This new class of public health professionals advocated for "scientific" interventions from laboratory discoveries. However, some municipalities attempted to bridge the social programs of the Progressives with clinical interventions.

## Neighborhood Health Centers
During the early years of the twentieth century, power over urban programs shifted from the federal government and state capitals to municipal governments. One example of this "home-rule" shift was the creation of neighborhood health centers that were financed by federal matching grants through the Maternity and Infancy Protection Act, also known as the Sheppard-Towner Act (Rosen 1971). These centers attempted to bring clinical and social services to the poor, instead of forcing needy residents to travel to faraway central offices. Health centers were started in predominantly immigrant neighborhoods of Milwaukee and Philadelphia, the Mohawk-Brighton district of Cincinnati, New York's Lower East Side, and the West End of Boston (Nelson 1919). One of the only community health centers to serve African-Americans was started in Atlanta by a women's

club called the Neighborhood Union (Smith 1995). By 1916 over fifty-six milk stations in New York City supplied clean dairy products, were staffed with visiting nurses, and acted as maternal, infant, and child care centers (Duffy 1990). In a radical move for the time, a Jewish physician was appointed to the health center in New York's Lower East Side because he was seen as someone who could best relate to the local culture (Rosen 1971).

A central feature of the health center was the creation of block committees with community representatives. These committees met regularly and provided an opportunity for residents to directly participate in community affairs, while also utilizing the professional skills of the health center's physicians and nurses (Sparer 1971). Block workers represented residents and visited families, keeping them in touch with center programs and raising their concerns at meetings (Kreidler 1919). Another committee run by the health center, the occupational council, organized local business and professional groups and gathered their input and support for the work of the center. Both committees acted as neighborhood planning bodies, since no new activities were undertaken in the neighborhood until they had the support of the two councils (Gillette 1983). Neighborhood health centers were a one-stop location for clinical care, community resources, and intensive participation by and involvement of local residents (Bamberger 1966).

While merging social and physical planning with health services for the poor, neighborhood health centers declined rapidly after World War I. Criticism by physicians and the powerful American Medical Association, who accused the centers of practicing "socialized medicine," diminished their political and financial support (Rosen 1971). Federal matching funding for neighborhood health centers ended when the Sheppard-Towner Act was allowed to expire in 1929. The decline of the neighborhood health center represented a more general trend in this era of private interests, whether they be of physicians or factory owners, pressuring the state not to intervene in the affairs of "free" markets.

**The Early Controversy in Professional Planning: Design or Social Justice?**
The private sector saw an opportunity to profit after the 1893 World's Columbian Exposition in Chicago and took the lead in promoting a city-wide plan to construct a network of parks, major roads, public buildings, art, and an amusement park (Hall 1996). The plan, released in 1909 by Daniel Burnham[13] and Edward Bennett, became known as the *Plan of*

*Chicago*, and ushered in the City Beautiful movement in American planning (Peterson 2003). According to Scott (1971:45–46), early city planning ideals raised tensions with those of sanitarians and other Progressive Era reformers:

The City Beautiful movement was a continuation or broadening of the park and boulevard movements, augmented by a fresh interest in malls, lordly public building, and all the street furnishings—fountains, ornamental benches, statues, and memorials—common in European cities. The emphasis on aesthetics tended to negate an earlier, more humanitarian tone and was almost certain to alienate some social workers, tenement-house reformers, and budding sociologists, yet without this reorientation America might not have entered the twentieth century with the prospect of evolving a new municipal function of city planning and a new professional corps dedicated to improving the city.

The Chicago Exhibition was an important event in the birth of the profession, but it was also noteworthy for its exclusion of African-Americans. Ida B. Wells, Frederick Douglass, and others, would publish a scathing critique of the Chicago World's Fair, *The Reason Why the Colored American Is Not in the World's Columbian Exposition*, where Wells would note in the Preface:

Columbia has bidden the civilized world to join with her in celebrating the four-hundredth anniversary of the discovery of America. . . . At Jackson Park are displayed exhibits of her natural resources, and her progress in the arts and sciences, but that which would best illustrate her moral grandeur has been ignored. The exhibit of the progress made by a race in 25 years of freedom, as against 250 years of slavery, would have been the greatest tribute to the greatness and progressiveness of American institutions which could have been shown the world. . . . Why are not the colored people, who constitute so large an element of the American population, and who have contributed so large a share to American greatness, more visibly present and better represented in this World's Exposition?

City Beautiful advocates did not mount a response to Wells, and the new American profession emerged with the mission of designing beautiful and efficient cities.

However, supporters of a social justice agenda for city planning, particularly Benjamin Marsh and the CCP, continued to insist that the new profession should directly address the well-being of the urban poor, and demanded that professionals advocate for the creation of separate zoning districts for factories, new public housing to relieve overcrowding, and,

**Table 2.2**
Marsh's data on the average death rates in selected American cities

| City | Average death rate per 1,000 inhabitants for 1901 to 1905 |
| --- | --- |
| New Orleans | 22.6 |
| San Francisco | 20.9 |
| Pittsburg | 20.7 |
| Washington | 20.6 |
| Baltimore | 19.7 |
| Cincinnati | 19.3 |
| New York | 19.0 |
| Boston | 18.8 |
| Philadelphia | 18.2 |
| St. Louis | 17.8 |
| Buffalo | 15.5 |
| Cleveland | 15.5 |
| Detroit | 15.2 |
| Chicago | 14.3 |
| Milwaukee | 13.2 |

Source: Marsh (1909:14).

perhaps most controversial, new taxes to control real estate speculation in cities. Marsh justified his social justice agenda for city planning by arguing that human health in urban areas was inequitably distributed, publishing data on death rates according to the population density of neighborhoods in New York City and by comparing mortality rates across American cities (table 2.2). Marsh also argued in his book, *An Introduction to City Planning* (1909), that the planning profession ought to be judged on whether or not interventions improve the health of the least-well-off city dwellers, not on designing aesthetically pleasing and efficient cities, noting:

[N]o city is more healthy than the highest death rate in any ward or block and that no city is more beautiful than its most unsightly tenement. The back yard of a city and not its front lawn is the real criterion for its standards and its efficiency. . . . It compels a departure from the doctrine that government should not assume any functions aside from its primitive and restrictive activities and boldly demands the interest and effort of the government to preserve the health, morals and efficiency of the citizens equal to the effort and the zeal which is now expended in the futile task of trying to make amends for the exploitation by private citizens and the wanton disregard of the rights of many. (Marsh 1909:27)

Yet it wasn't Marsh's human health agenda but rather his taxation and government regulatory reforms that elicited the most passionate responses from his supporters and critics. Financier Henry Morgenthau, in a speech at the first national planning conference, proclaimed that planners "have had a moral awakening . . . there is an evil [congestion] which is gnawing at the vitals of the country . . . an evil that breeds physical disease, moral depravity, discontent, and socialism—and all these must be cured and eradicated or else our great body politic will be weakened" (Proceedings of the First National Conference on City Planning 1909: 59). Nelson Lewis, author of one of the first city planning texts entitled, *The Planning of the Modern City*, noted:

There are many who believe that the chief purposes of city planning are social, that the problems of housing, the provision of recreation and amusement for the people, the control and even the ownership and operation of all public utilities, the establishment and conduct of public markets, the collection and disposal of wastes, the protection of public health, the building of hospitals, the care of paupers, criminals and the insane, and all of the other activities of the modern city are all a part of city planning. All of these, however, are matters of administration rather than of planning. . . . (1916:17–18)

It was Olmsted Jr. who would have the greatest influence on the profession through his national stature as chairman of the second national planning conference. In addition to his keynote speech outlining the direction of the new field described in the opening of this chapter, Olmsted Jr. would further marginalize the social justice agenda by removing the theme of "the problems of congestion" from the conference title. By the fifth national conference in 1913, entitled "The City Scientific," Olmsted Jr. and his supporters had successfully defined the burgeoning field as technocratic, and professionals were debating how to incorporate new scientific and technical tools into their practice of analyzing and designing efficient cities (Fairfield 1994; Petersen 2003).

As early planners sought to carve out their niche as social scientists, they were aided by new techniques that allowed for the gathering and use of statistical data to "scientifically" diagnose urban problems and devise rational responses (Boyer 1983). Influential business interests of the day would also sway city planners to adopt the scientific management practices of Taylorism (Haber 1964). However, disagreement continued, this time over the turn toward technocratic decision making. John Nolen, a city planner from Boston and one-time president of both the American City Planning Institute and the National Conference on City Planning, urged planners to pay attention to the processes behind their work, not just the outcomes, and was an early advocate for citizen involvement in planning decision making (Nolen 1924).

## Zoning and Public Health
Under pressure from private landowners to prevent noxious industries from locating in residential districts or near exclusive shopping areas where they had invested, American city planners extended Taylorist notions of scientific efficiency in adopting a hierarchical ordering of land uses (Ford 1915). American zoning ordinances borrowed from German ideas that divided cities by districts based on land use and housing type and built on nuisance laws used to protect public health by limiting odors, smoke, fumes, noises, and other noxious emissions from urban industries (Logan 1976). New York City developed the first citywide zoning code in 1916 that specified building heights and setbacks and created residential, commercial, and industrial zones (Willis 1992).

Zoning ordinances were couched as both protecting public health and benefiting private landowners. In affirming the right of local governments to separate residential and industrial land use, the Supreme Court noted in the 1926 Euclid v. Ambler (272 US 365, 391) ruling:

The decisions enumerated in the first group cited above agree that the exclusion of buildings devoted to business, trade, etc., from residential districts, bears a rational relation to the health and safety of the community. Some of the grounds for this conclusion are promotion of the health and security from injury of children and others by separating dwelling houses from territory devoted to trade and industry; suppression and prevention of disorder; facilitating the extinguishment of fires, and the enforcement of street traffic regulations and other general welfare ordinances; aiding the health and safety of the community, by excluding from residential areas the confusion and danger of fire, contagion, and disorder, which in greater or less degree attach to the location of stores, shops, and factories.

Zoning also increased the likelihood that certain types of development would occur on specific parcels of land. By combining human health and development arguments, zoning, according to Mel Scott (1971:192), "was the heaven-sent nostrum for sick cities, the wonder drug of the planners, the balm sought by lending institutions and householders alike." Yet, in practice, zoning tended to preserve the status quo through "exclusionary" zoning and deed restrictions, or restrictive covenants, both acting to per-petuate Jim Crow segregation (Babcock 1966:116). Zoning was also used by suburban planners to mandate minimum lot size, housing type, and house size in order to keep out lower income people, the majority of whom were immigrants and southern African-Americans coming north during the Great Migration (Lemann 1991). Extending Scott's (1971) use of health metaphors, zoning effectively "immunized" wealthy and white populations from having the poor and African-Americans live in their neighborhoods.

While American zoning was inspired by German planning models, British town planners were influencing a new, regional perspective that aimed to integrate city planning with principles from ecology. The Garden City movement, advanced by Europeans such as Ebenezer Howard and Patrick Geddes, called for a series of human-scale urban areas that were small and dense enough for residents to walk to most services and con-tained ample green-space within the city limits. The Garden City ideal attempted to create a network of medium-sized cities in a region, linked by high-speed rail and roadway systems that avoided the congestion plagu-ing large cities but took advantage of the efficiencies that urban life offered (Haar and Kayden 1989). Following the model of Letchworth and Welwyn Garden City in Hertfordshire, England, American planners designed and built Radburn, New Jersey, in 1929, and created the "greenbelt" towns of Greenbelt, Maryland, Greenhills, Ohio, and Greendale, Wisconsin.

## The Neighborhood Unit

Another land use idea from this era, also couched as a way to improve the quality of urban life and bring more order to American cities, was the "neigh-borhood unit" concept. The neighborhood unit, proposed by Clarence Perry (1929:98), was an urban design scheme centered around a primary school, where:

A population of 5,000 to 6,000 people and 800 or 1,000 children of elementary school age . . . [living] in single-family-per-lot sections requiring an area of about 160 acres . . . is a description of the physical environment that is best adapted, in my opinion, for the growing of an urban neighborhood community.

Reflecting an urban form similar to the Garden City ideal, the interior of the neighborhood unit consisted of a street pattern that encouraged pedes-trian circulation and reduced street congestion caused by automobiles, while the periphery of the unit consisted of businesses located at traffic intersections. While Perry's scheme was hailed as a design that might optimize space for the efficient delivery of services, provide for a safe residential environment, and encourage the social values of the day, the neighborhood unit was also criticized by some for ignoring the social, economic, and political complexities of urban living and for being a plan that would ultimately promote economic residential segregation (Isaacs 1948).

## The Science of Representing the City
The early years of twentieth century city planning and public health gave rise to new understandings of representing the city. Drawing from normative values supposedly inherent in science, including rationality, emotional neutrality, universalism, and disinterestedness, urban planners began to frame their work as representing cities that could be built anywhere. The City Beautiful, the Garden City, the Neighborhood Unit, and the Chicago School concentric zone model, popularized in 1925 by Robert E. Park and Ernest W. Burgess in their sociological work *The City*[14] (figure 2.2), were all new city representations that emerged during this era, and each offered an ideal that tended to ignore the often contested, gendered, variegated, and value-laden characteristics of cities. By leaving out the distinctive virtues of particular places in a bid for universal applicability, these representations of the city were intended to be credible and capable of being applied regardless of time and place, social and physical geography, or political and administrative organization—much like laboratory science. In fact Chicago school texts often refer to the city as a "social laboratory" or "out-of-door laboratory" (Park 1929:1) and characterize the ghetto as a "laboratory specimen" where the social engineer engages in prediction, "diagnosis and treatment" of the city's ills (Wirth 1928:287). At the same time these "scientifically" grounded representations were resonating with urban planners and other social scientists, public health embraced the laboratory science of bacteriology, where findings were also not specific to place or context conditions but rather aimed at generating universal truths (Tesh 1988). Thus the popularity and legitimacy of laboratory science in public health offered planners a new frame for representing the city.

Reflecting the rules for generating credible results in a lab, planners offered design schemes that aimed to gain exquisite control over the objects of their analysis by selecting what data were let in and segregating out potential "contaminants"—both natural and human. The one-size-fits-all

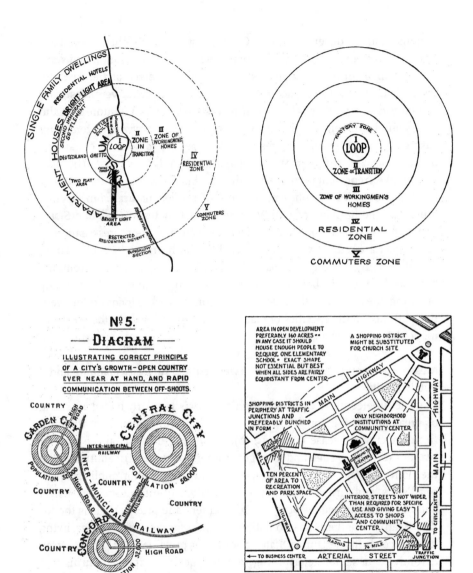

**Figure 2.2**

Representations of the city: Here and anywhere

Sources: *Top left*: Park and Burgess Map of Chicago; *top right*: their generalized city map (1925:51, 55). *Bottom left*: Ebenezer Howard's Garden City (Howard 1965); *bottom right*: Clarence Perry's Neighborhood Unit (Perry 1929).

designs of the Concentric Zone, Garden City, and Neighborhood Unit models reflected common laboratory practices of mechanization and standardization in order to create distance between the researcher and the researched. Laboratory spaces, like the urban models, were designed similarly to allow other scientists at diverse locations to assume that the background ambient conditions were equivalent everywhere, removing suspicions that experimental results might be due to some peculiar and unannounced environmental factor (Gieryn 1999; Latour 1987). The "laboratory-like" representation of cities during this era was accompanied by a new view of cities as coherent systems of unified natural components, much like the human body. As Richard Sennett notes in *Flesh and Stone: The Body and the City in Western Civilization* (1994), the representation of the city as a circulatory system much like the human blood circulatory system emerged alongside bacteriology. As nonspecific interventions became the norm in both early twentieth-century public health and city planning, the science of the fields shifted from an earlier focus on interventions attuned to the specifics of places and neighborhoods to those reflecting a placeless universalism.

## Measuring Health Outcomes: Early Twentieth-Century City Planning and Public Health

The late nineteenth to early twentieth century is regularly hailed as a time of great progress in public health, particularly for reducing death rates from infectious disease (Duffy 1990). Of course, this was also a time of virulent racism, as state and local governments denied African-Americans the right to vote, forced them to use separate and inferior public services of all sorts, and turned a blind eye to campaigns of intimidation, violence, and murder launched by local law enforcement and groups such as the Ku Klux Klan. Since there was no national system for collecting or classifying death records in the United States prior to 1933 (Haines 2001), there is no definitive data set for determining whether "health" improved during this time for all population groups. Kuznets (1965) calculated the crude death rate for whites by decade between 1875 and 1920 and suggested that mortality did decline steadily over this period. Edward Meeker (1972) used data from city offices of vital statistics to calculate death rates for specific diseases in New York, Boston, Philadelphia, and New Orleans between 1864 and 1923. These data suggest that declines in infectious disease deaths contributed to an overall lowering of mortality in some major cities (table 2.3). Yet, these data may be masking heterogeneity by age, class, and

**Table 2.3**
Disease-specific death rates for New York, Boston, Philadelphia, and New Orleans

| Disease | Average death rate | |
|---|---|---|
| | 1864–1888 | 1889–1913 |
| Consumption | 365 | 223 |
| Stomach and intestinal | 299 | 196 |
| Scarlet fever | 66 | 19 |
| Typhoid and typhus | 53 | 25 |
| Smallpox | 40 | 2 |
| Cholera | 8 | 0 |
| Diphtheria | 123 | 58 |
| Yellow fever | 14 | 1 |
| Total for group | 964 | 524 |
| Crude death rate | 2570 | 1890 |

Source: Meeker (1972:365).

ethnicity, and statistics do not specify the reasons behind these apparent declines.

Were city planning and public health interventions responsible for these declining death rates? One explanation posited that large-scale planning and public health innovations and infrastructure projects, including clean water technologies, citywide sanitation programs, milk pasteurization, and meat inspection, were the source of health improvement. However, others would later argue that increased wealth and nutrition were responsible (McKeon 1976), while still others argued that advances in medical care combined with individual hygiene practices, such as hand and food washing, explained declines in mortality. While the debate remains unsettled, the latter half of the twentieth century saw the rise and dominance of the medical model, and this paradigm would further distance public health from city planning.

### 1930s to 1950s: The Biomedical Model and Pathogenic City

The driving theory in public health shifted again during the pre-WWII era to the *biomedical model* of disease. This model attributes morbidity and mortality to molecular-level pathogens brought about by individual lifestyles, behaviors, hereditary biology, or genetics, and it altered attention in public health to personal "risk factors" such as smoking, diet and exercise (Susser and Susser 1996). However, New Deal programs kept public health activities linked to spatial and social planning, as new federal agencies were created to rebuild public health infrastructure such as drinking water and sewer systems, clinics and hospitals, and to develop new sources of electricity (Grey 1999). The New Deal also provided federal funding for municipal planning and health departments, ushering in the era of the "bureaucratic city" where a new set of impersonal public institutions, staffed by newly credentialed professionals, laid claim to expert interventions. As separate municipal departments for everything from sanitation to sewerage to smoke control were created, distinct professional and academic boundaries followed (Peterson 2003). Cities such as St. Louis and Pittsburgh established their own ordinances and a smoke inspector's office to reduce smoke (Stradling 1999). However, the city's efforts were short-lived as the Pennsylvania Supreme Court ruled that only the state legislature, not city governments, had the authority to create smoke abatement laws (Tarr and Lamperes 1981).

Despite the rise of the biomedical view, some researchers in public health returned to investigating the links between economic deprivation, bodily characteristics, and health. This theme played a central role in the 1933 US report *Health and Environment*, prepared by Edgar Sydenstricker for the President's Research Committee on Social Trends. Sydenstricker argued that it was wrong to focus analyses of the human health impacts of the Depression on mortality because causes of death rarely operate instantaneously (except for fatal injuries, homicide, or suicide). The health impact of social inequality, claimed Sydenstricker, would be expected to first manifest itself in changes in morbidity, not mortality. Sydenstricker conducted a ten-city study of the health impact of the Depression, providing evidence of how poverty and extreme material deprivation had acute effects on morbidity while also generating some of the first large-scale evidence of black to white inequalities in health (Sydenstricker 1934).

## Public Health and the Neighborhood Unit
Clarence Perry's neighborhood unit idea took hold with planners and developers and, in perhaps the most striking linkage between planning and public health of the early twentieth century, the American Public Health Association's Committee on the Hygiene of Housing. The APHA committee adopted the neighborhood unit design scheme as the basis for two reports; one, in 1938, *Basic Principles of Healthful Housing*, and a second in

1948, *Planning the Neighborhood.* The earlier housing guide detailed thirty essential health aims that were believed to be the minimum required for the "promotion of physical, mental, and social health, essential in low-rent as well as high-cost housing, on the farm as well as in the city dwelling." The latter document set standards for the "environment of residential areas," defined as "the area served by an elementary school," and emphasized that:

No perfection in the building or equipment of the home can compensate for an environment which lacks the amenities essential for decent living. We must build not merely homes but neighborhoods if we are to build wisely for the future of America. . . . [T]he effects of substandard environment extends beyond direct threats to physiological health, and involves . . . significant detriments to mental and emotional well-being. (APHA 1948:vi–vii)

Significantly both the 1938 and 1948 documents recognized the existence and persistence of health disparities in poor neighborhoods and how stigma might influence health status:

[T]he mere elimination of specific hazards in poor neighborhoods falls short of the real goal of planning an environment which will foster a healthy and normal family life . . . a sense of inferiority due to living in a substandard home may often be a more serious health menace then any unsanitary condition associated with housing. (1948:vii)

The APHA committee stopped short of recognizing that widespread residential segregation might contribute to poor health, stating: "Further research is needed to determine to what extent housing segregation or housing aggregation of differing population groups may create mental tensions or otherwise affect health" (1948:2).

Banerjee and Baer (1984), in a detailed review of *Planning the Neighborhood,* observed that the APHA guidelines were instantly influential because most practitioners presumed that the design standards it offered linked the built environment with health concerns at a time when no other similar standards existed. However, they also note that since most of the "neighborhood effects" described with numerical precision in the APHA report could not be nor had yet been empirically measured, the precision of the recommendations were artificial at best and tended to reflect the opinions of a select group of experts (Banerjee and Baer 1984:24–25). Other critics of *Planning the Neighborhood* challenged its physical deterministic orientation, suggesting that the social health of a place may not match up neatly with the confines of the neighborhood unit. Yet, as Fischler (1998:390) has noted, the APHA adoption of the neighborhood unit and publication of specific healthy design standards "represent the culmination of a search for scientific methods to secure collective well-being. They are the fullest expressions of the welfare state in the field of urban development."

### Housing and Urban Renewal
While the neighborhood unit and *Planning the Neighborhood* guidelines remained influential with planners, another set of policies geared toward housing, slum removal, and highway construction would also have a significant impact on the health of urban populations during this era (Fullilove 2004; Hirsh 1983; Mohl 2000). By 1931 a group of influential women aimed to reignite the American public housing debate responding, in part, to the lack of a national housing movement and increasing slum populations (Wood 1931). Led by Catherine Bauer, the director of the Labor Housing Conference, and Mary Simkhovitch, these women organized the National Public Housing Conference (Bauer 1945). Also attending the public housing conference was Edith Elmer Wood, a member of the New Jersey State Housing Authority. Drawing inspiration from European public housing programs, Bauer and Wood argued for a greater federal government role in building housing for the poor that was safe, affordable, and constructed in modernist, high-rise buildings on super-blocks (Pluntz 1990). The conference appeased a wide range of groups by calling for the creation of a single federal housing agency while simultaneously acknowledging that housing was, and should remain, a local matter that ought to be integrated into such local government functions as city development and planning (Scott 1971:326). A key aspect of this group's public housing program was the clearance of existing slums followed by the construction of government-subsidized low-cost housing. Perhaps ironically, these public housing advocates generated much of the language and political momentum behind the Wagner-Steagall Housing Act of 1937, particularly its slum clearance provisions, and other similar housing legislation of the 1930s and 1940s (Oberlander and Newbrun 1999).

The federal insurance of home mortgages began in 1934 through the Federal Housing Administration (FHA), targeting new single-family suburban homes. The FHA also issued technical guidelines for neighborhood design, and the 1936 bulletin *Planning Neighborhoods for Small Houses*

(FHA 1936) rejected the urban grid pattern and instead mandated that new residential subdivisions, in order to take advantage of federally insured mortgages, be designed using cul-de-sacs and curvilinear streets. These federally mandated suburban design patterns would set the stage for late twentieth-century suburban sprawl (Fishman 2000).

The Federal Housing Act also refused to insure mortgages for older houses, effectively "redlining" inner-city neighborhoods out of the program (Hirsh 1983). White racism in housing was perpetuated by the planning field's acceptance and perpetuation of this de facto policy of segregation (Abrams 1955). Federally subsidized mortgages often required that property owners incorporate restrictive covenants into their deeds. The federal government consistently gave black neighborhoods the lowest rating for purposes of distributing federally subsidized mortgages (Massey and Denton 1993:52). The Federal Housing Administration, which insured private mortgages, advocated the use of zoning and deed restrictions to bar undesirable people and classified black neighbors as nuisances to be avoided along with "stables" and "pig pens" (Abrams 1955:231). Not surprisingly, "[b]uilders . . . adopted the [racially restrictive] covenant so their property would be eligible for [federal] insurance," and "private banks relied heavily on the federal system to make their own loan decisions. . . . Thus the federal government not only channeled federal funds away from black neighborhoods but was also responsible for a much larger and more significant disinvestment in black areas by private institutions" (Massey and Denton 1993:52). Although the federal government ended these discriminatory practices after 1950, it did nothing to remedy the damage it had done or to prevent private actors from perpetuating segregation until much later.

The Housing Act of 1949 institutionalized urban renewal, where municipalities began razing "slum" neighborhoods and displacing thousands of poor, largely African-American residents (Von Hoffman 2000; Weiss 1980). Urban renewal was a program and theory that aimed to remove downtown blight—still viewed as the cause of moral evil and the breeding ground for disease—and rebuild whole sections of the city using the best of modern technology and scientifically rational design (Fishman 2000). Yet urban renewal tended to only increase poverty for residents of poor neighborhoods because their homes were replaced with either inadequate public housing or, as was more often the case, private real estate developers acquired the downtown land cheaply and opted not to build new housing but expensive high-rise office towers (Weiss 1980). Not only were neighborhoods physically fractured, but social and emotional ties, trust, and notions of collective efficacy were also severed by urban renewal, further diminishing the health-promoting resources available for African-Americans (Fullilove 2004). Shut out from most new suburbs, African-Americans were denied other health benefits that can come with homeownership, such as capital accumulation, access to better-funded schools, and participation in the growing suburban economy.

By the 1956 passage of the Federal Aid Highway Act, the field of planning had not only ignored the public health impacts of its programs but had perpetuated the widespread destruction of the nation's poorest inner-city neighborhoods (Mohl 2000). In January 1945 the infamous Robert Moses captured the sentiment among elitist planners in an *Atlantic Monthly* article entitled "Slums and City Planning," stating that "there has to be modern roads and modern harbors and somebody's got to build it and, in order to get things done, and done properly, people must be inconvenienced who are in the way" (Moses 1945:63).

### De-industrialization, Cities, and Racial Disparities

By the 1950s the postwar economic growth had slowed and the unequal distribution of the "affluent society" became increasingly apparent. Midwestern and northeastern cities began losing hundreds of thousands of entry-level manufacturing jobs in such industries as textiles, electrical appliances, motor vehicles, and military hardware (Sugrue 1996). Automated production and plant relocation to suburban and rural areas proceeded with the full support and encouragement of the American government. Federal highway construction and military spending facilitated and fueled industrial growth in nonurban areas. Yet economic inequality remained largely off the agenda of politicians and scholars until books like Michael Harrington's *The Other America* (1962), which documented a world of skid rows and Black ghettos.

Three interrelated political and cultural assumptions about the urban economy helped shape public policy during this period. The first was a near orthodox faith in neoclassical economics that interpreted the structural changes of the postwar era as temporary dislocations, and looked to national aggregate indicators of economic prosperity rather than to regional variations. Second was the use of the "manpower" idea to explain unemployment as the result of individual educational or behavioral deficiencies while at the same time deemphasizing the structural causes of joblessness.

A third ideology was a federal government optimism about the capacity of the private sector to absorb surplus labor. The result was continued divestment from and a lack of political attention to the economic and racial well-being of most American cities (Weir 1994).

Economic inequality and white flight from cities was compounded by racism that perpetuated residential segregation (Sugrue 1996). African-Americans in every major city found themselves entrapped in rapidly expanding, yet persistently isolated urban ghettos. Life in inner cities during this era was characterized by a series of life hazards that included widespread joblessness, decaying infrastructure, white stereotypes, and stigmatization of blacks, leading some to define urban residents as America's "outcasts" (Wacquant 1993).

By the end of this era both urban planning and public health were in crisis. Urban renewal highlighted the impotence of physical planning to improve the social, economic, and health conditions of urban residents. The theme of the 1957 annual meeting of the American Public Health Association was "Is Public Health in Tune with the Times" (Duffy 1990)? Declining health for minorities during this period coupled with sustained urban divestment heightened racial tensions and responses ranged from rioting to the organizing of new social movements to challenge state-centered planning.

## 1960s to 1980s: Crisis and the Activist City

By the 1960s planning was grappling with widespread social unrest and the field was hard-pressed to respond to activists' claims that large-scale public development projects and modernist designs that accompanied urban renewal projects were not any better than piecemeal changes that built on the existing fabric of older neighborhoods (Goodman 1972). The federal government, already encouraging the private sector to take control of central business district development in cities, passed the Urban Development Action Grant in 1977, which included tax exempt municipal bonds and changes in the federal tax code to further encourage the creation of quasi–Public Redevelopment Corporations to operate in most declining American cities. This legislation represented an important formalization of private control over key areas of municipal policy. Yet, as Thomas J. Sugrue (1996:271) noted in *The Origins of the Urban Crisis: Race and Inequality in Postwar Detroit*:

Celebrated public–private partnerships, including the Ford-financed Renaissance Center hotel and office project, and the General Motors Poletown plant, have done little to enlarge the city's employment base, and have drained city coffers of more tax money. The bleak landscapes and unremitting poverty of Detroit in the 1970s and 1980s are the legacies of the transformation of the city's economy in the wake of World War II, and of the politics and culture of race that have their origins in the persistent housing and workplace discrimination of the postwar decades. What hope remains in the city comes from the continued efforts of city residents to resist the debilitating effects of poverty, racial tension, and industrial decline.

Activists also challenged public health professionals to address why, in the face of rising economic prosperity and improvements in medical technology, inequalities in health persisted particularly for the urban poor and people of color (Krieger 2000)? For example, in 1960 the infant mortality rate was 44.3 per 1,000 for African-American babies and 29.2 for whites (Satcher et al. 2005:459).

President Johnson's War on Poverty programs, along with the passage of Medicare and Medicaid, addressed some of the health care needs of the elderly and poor. One program of the War on Poverty created neighborhood health centers (Sparer 1971). Organized by the newly created Office of Economic Opportunity, neighborhood health centers again linked clinical care, childhood education, and community involvement (Lefkowitz 2007). However, citizen activism, not programs from the professions, forged the strongest links between planning and public health during this era.

Civil Rights activists organized in urban areas to link social, environmental, and health justice. For example, the Young Lords, a group of New York City Puerto Rican activists in "El Bario" or East Harlem, organized street cleanups after the sanitation department refused to collect neighborhood garbage for weeks. The group convinced local health professionals to train lay residents in the techniques of door-to-door lead-poisoning screening and tuberculosis testing (Abramson et al. 1971). Reminiscent of the Progressive Era, the Lords started day care programs in local churches, provided breakfast in neighborhood schools, organized tenants to demand housing improvements, and occupied a neighborhood hospital to highlight its inadequate service to the local population. The Young Lords combined local knowledge with professional techniques to address health disparities in their neighborhood and showed that contrary to dominant professional beliefs at the time, urban neighborhoods were not places of total disorder requiring "expert-derived rational designs" imposed on them without their consultation (Melendez 2003).

The public dissatisfaction with planning was captured in the now classic critique of modern planning, Jane Jacobs's (1961) *The Death and Life of Great American Cities*. According to Jacobs, the mega-block projects of urban renewal were destroying the aspects of neighborhoods that made them livable, such as human-scale streets that encouraged connection to and contact with one's neighbors. For Jacobs, a healthy community was as much determined by social characteristics as physical, where neighbors and strangers constantly interacted in an "urban ballet" of familiarity and chance encounters (Jacobs 1961:65).

Environmental health was met with an equally influential book, the 1962 publication of Rachel Carson's *Silent Spring*. Carson challenged the "better living through chemistry" ideal of the time that viewed industrial chemicals as largely benign. Writing about the harmful effects that chemicals such as DDT were having on ecosystems—"silencing the songbirds"—Carson re-popularized nineteenth-century themes linking industrial pollution and environmental health (Gottlieb 1993). Perhaps as important, Carson's work challenged the dominant idea in planning and public health that advances in science and technology were unquestionable signs of progress, in the public interest, and would improve human health. Yet some have noted that Carson's consumer-oriented focus on the ecology of suburban spaces and federal wildlife refuges made the bodies of farm workers and inner-city residents relatively invisible to the growing environmental movement (Lear 1997).

By 1970 the Nixon administration began redirecting resources away from inner cities to the suburbs through block grants, dismantling Model Cities programs, and instituting "benign neglect."[15] Benign neglect gave affirmative signals to cities, such as New York, to adopt policies such as "planned shrinkage," where essential services, such as libraries, fire protection, and public transportation were withdrawn from designated "sick" neighborhoods and redirected to "healthier" ones (Fried 1976; Roberts 1991). As ghettos were left to burn, businesses fled and essential retail outlets, such as supermarkets, adapted their operations to fit their new suburban locations.

During this same period in the late 1960s and early 1970s, some of the twentieth century's most significant environmental legislation was passed. In addition to creating the US Environmental Protection Agency and Occupational Health and Safety Administration, Congress would adopt the

National Environmental Policy, Clean Air, and Clean Water Acts and begin to phase out lead in gasoline all during the first years of the 1970s. A proposed National Land Use Planning Act was defeated in 1974, but its debate as "jobs versus the environment" acted to split a coalition of urban African-American activists that would hold through much of the next two decades (Weir 2000). However, by the end of this era, the Centers for Disease Control recognized that improving urban health required attention to more than just the physical characteristics of neighborhoods, but also to the social and psychological implications of housing, removal, and relocation (Hinkle and Loring 1977).

**A Global Movement for Healthy Cities**
In the early 1980s academics and activists around the world met with the idea of reconnecting cities and public health. The World Health Organization, Office for Europe, created the Healthy Cities Project in 1986 (WHO 1988). The movement aimed to get cities to commit to developing a healthy city plan and to build networks of cities and towns committed to health (Tsouros 1994). In the United States, the Coalition for Healthier Cities and Communities was started in the 1990s and aimed to get city and county health departments to embrace the broad view of health reflected in the European healthy cites movement (Norris and Pittman 2000). By 1993 the International Society of City and Regional Planners (ISOCARP) congress focused on reconnecting planning and public health, and was entitled, "City-Regions and Well-Being: What Can Planners Do to Promote the Health and Well-being of People in the City-Regions?"

Importantly the Healthy Cities movement of the World Health Organization began to reconnect city planning and public health in a number of ways. First, participating cities were required to develop a health profile and a city health plan. Second, cities had to demonstrate how they would achieve their plan, noting linkages across political agencies and changes in resource allocations. Finally, participating cities were required to establish and staff a Healthy City Office within municipal government to be responsible for reporting on progress toward specific objectives outlined in the City Health Plan, producing a City Health Development Plan, and committing the city to internal and external monitoring and evaluation (Barton and Tsouros 2000). More generally, the Healthy Cities movement highlighted the critical role local government can play in promoting the global health agenda of the WHO and aimed to transcend the traditional boundaries of the agencies and participants that ought to take part in health promotion. However, De Leeuw and Skovgaard (2005) note that evaluations of Healthy Cities projects have been difficult and suggest mixed results, in part due to the lack of agreement over appropriate evidence and indicators but also due to limited implementation of plans within city governments.

## 1990s to Twenty-first Century: Toward the Healthy and Equitable City

The Healthy Cities Movement is part of a series of international efforts to promote health equity. The 1980 publication in Britain of the *Inequalities in Health Report* (commonly referred to, using the lead author's name, as the Black report) ignited international debate over the social and economic determinants of health inequities (Townsend and Davidson 1982). After the 1988 release of the US Institute of Medicine's *Committee for the Study of the Future of Public Health* report, leaders in the field agreed that the nation's public health activities were in disarray and that the field needed to refocus its efforts to address the growing inequalities in health across population groups (IOM 1988). A 1998 publication in Britain, the *Acheson Report*, again highlighted that action was urgently needed across sectors of government and society to address rising health inequities and that medical care alone was insufficient to reverse this alarming global trend (Acheson et al. 1998).

These and other reports helped researchers re-conceptualize explanations for the *distribution* of disease across populations in order to explain health disparities, energizing the field of social epidemiology (Berkman and Kawachi 2000). Social epidemiologists pushed public health to reconsider how poverty, economic inequality, social stress, discrimination, and other social and economic inequalities act as the "fundamental causes" of health disparities (Link and Phalen 2000). In 2006 the US Department of Health and Human Services developed a national Action Agenda for the Elimination of Health Disparities, with the impact of the "built environment" on vulnerable populations emerging as one of four top priorities of the federal agency (www.omhrc.gov). But, by the end of the twenty-first century a split emerged in public health between those emphasizing the biomedical model and focusing on treating individual disease "risk factors" and social epidemiologists who emphasized nineteenth-century ideas of improving neighborhood conditions, eliminating poverty, and enhancing social resources for health (Fitzpatrick and LaGory 2000; Geronimus 2000; Krieger 2000).

The American professions of city planning and public health had emerged with similar objectives in the late nineteenth century, slowly split during the twentieth century, and encoded institutions of science and urban governance along the way. Yet the separation between the fields was never absolute; events and practices throughout the twentieth century linked ideas and work in the two fields in various ways. However, by the twenty-first century, the disconnect between environmental health and urban planning decision making was increasingly recognized by researchers and practitioners as a serious impediment to addressing health disparities, particularly in cities, and efforts were underway to reconnect the fields (Frumkin et al. 2004; Frumkin 2005).

# 3   Urban Governance and Human Health

Imagine that a new development consisting of a convention center, market rate housing and retail space is proposed for the downtown area of your city. Proponents argue that the project will revitalize vacant and underutilized land, increase city tax revenues, and provide much needed jobs for local residents, particularly low-income people of color currently living in the downtown area. Opponents of the project are concerned that existing residents and businesses may be indirectly displaced from rising property values, that air pollution and noise will increase, and the new service-sector jobs will not pay a living wage. Your city's planning department is set to review the project. How might existing planning processes review the positive and negative human health impacts of this project?

## Environmental Assessment and Human Health

The planning department in your city would likely have to perform an environmental impact assessment (EIA) for this project. Emerging out of the National Environmental Policy Act (NEPA) of 1969, environmental assessment directed federal agencies to essentially "look before they leap" and review potential impacts "to the environment and biosphere and stimulate the health and welfare of man" (Sec. 2, 42 USC § 4321). The federal statue gave rise to "little NEPAs" in dozens of states, countries and international organizations. As the practice of environmental review evolved, a set of guidance documents within local, state, and federal government agencies emerged, followed closely by legal challenges and court interpretations of the statute, such as what counts as an environmental impact (Karkkainen 2002).

Planners in your city would likely organize their review around a set of environmental impacts categories. The typical categories in an environmental review are related to land use (i.e., does the project comply with existing zoning or other land use controls?), environmental pollution (i.e., how might air quality be impacted due to increased traffic?), and social and/or community character (i.e., will the size or design features of the project have an adverse impact on the surrounding community?). While the process is called an environmental review, the definition of environment is broad, and often includes physical hazards, such as noise, air, water, and soil pollution; energy, water use, and waste disposal; built environments of housing, parks, schools, streets, and other infrastructure; economic environments such as employment and housing affordability; and sociocultural environments such as historic resources and community aesthetics.

In 1997 the Council on Environmental Quality issued guidance to incorporate environmental justice into NEPA reviews, directing agencies to include minority and low-income populations in the assessment process; "analyze human health, economic, and social effects" (CEQ 1997:4) of actions on minority, low-income and Indian tribe populations, and recognize that impacts in these communities "may be different from impacts on the general population" due to a community's distinct circumstances and cultural practices (CEQ 1997:14). States from New York to California initiated processes to draft environmental justice guidance into their environmental review laws.[16] Despite the call for clear guidance, analyses of how a project, plan, program, or policy might positively or adversely influence the public's health, especially that of the poor and people of color, remains limited or nonexistent within laws governing existing environmental review processes. This was confirmed most recently by the US Environmental Protection Agency's Office of Inspector General in a scathing report reviewing the agency's oversight and implementation of numerous environmental justice directives (OIG 2006).

While the public health and environmental justice sections of an environmental review direct agencies to consider how a project may adversely impact human health, these reviews are rarely conducted, and this is only partially due to the fact that there is limited or no guidance from state and federal agencies (Steinenmann 2000). When public health is assessed, the focus is often only on whether a project or plan will meet a health-based environmental regulatory standard. In addition most environmental review processes tend to rely on risk assessment for analyzing potential public health impacts (BMA 1998). The risk assessment process typically generates a quantitative probability of a single health outcome such as cancer from exposure to a single toxin over one lifetime and routinely fails to consider potential disproportionate impacts on the poor or people of color (Kuehn 1996). Chronic illnesses, the multiple and cumulative exposures that humans experience in their daily environments, and the broad social determinants of health are also ignored in most quantitative risk assessments. As a result city planning processes that use environmental impact assessment rarely engage with the multiple physical, social, and economic forces that are suspected of being major influences on human well-being and key drivers of health inequities in cities (Lawrrence 2003; Geronimus 2000; Wilkinson 1996).[17]

The lack of broad public health analyses within planning processes is significant because many land use projects and urban plans influence the social and economic circumstances, or factors outside the health care system, that tend to be beyond individual control but significantly affect human well-being. The socioeconomic circumstances of individuals and groups are equally or more important to health status than medical care and personal health behaviors, such as smoking and eating patterns (Evans et al. 1994; Yen and Syme 1999). These influences on well-being are commonly referred to as the social determinants of health (SDOH), and according to the World Health Organization, they adversely impact health through such social forces as unsafe and insecure living and working conditions combined with the "worries and insecurities of daily life and the lack of supportive environments" (Wilkinson and Marmot 2003). The social determinants of health can act positively or negatively on well-being, and high on the list are long-term social disadvantage, social and psychological environments, early childhood environments, work, unemployment and job insecurity, friendship and social cohesion, social exclusion, alcohol and other drugs, and access to healthy food and transport systems (WHO 2008). The SDOH have a direct impact on the health of individuals and populations, are the best predictors of individual and population health, structure lifestyle choices, and interact with each other to produce health and drive health inequities (Acheson et al. 1998; Evans et al. 1994; Adler and Newman 2002). While many social determinants of health are expressed at the community or neighborhood level (i.e., affordable housing, access to healthy food and transportation, social connections with others) and could be assessed within existing environmental review processes, typical impact assessments have adopted standard practices that regularly fail to consider these important determinants of well-being (see table 3.1).

**Table 3.1**

Typical environmental impact assessment categories and the social determinants of health

| Analytic category | Typical analytic content | Examples of social determinants analytic content |
|---|---|---|
| Environmental quality | • Emissions to air, soil, water, etc.<br>• Pollutants evaluated against regulations and/or discharge requirements | • Cumulative burdens from exposure to multiple hazards across different media<br>• Impacts on vulnerable populations such as the elderly and asthmatics |
| Transportation | • Vehicle level of service<br>• Transit system capacity | • Transit access to job centers, goods, services, and health care<br>• Pedestrian safety/injuries<br>• Pedestrian and bicycle opportunities for physical activity |
| Land use | • Compliance with existing zoning code<br>• Consistent with published area or general plan | • Business displacement<br>• Parks/recreation uses that can support social interaction<br>• Access to retail food outlets, farmer's markets, and community gardens |
| Community/ cultural facilities | • Population/ demographic analysis<br>• Impacts on historic sites/resources<br>• Impacts to community centers | • Does the project promote or stymie social connections among residents?<br>• Can project help build capacity within existing civic organizations?<br>• Will the project impact violence and social stress? |
| Housing | • Meet existing/ projected housing demand<br>• Direct displacement of housing and/or people | • Will the project result in direct or indirect residential displacement/ gentrification; racial residential segregation and social exclusion; or increase or decrease the supply of affordable and safe housing within the region? |
| Environmental justice | • Disproportionate pollution burdens on the poor and people of color | • Promote safe, living-wage jobs<br>• Meaningful participation in decision making<br>• Equal access to quality educational opportunities, especially for children |

## Politics of Environmental Health Reviews

Let us return to our hypothetical development project to examine why focusing on changing the analytic categories of processes like environmental impact assessment is a necessary but insufficient step in moving toward a new politics of healthy city planning. Remember that in our development scenario, planners seemed to enter the process after the project was proposed. By this time in a development project or land use plan, key decisions from design to financing to political support would likely have already been made. Yet planners and city planning processes more generally can have influence over shaping projects and plans before an environmental review is triggered. For instance, your city's general plan, which acts as a multi-year land use and development blueprint, might have encouraged or provided incentives for downtown development. Your zoning or tax codes might have also encouraged the size and scope of the downtown development project. For example, your city, county, or state might have a strategic plan for attracting tourism revenues that includes tax breaks and other incentives for the downtown development.

In these and other ways planning processes beyond environmental impact assessment act to influence the scope, location, and scale of development in cities.[18] Urban planning processes are also embedded within the broader politics of the city as planners might work to realize the goals and objectives of elected and appointed officials, respond to concerns expressed by individuals and interest groups, promote economic efficiency, and/or social justice. The classic constraint on city politics is the "growth machine," where elite interest groups align to promote economic development over other urban policy objectives by arguing that development brings the tax revenue necessary to keep a city running (Molotoch 1976). Planning processes are also often closely aligned with promoting private development and control of land through such mechanisms as targeted public investments, privatization of utilities and other services, public–private development partnerships that can reduce financial risks for private investors, and noneconomic incentives that expedite or waive review and permit processes. Yet the planning process might also demand that the private sector contribute to social and public needs, such as by requiring development impact fees or affordable housing as part of the zoning code or the development review process (Krugman 1998).

The politics of planning is further complicated by democratic demands on the field. The environmental impact assessment process for our hypothetical development, would include at least three, often legally required, opportunities for public participation: (1) during the draft "scoping session" that determines the content of the analytic categories; (2) after the initial draft environmental impact report is issued, and (3) after the final draft environmental impact report is issued. These opportunities for public involvement are often limited to public hearings and written comment periods and are regularly criticized for limiting meaningful opportunities for participation by all members of the public (Petts 1999). But even within these constraints planners can make decisions over the democratic character of planning by doing such things as shaping meeting agendas, timing of meetings, availability of translation services, methods of public deliberation, and processes of resolving controversies and reaching agreement (Forester 1999).

Thus planning processes include a range of often discretionary decisions over the values that a project or plan should promote, how accountable projects and plans are to varying interests, the analytic content and breadth of analyses, and the timing and scope of participation by public and private sector actors and organizations. Since urban planning's history is littered with stories of displacement, power politics, racism, cultural discrimination, and botched attempts at addressing community issues, planning processes also often struggle with how or whether to address the past while orienting action toward the future. The discretionary, value-laden, and public qualities of planning processes suggest that they are a central feature of urban governance.

## Planning Process as Urban Governance

The discretionary decisions, value judgments, and participatory processes in planning comprise a set of institutional urban governance practices. By institutions, I mean not just the formal organizations or rules, such as a planning agency or the rule of law, that shape urban policy decisions but also the set of informal norms, practices, and behaviors that evolve over time and shape public decisions ranging from what counts as appropriate evidence to who gets invited to policy setting discussions. An institutionalist view of planning as urban governance aims to highlight the interrelations between "episodes" of micro-practices, or governance, and the broader socioeconomic and political contexts that influence these practices (Healey 1999).

Central to the institutionalist view of planning is the notion of governance (Innes 1995). The term urban governance is broadly understood as attentive to the relationships between the overlapping spheres of political, economic, and social life in places, namely the city, and how these spheres aim to influence collective action (Cars et al. 2002). Governance is inherently about struggle and conflict, often among institutions and organizations interested in perpetuating the status quo or taking a new, often uncharted and more risky path. Governance, as used here, is defined as "the establishment and operation of social institutions or, in other words, sets of roles, rules, decision making procedures, and programs that serve to define social practices and to guide interactions of those participating in these practices" (Young 1996:247). In other words:

Politically significant institutions or governance systems are arrangements designed to resolve social conflicts, enhance social welfare, and, more generally, alleviate collective action problems in a world of interdependent actors. Governance, on this account, does not presuppose the need to create material entities or organizations—"governments"—to administer the social practices that arise to handle the function of governance. (ibid.)

Indeed the governance view of planning highlights the particular, often explicit, discourses of day-to-day struggles over specific decisions, as well as the more implicit ideologies behind planning practice that transcend particularity, such as neoliberalism or social justice (Nussbaum 2000). The governance view, as conceived here, emphasizes both the processes of planning—the how—and the substantive content and outcomes of these processes—or the distributions of who gets what and when.

By being attentive to more than just the formal processes of spatial planning—such as environmental impact assessment, general plan making, zoning regulations, and other land use planning processes—the urban governance view of planning can engage in an analysis of the forces, both micro and macro, that influence how existing processes, content, and outcomes of spatial planning came to be in the first place and whether and how shifts in power, resources and discourses might act to change these practices (Huxley and Yiftachel 2000). Healthy urban governance is a means toward an end—health equity in this case—and involves critically interrogating whether the taken-for-granted ways of seeing, knowing, and doing in city planning can promote equity. More specifically, such transformative practice involves engaging with:

the governance practices that currently exist and to help governance communities concerned with place qualities to develop different approaches where these are seen to be failing. This involves attention to both discourses and practices; to what already exists, what is emerging and what might possibly emerge in a specific context. In this way, combining analysis with critical evaluation and creative invention, normative precepts should not float away into abstract generalizations, but be grounded in the particularities of specific times and places. (Healey 2003:116)

According to Patsy Healey, professor emeritus in the School of Architecture, Planning and Landscape at the University of Newcastle upon Tyne, the politics of planning is simultaneously about addressing the qualities of place, the processes of decision making that influence these qualities, and grappling with the macro-policy constraints and opportunities that influence local decision making (Healey 2007). Moving toward the healthy city requires a politics of healthy planning that engages with both the *substantive content* of what contributes to human well-being (the substance of health) and the *processes* that make everyday decisions about how or whether to consider these substantive issues (institutions and governance).

### Planning Practice and Human Health

How might the politics of planning, or the urban governance view described above, help us better understand the ways *planning processes* surrounding our hypothetical downtown development might positively and negatively influence human health? In the next section, I compare how typical development planning processes and what I'll call the "healthy urban governance" approach would approach the likely human health impacts of potential noise pollution from our downtown development. I emphasize that both implicit overarching ideologies toward development and environmental impacts and standard operating procedures that have become institutionalized over time act synergistically to direct planning processes away from meaningfully considering the social determinants of health.

While noise is one of the most often cited nuisance complaints in cities, planning processes rarely consider the human health impacts from environmental noise (Passchier-Vermeer and Passchier 2000; Stansfeld et al. 2000). If a planning process were to review the impacts of noise, analysts would likely start by estimating or measuring the existing background noise and then model or predict the likely increase in noise pollution from the development project. The modeling might include increases in noise from vehicular traffic, pedestrians, nightclubs, heating and ventilation equipment, and other noise-producing activities. To determine whether the new development would produce a significant noise impact, analysts would likely use a noise standard of some decibel level over a certain period of time (often during sleeping hours) that is codified in a local environmental regulation. If such a standard does not exist, analysts might find a threshold in the scientific literature that is thought to be the maximum allowable decibel level for certain activities, such as sleeping. If the background measures of noise and the predicted increase meet the threshold, an environmental review would likely rule that there is no significant impact.

Under the "healthy urban governance" view, analyses and potential remedial action would differ both procedurally and substantively. Analyses might start by asking whether the noise might be eliminated or mitigated, even before measurement and examining appropriate thresholds. If noise is inevitable, analysts working under the social determinants and governance view of planning would examine who (which population groups: youth, elderly, etc.) is impacted and at what times of the day or night? In order to answer these and other contextually specific questions, analysts might use surveys, interviews, or focus groups with local residents to learn more about existing and future noise impacts on the local population.

A healthy urban governance approach would also require that analysts trace the multiple and overlapping health effects of noise pollution. For example, noise pollution can contribute to sleep deprivation, a significant health effect. Sleep loss can contribute to added stress, another contributor to poor health and a factor that can adversely impact family and interpersonal relationships and/or school and job performance. For example, stress can trigger asthma and compromise the immune system. Stressful interpersonal relationships might increase the prevalence of domestic and neighborhood violence, and/or unhealthy stress-related behaviors such as overeating, smoking, and drug or alcohol abuse. These behaviors contribute to liver, lung, and cardiovascular disease and increase heart damaging hypertension. Poor workplace performance can contribute to decreased wages or job loss, both of which might lead to trade-offs over paying for rent, food, transportation, or health care. This scenario is not meant to imply that planning processes that fail to consider the cascading impacts from noise pollution are to blame for these outcomes. Rather, this chain of events suggest that planning processes must be critically examined for *how* they can directly and indirectly influence a range of health outcomes and what planners can do to avoid the physical, social, and economic conditions that contribute to health inequities. I offer a brief review of how the healthy urban governance paradigm differs from most current planning practices, especially environmental review processes, in the next section and summarize these differences in table 3.2.

### Air Quality

Almost all urban development has some adverse impact on air quality, from localized particulate pollution to regional ozone pollution to carbon dioxide emissions that contribute to climate change. As described above, the typical planning process analyzes one pollutant at a time and rarely considers the multiple outdoor and indoor air pollutants that can adversely impact vulnerable population groups, such as the elderly, pregnant women, and children. In addition planning processes tend to only consider the proposed project under review, not how the new project might combine with other facilities in the same area (as well as mobile or vehicular sources of pollution) to create a cumulative air quality burden on the surrounding population.

Instead of analyzing one facility and pollutant at a time, the governance view of planning might use spatial analyses to capture cumulative air pollution burdens. New monitoring protocols, where pollution is measured at multiple locations across a neighborhood, would then be required to ensure that planning processes have adequate data to conduct cumulative exposure analyses. Urban planning processes might also consider hazardous air pollutants or air toxics, which the US EPA has identified as adversely influencing a range of human health outcomes from carcinogenesis to asthma.[19] Local concentrations of hazardous air pollutants, like other harmful air pollutants, tend to be located in low-income communities of color (Payne-Sturges et al. 2004). The California Environmental Protection Agency has studied the links between concentrations of air toxics in cities and land use policies, noting that these pollutants are routinely ignored in environmental review processes (Cal EPA 2005). Healthy city planning would analyze these air toxics, assess whether certain land uses and practices, such as zoning, are exacerbating pollutant concentrations in communities of color, and devise interventions to prevent their release in the first place. Healthy urban governance would also assess whether there is a cumulative burden of multiple air pollutants in an area and whether air

**Table 3.2**
City planning processes and human health impacts

| Health resource | Social and physical influences on health | Example of healthy planning processes |
|---|---|---|
| Environmental quality, including noise, air, soil, and water pollution | • Vehicle emissions exacerbate respiratory disease and increase cardiopulmonary mortality, while indoor allergens exacerbate asthma<br>• Chronic noise exposure adversely harms sleep, temperament, hearing, and blood pressure, all of which can lead to developmental delays in children<br>• Trees and green space remove air pollution from the air and mitigate the urban heat island effect | • Ongoing environmental monitoring at the "street-level" to capture cumulative exposures, especially in low-income/people of color communities<br>• Productive and appropriate re-use of previously contaminated sites, or brown fields<br>• Eliminate risk assessment as the only environmental health analytic tool<br>• Enforcement and expansion of urban lead abatement programs |
| Access to high-quality transit and safe roadways, sidewalks, and bicycle lanes | • Vehicle/pedestrian injuries are most severe where sidewalks and crosswalks are nonexistent<br>• Sidewalks and bicycle lanes facilitate physical activity, reducing heart disease, diabetes, obesity, blood pressure, osteoporosis, and symptoms of depression.<br>• Public transit provides access to employment, education, parks, and health care services | • Coordinated transportation, land use, housing, economic development, and public health strategies<br>• Transit plans that serve and link isolated, low-income communities throughout a metropolitan region<br>• Traffic calming, bicycle and pedestrian circulation plans |
| Access to quality child care, education, and health care facilities | • Quality child care can build disease immunities and increase likelihood of future educational attainment and earnings<br>• Education can enhance health literacy about preventative behaviors and services<br>• Timely access to primary health services prevents serious illness | • Reforms to school financing to create more equity in urban school funding compared to suburbs<br>• Land use/zoning rules requiring employers of certain size to provide child care and income supports for employees with newborns<br>• Planning "safe routes" to schools<br>• Planning neighborhood health centers |

**Table 3.2**
(continued)

| Health resource | Social and physical influences on health | Example of healthy planning processes |
|---|---|---|
| Affordable, safe, stable and socially integrated housing | • Crowded and substandard housing conditions increase risks for infections, respiratory disease, fires, and stress<br>• Unaffordable rents or mortgages result in trade-offs among housing, food, and medical care<br>• Racial residential segregation limits economic and educational opportunities, concentrates disadvantage, and increases social distance between racial/ethnic groups | • Integrated local and regional plans for new public and affordable housing<br>• Zoning and local tax incentives to upgrade older housing to new "green" and healthy standards<br>• Include and increase inclusionary housing requirements in zoning code<br>• Local and regional plans for racially and economically integrated neighborhoods |
| Access to safe and quality open space, parks, cultural and recreational facilities | • Clean and safe parks can increase the frequency of physical activity<br>• Cultural activities can promote cross-cultural understanding, decrease violence, and enhance social cohesion | • Park and open space plans that account for distribution of access across neighborhoods and recreation/activity needs for specific cultural and ethnic populations<br>• Zoning requiring school playgrounds and facilities to be open to public use outside school hours |
| Employment providing meaningful, safe, and living wage jobs | • Higher income is associated with better overall health, reduced mortality, and higher emotional stability<br>• Unemployment is a source of chronic stress, while job autonomy increases self-esteem | • Living wage requirements within zoning code or other city policies<br>• Zoning incentives for locally owned and operated businesses<br>• Local land use plans that promote "green collar" jobs through partnerships between public, community-based and private sectors |

**Table 3.2**
(continued)

| Health resource | Social and physical influences on health | Example of healthy planning processes |
|---|---|---|
| Access to affordable and quality goods and services | • Neighborhood grocery stores support nutritious diets<br>• Local financial institutions help families create and maintain wealth | • Zoning rules that target retail needs of an area, such as grocery stores and financial institutions, and limit the concentration of liquor and fast food stores<br>• Zoning that limits targeted advertising of tobacco and alcohol products<br>• Land use plans for urban organic agriculture and farmers markets |
| Protection from crime and physical violence | • Indirect effects of violence and crime include fear, stress, anxiety, and unhealthy coping behaviors, overeating, smoking, and alcohol/ drug abuse<br>• Fear of crime can force children to stay indoors, increasingly exposure to toxic indoor air and allergens, and limiting physical activity outside | • Plans that increase street activity and provide adequate lighting<br>• Planning for community facilities for youth and job training<br>• Community policing |
| Social cohesion and political power | • Physical and emotional support buffers stressful situations, prevents isolation, contributes to self-esteem and reduces the risk of early death.<br>• Stress from severed/lack of social ties/support can contribute to low birth weight, increasing risk of infant death, slow cognitive development, hyperactivity, overweight, and heart disease | • Public participation plans meaningfully include community members, especially marginalized and disadvantaged groups<br>• Governmental commitment to implement procedural and distributive goals of environmental justice<br>• Effective participation of marginalized groups in governance can shift balance of decision-making power and ensure that basic needs are served |

pollution is combining with other environmental stressors, such as noise pollution, to burden particular places and population groups.

## Pedestrian Injuries and Activity

Pedestrian conflicts with motor vehicles are one of the leading causes of injuries in urban areas. When a new development project includes housing and commercial activity, pedestrian traffic increases, and this can lead to an increase in conflicts with vehicles and related injuries. Locating development in areas with high traffic volumes can also exacerbate injuries. However, greater pedestrian activity can promote physical activity that reduces heart disease, stroke, and mental illness (Chu et al. 2004). Creating new opportunities for pedestrian activity can also improve well-being by increasing the likelihood of social interactions that can reduce feelings of isolation (Addy et al. 2004).

Planning processes, from transportation, park, and open space plans to streetscape and bicycle path designs, not only need to examine their positive and negative influences on pedestrian injuries and activity but also need to recognize that not all population groups have the time or resources to take part in recreational activities outside of their daily routines. The governance view of planning combines analyses of the physical features that might promote activity with social, cultural, and economic assessments of the resources, norms, and values different groups might place on physical activity. Healthy urban governance would focus on how to integrate opportunities for safe physical activity into everyday life tasks.

## Transit and Land Use Sprawl

Inner-city or "in-fill" development can reduce suburban sprawl and related health impacts, such as the loss of open space, longer commute times, less time with family, increased air pollution, and greater transportation costs due to longer commutes (Ewing et al. 2003; Frumkin 2002). Well functioning transit that serves all population groups and areas of a city—regardless of class—can reduce health inequities while also improving regional air quality for all groups. Lack of adequate public transit can increase stress and reduce time with family and building social relationship, as commuters are forced to spend more time in their cars (Dora and Phillips 1999). Public transit also improves health by providing a vital means for many to get to work, school, child care, grocery stores, banks, and health care, especially for low-income populations that have low rates of car ownership (Besser and Dannenberg 2005). For the elderly and disabled populations, the absence of or limited access to public transit can create barriers to participation in community and civic life, often contributing to depression and social alienation (Cunningham and Michael 2004).

Transportation planning, as discussed in chapter 2, has a history of being detrimental to urban health, by doing such things as constructing highways that bifurcate communities, destroying health supportive family and social ties, and, in some cases, limiting physical access to essential goods and services (Fullilove 2004; Mohl 2000). Healthy urban governance would assess which populations groups and areas are served by transit and transportation plans and whether currently underserved groups will have greater access to essential health-supportive needs, from grocery stores and financial institutions to employment centers and health care facilities.

### Education and Child Care
More years of education not only protect against almost every adverse health outcome, but higher education is also strongly correlated with higher incomes (Adler and Newman 2002). Incomes for workers with less than a college degree have stagnated or decreased since the 1980s (Mishel et al. 2007). Yet, as with many other issues, educational attainment and adult wealth is often influenced by early-life events. Children from wealthier families tend to enjoy high-quality preschool education, which puts them at an advantage in kindergarten, and these same children tend to continue to reap advantages as they move through the education system and enter the job market (Case et al. 2005). Due to social stress, discrimination, poor access to nutrition and pre-natal care, toxic exposures in the home environment, and other factors, low-income populations and people of color tend to have babies with low birth weights (Collins et al. 2004). The consequences of low birth weights include slow cognitive development, hyperactivity, breathing problems, and greater likelihood of being overweight and having heart disease later in life (Galobardes et al. 2004). Low birth weight is also thought to adversely affect academic achievement and attainment later in life (Conley and Bennett 2000). Disparities in public spending on education, school quality, and educational achievement closely track disparities in health (Lynch 2003).

While educational attainment is regularly understood as a key driver of well-being and linked to health disparities, city planning processes regularly fail to consider urban educational quality as an "environmental impact" or an indicator of the success or failure of the field.[20] A healthy urban governance approach would analyze existing school quality, performance, and future needs, critically evaluate the role of land use policies in shaping educational outcomes, and ensure that development decisions across a city include commitments to providing space for child care facilities and resources to improve existing schools.

## Housing and Residential Environments

The human health impacts of housing range from direct influences such as exposures to lead paint, mold, pesticides, and indoor air pollution to indirect influences such as the stress of displacement, increased social segregation, and decreased wealth as a greater proportion of income is spent on housing (Krieger and Higgins 2002). Indoor allergens, such as mold and cockroach dander, exacerbate asthma in children. Unaffordable housing can force low-income populations to accept unsafe or crowded housing, which increase the likelihood of fatal fires, and exposures to environmental hazards, such as inadequate heating, lead-based paint, unprotected windows, and inadequate ventilation. When housing costs are high, members of low-income households often work long hours and multiple jobs to afford rent, limiting the time available for sleep, recreation, and family. Spending more of household income on rent often means doing without other health-promoting necessities such as food, clothing, transportation, and health care.

## Racial Residential Segregation

Racial residential segregation is the most detrimental housing-related influence on health inequities in the United States (Acevedo-Garcia et al. 2003; Williams and Collins 2001; Massey and Denton 1993).[21] Williams and Collins (2001) suggest that racial residential segregation adversely impacts overall mortality, birth outcomes, rates of tuberculosis, and depression for people of color by (1) concentrating poverty, (2) reducing access to quality education, (3) limiting well-paying employment opportunities, (4) increasing resident exposures to dangers and toxins, ranging from violence and crime related stress to concentrations of polluting facilities, and (5) limiting access to essential services like grocery stores, banks, and basic medical services. While segregated neighborhoods may also provide some health-supportive protections, such as social support and kin-care networks, and reduce exposure to chronic discrimination (Geronimus and Thompson 2004), racial residential segregation is suspected of being a key driver for understanding and addressing health inequities in the United States (Avecedo-Garcia 2004; Morello-Frosh and Jesdale 2006).

Healthy urban governance recognizes that racial residential segregation is the result of historical and contemporary policies, such as the GI Bill and federal home mortgage subsidies, which allowed white Americans to take advantage of opportunities while restricting participation by people of color, mostly African-Americans. As chapter 2 reviewed, the Federal Housing Administration supported the sale of new homes in racially homogeneous white suburban neighborhoods while also encouraging home buyers to adopt racial covenants that precluded the sale of subsidized homes to nonwhites (Frug 1999). While both racial covenants and racist mortgage insurance policies were declared unconstitutional in 1948, their legacy prompted private companies to engage in redlining practices and subprime lending that continue to shape housing market outcomes in the twenty-first century (Bajaj and Story 2008).

Segregated communities are also health-damaging because they stymie social relationships among different groups, increasing so-called social distance (Frug 1999). Massey and Denton (1993:2) captured the multiple overlapping impacts residential segregation can have on well-being by noting that:

Housing, after all, is much more than shelter: it provides social status, access to jobs, education, and other services. Residential segregation is self-perpetuating, for in segregated neighborhoods the damaging social consequences that follow from increased poverty are spatially concentrated . . . creating uniquely disadvantaged environments that become progressively isolated—geographically, socially, and economically—from the rest of society.

While housing policy is a central focus of city planning activities, analyses and plan-making rarely consider how characteristics of the residential environment—from housing quality and affordability to levels of segregation to the proximity of employment and services to housing—combine to influence human health. Residential environments include the locational attributes of housing *and* the physical and social attributes of its surroundings as well as the "acts of residence" together as a set of relationships (Hartig and Lawrence 2003). Residential environment and health is a much more inclusive term than "housing and health" and captures the interactions between built structures' occupants and their activities, between the meanings assigned to "home" and the influence of neighboring physical and social characteristics and forces. Embracing healthy urban governance means focusing on improving residential environments, not just building "healthy housing."

## Open Space, Parks, and Recreation

Safe and easily accessible spaces to walk and recreate are likely to increase regular physical activity. Physical activity can reduce the risk of developing heart disease, diabetes, osteoporosis, and obesity; lower blood pressure; relieve symptoms of depression and anxiety; and prevent the likelihood of mental illness (Diez Roux et al. 1997; 2001; De Vries et al. 2002). Parks and open spaces can provide a place for social interaction, which can reduce depression. Trees and green space also improve the physical environment by removing pollution from the air and reducing the impacts of extreme heat event in cities, or urban heat islands, that result in heat-related mortality and morbidity related to heat stroke, exhaustion, and cardiovascular and respiratory stress (Semenza et al. 1999). Healthy urban governance would emphasize more than just the presence or absence of open space and its proximity to residents but also whether the space is conducive to use by local populations. This assessment should include such questions as whether the park or playground is safe, clean, and maintained well; serves a range of users; and includes locally relevant programming (sports, cultural activities, etc.)?

## Employment and Economic Opportunities

Employment, income, and wealth, or class, are perhaps the most often cited nonmedical determinant of health and explanation for persistent health inequities (Acheson et al. 1998; Kaplan et al. 1996; Kawachi and Kennedy 1999; Wilkinson 1996). Unemployment not only reduces material resources but is a source of chronic stress and low self-esteem; meaningful employment can help promote self-identity and a sense of control (Fone and Dunstan 2006). Nonphysical job stressors such as excessive work load, shift work, low control, threats of pay cuts or job loss, and conflicts between family obligations and work demands contribute significantly to poor physical and mental health, most acutely for the working poor (Marmot et al. 2005). Since health insurance is often tied to employment in the United States, quality health care is often linked to secure and stable employment. Higher incomes allow some groups to sort themselves into "health protective environments," away from the noise and toxins of industries and highways and into communities with quality public services and amenities, including police and emergency services, education, and other physical and social infrastructure. Accumulated wealth and assets protect families against short-term economic instability and related physical deprivation and psychosocial stress that can adversely impact health.

The economic "environment" also influences well-being. Neighborhoods with high concentrations of liquor stores also have high rates of addiction. However, local businesses can act as sources of employment, culturally appropriate foods, and other services. Displacement of local businesses can adversely impact health by altering the availability and affordability of essential goods and services and the type of local employment possibilities. Business displacement can also contribute to physical blight—the tooth-gaped landscape all too common in poor neighborhoods where widespread property abandonment has taken hold. Property abandonment can adversely influence health by increasing the likelihood of illegal dumping of garbage and hazardous wastes, increased criminal activity, and injection drug use (Wallace and Wallace 1990).

While many planning processes aim to spatially assess socioeconomic conditions, and special economic investment districts are a tool increasingly used by planners to stimulate investment in low-income communities, these and related economic planning processes rarely evaluate their impacts on human health. Healthy urban governance would attach health protective measures to economic development decisions, such as requiring employers to pay a living wage and to provide health insurance and paid sick days for employees. Healthy urban governance would also pay explicit attention to who (the chronically unemployed, low-skilled workers, etc.) might benefit from economic development and employment decisions. For example, healthy urban governance might explore ways that economic development decisions could promote "green collar jobs," or new employment opportunities in disadvantaged neighborhoods that offer workers living wages, safe working conditions, and chances for advancement and allow workers to contribute to the environmental health of their communities such as through recycling, organic urban agriculture, auditing and retrofitting buildings to be more energy-efficient, and installing and maintaining renewable energy-generating technologies (Jones 2008). According to Van Jones (2008:12):

[A green-collar job is a] family-supporting, career-track job that contributes to preserving or enhancing environmental quality. Like traditional blue-collar jobs, green-collar jobs range from low-skilled, entry-level positions to high-skill, high-paid jobs . . . we should never consider a job that does something for the planet and little to nothing for the people or economy as fitting the definition of a green-collar job. . . . We must ensure that all green-collar-job strategies provide opportunities for low-income people to take the first step on a pathway to economic self-sufficiency and prosperity.

## Goods, Services and Health Care

Good health is also influenced by access to quality goods and services, including nutritious and affordable food, child care, social services, financial institutions, and health care facilities (Cummins et al. 2005). Access to full service and affordable grocery stores and farmer's markets can increase the likelihood that local people will eat nutritious food, while a plethora of liquor stores and junk-food outlets decrease the likelihood of healthy eating (Flournoy and Treuhaft 2005). Local financial institutions, such as banks not check-cashing storefronts, help families and small businesses gain access to credit that can create and maintain wealth. The location of hospitals and clinics in an area increase the likelihood that residents will seek acute and preventative care and avoid serious hospitalizations (AHRQ 2005).

Healthy urban governance focuses on the policies and land use decisions that have acted to discourage the siting of libraries, grocery stores, banks, and hospitals in low-income neighborhoods while encouraging a plethora of liquor stores and fast food restaurants in these same places. Healthy urban governance would include analyses that aim to connect the availability of and access to essential goods and services with transportation planning and housing decisions both within a city and across an entire metropolitan region. Healthy urban governance would also consider practices that couple the delivery of basic goods with medical or health-promoting services, particularly in low-income communities, such as programs that combine expanding urban agriculture with healthy cooking and nutrition education (Peoples Grocery 2008) and micro-credit programs where lenders also provide health care (Lashey 2008).

## Social Cohesion and Exclusion

Social cohesion or exclusion can influence well-being by encouraging or stymieing interpersonal relationships with family, friends, and/or neighbors. These relationships can promote health by providing physical and emotional support that buffer stressful situations, contribute to illness recovery, prevent isolation, and contribute to increased self-esteem (Adler and Newman 2002; McEwen and Seeman 1999). A social network might also offer health promoting information, such as where to find a good doctor or child care, upcoming employment and educational opportunities, or where to get the lowest price for a good or service, such as food or a new checking account. Social cohesion also includes participating in organizations, which can contribute to well-being by exerting collective power to influence a political decision, such as shaping a legislative agenda or stopping a development project deemed locally undesirable. Social support can serve as a buffer against race-related stress (Williams 1999) and stigmatization (Jones 2000). In a race-conscious society the stress-mitigation and access to power that social connections and social networks can provide for people of color act as a powerful determinant of health (Geronimus and Thompson 2004).

The public participation aspects of planning processes offer planners numerous opportunities to promote social cohesion and build social networks, particularly between disparate groups. Unfortunately, planners rarely see public participation processes as opportunities to build lasting social relationships and enhance community cohesion (Forester 1999; Healey 2003). Community involvement processes within planning have become exercises that aim to avoid conflict, limit public deliberation, and placate interest groups. Healthy urban governance would focus on expanding opportunities for meaningful public involvement and recast public participation as an opportunity to improve community health, not just the democratic character of public decisions.

The challenges for healthy urban governance are, first, to recognize that many local planning decisions and institutions shape the social determinants of health; second, to find new ways to incorporate analyses of the social determinants into existing planning practices; and third, to explore policy and decision-making alternatives that avoid the adverse health impacts of planning decisions and promote the conditions that contribute to positive health outcomes for all, but especially populations experiencing greatest social and health inequities. The next chapter explores these three challenges in more detail and offers a set of political frames for moving toward the healthy city.

# 4 Toward a Politics of Healthy City Planning

Incorporating the social and physical determinants of health into the healthy urban governance view of city planning will require a new politics of planning. As noted in chapter 2, very few historical practices have aimed to combine the social determinants of health equity with governance practices; many of the progressive urban reforms of the last century were top-down projects, not collaborations among different disciplines, professions, bureaucracies, community organizations, and the private sector. Recall from the historical review of the fields of planning and public health in chapter 2 that at least five interrelated forces helped to both separate the fields and remain encoded as contemporary barriers for moving toward a new politics of healthy city planning.

One of the first challenges for a new politics of healthy city planning is to avoid reacting to and removing urban problems and instead work to prevent harms in the first place. Yet preventative strategies will need to acknowledge and redress the uneven distributional impacts that removing environmental pollution, "blighted" infrastructure and "pathogenic people" has had on some urban neighborhoods. Urban policy and planning decisions have left a legacy of physical deprivation along with social and psychological scars for neighborhoods of the poor and people of color, and these issues must be addressed while also developing new strategies to prevent future harms.

A second challenge is for planners to temper their commitments to scientific rationality and technological determinism and recognize that the science underwriting healthy city planning will require new experimentation and innovation—in analytic methods and monitoring. This new science for healthy city planning will need to cross traditional disciplinary boundaries and be shaped as much by social commitments to equity as by available technologies. The new science of the city will need to be co-produced, where social and political commitments are viewed as not contaminating but enhancing the social and political relevance of regulatory science (Jasanoff 2004).

A third challenge for healthy city planning is to avoid moral environmentalism and physical determinism, or the notions that immoral behaviors are to blame for unsanitary and unhealthy environments and that physical changes to the built environment by themselves can change group behaviors. Planners of the healthy city must recognize that the physical environment is one, but not the only or most powerful, influence on human well-being. People cannot be portrayed as passive in environment-behavior relationships, just as political and social processes behind the shaping of physical environments cannot be neglected. Importantly the new politics of healthy city planning must treat the physical, social, and political aspects of places relationally, which means recognizing that places attain meaning and significance through the interactions and relations among all its constituent parts, not through any one part alone.

A fourth challenge for the new politics of healthy city planning is that focusing on either the "laboratory" or "field site" view of the city is insufficient for addressing urban inequalities and health disparities. As I showed in chapter 2, an overreliance on the "laboratory view" has caused many urban health interventions to overlook the particularities of places that can ensure policies are relevant to contexts and incorporate local knowledge. However, an overreliance on the "field-site" view of cities can limit the scaling-up of interventions and fail to take advantage of advances in medical and other technologies. Moving toward a new politics of healthy city planning requires critically embracing a population health perspective where planners, public health practitioners, and others work together to explain how place-based conditions are biologically embodied. As I discuss below, the embodiment idea brings together the laboratory view—by acknowledging the importance of biologic processes without equating "biologic" with "innate"—and the field-site view, by emphasizing that both physical and social contexts influence health outcomes while avoiding social determinism.

A fifth challenge for the new politics of healthy city planning is to address the disciplinary specialization, bureaucratic fragmentation, and professionalization currently plaguing both planning and public health and acting as a barrier toward crafting a coordinated, healthy city research and action agenda. New models of collaborative research and urban governance will

**Table 4.1**

Toward a politics of healthy and equitable city planning

| Unhealthy city-planning frame | | Healthy and equitable city-planning frame |
|---|---|---|
| Removal of hazards and people | ⟹ | Prevention and precaution |
| Overreliance on scientific rationality | ⟹ | Co-production of scientific knowledge New measurement and monitoring networks |
| Moral environmentalism and Physical determinism | ⟹ | Relational view of places |
| Laboratory view of city | ⟹ | Field site and laboratory view of population health and embodiment |
| Professionalization, fragmentation, and specialization | ⟹ | Cross-disciplinary collaborations and regional coalition building |

need to accompany the construction of new, cross-disciplinary and sector coalitions both within and outside government. Regional or metropolitan coalitions that can build on local knowledge and expertise will be critical in shaping new institutional practices for promoting healthy city planning. This chapter details the new political frames needed for moving toward the healthy city (table 4.1).

### From Removal to Prevention and Precaution

As discussed in chapter 2, during much of the nineteenth and twentieth centuries the fields of planning and public health responded to real or perceived urban health crises by *physically removing and displacing* wastes and people, primarily poor immigrants and African-Americans. This was evident from the waste removal programs of the Sanitary Era through the discriminatory housing and urban renewal policies of the postwar period. Policy makers often justified removal strategies by referencing dominant paradigms of disease causation of the day, such as miasma and contagion, and moving toward a new politics of healthy city planning will require a new paradigm of precaution and prevention.

The precautionary principle, now widely used to guide environmental health decision making in Europe,[22] may be a more appropriate social justice frame through which to grapple with contemporary challenges for reconnecting urban planning and public health. The precautionary principle is an analytic and decision-making framework that seeks to reduce or eliminate pathogenic exposures, to ecosystems and humans, by first asking whether a toxin or proposed policy is needed, setting environmental and public health performance goals with impacted stakeholders and collaboratively reviewing prevention scenarios, even in the absence of definitive proof of harm (Tickner and Geiser 2004). Drawing from the clinical notion of "first, do no harm," the precautionary principle challenges current environmental health regulatory models where the state is responsible for generating scientific proof of harm before taking regulatory action. Instead, the precautionary approach demands that preventive and protective action should be taken even in the face of uncertain science and that the burden of proof of safety rests with those who create risks. By requiring action in the face of uncertainty, the precautionary principle also demands that alternative courses of action are explored, often redirecting environmental health science and policy from describing problems to identifying solutions.[23]

Yet orientations to prevention, particularly in public health can differ radically. For example, the health departments of New York City and San Francisco have taken two very different orientations to preventing illness (table 4.2). In New York the health department set ten objectives, called Take Care New York, that focus on clinical activities and interventions. San Francisco developed a set of preventative strategies as part of a public process that focus on changing the structural conditions that contribute to poor health. Resources for prevention are likely to focus on very different interventions in New York and in San Francisco.

## Epidemic of People Removal: Incarceration and Foster Care

A preventative and precautionary framework might also address the modern urban "epidemics" of people removal, such as foster care and incarceration (Roberts 2003; Wacquant 2002). In 2000 African-American children were four times as likely as white children to be in foster care, and in cities such as Chicago and New York, African-American children are ten times as likely as white children to be in the child protection system (Roberts 2003). Many children of color grow up in neighborhoods where state supervision is commonplace, while relatively few white children do. Planners have yet to address how the spatial concentration of foster care is shaping how young people view themselves, their families, their communities, and their chances of living a life independent of state

**Table 4.2**
Approaches to preventing illness in New York City and San Francisco

| Take Care New York, 2004[1] | SF Department of Public Health, Prevention Strategic Plan, 2004 to 2008[2] |
| --- | --- |
| • Have a regular doctor or other health care provider<br>• Be tobacco free<br>• Keep your heart healthy<br>• Know your HIV status<br>• Get help for depression<br>• Live free of dependence on alcohol and drugs<br>• Get checked for cancer<br>• Get the immunizations you need<br>• Make your home safe and healthy<br>• Have a healthy baby | Advocate for policies such as:<br>• Living wages<br>• Employment development/full employment<br>• Results-based employment training<br>• Adequate supply of high-quality child care<br>• Improve quality and quantity of housing<br>• Strong social safety net<br>• Improved public transportation<br>• Increased public participation in political and social organizations<br>• Improved availability of respite services<br>• Equal and fair education policies |

1. New York City Department of Health and Mental Hygiene. 2004. *Take Care New York.* www.nyc.gov/html/doh/tcny/index.html.
2. San Francisco Department of Public Health. 2004. *Prevention Strategic Plan, 2004–2008.* www.dph.sf.ca.us/reports/prevplan5yr/prevPlan5yrMain.pdf.

supervision. Dorothy Roberts (2003) notes in her book, *Shattered Bonds: The Color of Child Welfare,* that the foster care system's urban racial geography has negative consequences by interfering with a community's ability to form healthy connections among its members and to engage in collective action. Such intensive, concentrated state regulation, Roberts argues, can disrupt family and community networks that prepare children for civic life and self-governance, all forces that act as powerful social determinants of health equity.

American jail populations reflect similar characteristics of the foster care system, as they are disproportionately young, urban, African-American, and Latino men. These same groups also have some of the poorest health outcomes in the United States. Incarceration has created a planning and public health challenge by spatially concentrating both the removal of young men from families and the workforce and the social stress that accompanies inmates' return to their neighborhoods (Conklin et al. 1998).

For instance, in New York City almost 70 percent of the 2002 jail population came from one of three neighborhoods, the South Bronx, Harlem, and Central Brooklyn, more than half are released and return to jail within the same year, and the city spends over $92,000 per year to incarcerate one person (Bloomberg 2003; NYC DOC 2003). The constant cycle of incarceration and reentry in New York and other urban areas has brought the health issues of prisons into the neighborhood, including infectious disease, addiction, mental health problems, and routine physical violence. Yet returning inmates face homelessness, family evictions from public housing, denial of food stamps, terminated Medicaid benefits, and regular workplace discrimination (Steinhauer 2004).

In New York City, a neighborhood-focused reintegration project, called the Community Reintegration Network, is working to address the strains on public safety, community health, family stability, and municipal budgets that come from neighborhood concentrations of former inmates (Von Zielbauer 2003). As a partner in this coalition, the Vera Institute of Justice launched Project Greenlight, which prepares inmates for release and reintegration by matching them with programs and organizations in their home community, including supportive and special needs housing, drug-treatment programs, job training, and health clinics (Brown and Campell 2005). While these initiatives aim to build one-stop locations for housing, job training, social, and health services, city planners have a unique opportunity to reconnect with the social justice roots of the profession by participating in community-based reentry programs and to offer their knowledge of spatial and social programming in helping reduce recidivism (Black and Cho 2004). In the twenty-first century foster care, incarceration, and community reentry must become planning and public health issues so that, for instance, municipal funds are redirected to provide the place-based housing, education, employment, and social services necessary to support neighborhoods that house foster children, prevent recidivism, and reduce the community impacts of foster care and incarceration.

## From Scientific Rationality to the Co-production of Scientific Knowledge

Scientific rationality and economic efficiency arguments acted to justify many urban health interventions during the nineteenth and twentieth centuries. Restoring order and normalcy to "pathogenic" cities with scientific methods and new technologies, often justified using cost–benefit analyses, was the driving paradigm in both fields. Science was viewed as "normal," or paradigmatic in the sense described by the philosopher of science Thomas Kuhn, where independent reviewers—recognized members of the scientific specialty within which normal science was conducted—were employed to help ensure that researchers were applying the standards of their field rigorously, consistently, and without bias or deception.

Yet healthy city planning will require evidence from a range of disparate disciplines and includes a high degree of uncertainty with regard to the causal mechanisms between exposures and health outcomes. As noted earlier, healthy city planning will also need to transcend traditional disciplinary boundaries and experiment with new analytic methods and an unconventional evidence base to make timely, politically sensitive decisions. All these characteristics encompass what Funtowicz and Ravetz (1993) have called "post-normal" science. In post-normal science, social and public policies ask questions of science that conventional scientific methods alone can not answer and instead, policy decisions must rely on new science that:

1. crosses disciplinary lines;
2. enters into previously unknown investigative territories;
3. requires the deployment of new methods, instruments, protocols, and experimental systems; and
4. involves politically sensitive processes and results (Jasanoff 1990).

Healthy city planning requires a new orientation to science that embraces these characteristics and aims to incorporate them into the analytic and intervention process.

The co-production framework offers one such orientation to science that aims to embrace the social, uncertain, and emergent characteristics of healthy city planning. The co-production idea suggests that science and technology are not "contaminated" by input from social and political institutions and actors, but rather that science and technology should be understood as embedded in "social practices, identities, norms, conventions, discourses, instruments, and institutions—in short, in all the building blocks of what we term the social" (Jasanoff 2004:3). Co-production aims not only to bring the social back into science policy making but also to explore how this knowledge is applied, stabilized, and institutionalized over time, and as such is a critique of the realist ideology that persistently separates the domains of nature, facts, objectivity, and reason from those of culture, values, subjectivity, and emotion in policy and politics more generally.

The frame of co-production aims to open up how authoritative technical knowledge is produced in society and gets stabilized and institutionalized over time so that it becomes a "given" or taken for granted truth. Co-production also extends Habermas's (1975) critical discussion of "decisionism", or a model where policy processes are conceptualized as a series of completely unrelated decisions over issue meaning, authority, and legitimacy, each one of which has no interaction with any other. Instead, co-production aims to problematize the origins and substance of the meanings of policy issues, who was included or left out of generating these meanings, and builds on constructivist work in the social sciences highlighting that scientific legitimacy is simultaneously a social, political, and material phenomenon, none of which can be disentangled from the other (Hacking 1999). The notion of co-production also aims to extend analyses within the interpretive turn in the social sciences, particularly poststructuralist frameworks, by highlighting the often invisible role of knowledge, expertise, technical practices, and material objects in shaping, sustaining, subverting, or transforming relations of authority, particularly that of the state (Scott 1998).

Co-production as used here should not be viewed as a full fledged theory—claiming law-like consistency and predictive power—but rather as an idiom, or a way of interpreting and accounting for complex phenomena so as to avoid the strategic deletions and omissions of most other approaches to understanding the roles of the public and nondisciplinary actors in science policy (Jasanoff 2004:3). For example, Hacking (1999) describes how the American legal and policy processes created new "social kinds" of child abuse and "recovery memory" in response to specific cultural anxieties of the 1980s and, in the process, generated "objective" evidence of these phenomena. In another example of co-production, Evelyn Fox Keller (1985:131) showed how concepts central to the practice of science, such as objectivity and disinterestedness, came to be gendered as masculine through centuries of rhetorical usage and that the construction of the "laws of nature" have political origins. Thus a central aim of the co-productionist framework is to help clarify how power originates, where it gets lodged, who wields it, by what means, and with what effect within the complex network of science policy making (Wynne 2003).

### New Measurement and Monitoring Networks
One application of the co-production idea for healthy city planning practice is through new forms of measurement and monitoring of health equity

in places and for populations. In West Oakland, California, a coalition of residents formed a partnership in 2000 with a nonprofit technical assistant organization called the Pacific Institute and created the West Oakland Environmental Indicators Project (WOEIP) in order to measure and track the hazards the community faced (Pacific Institute 2003). According to Dr. Anthony Iton, director of the Alameda County Health Department, West Oakland has one of the greatest air pollution burdens compared to almost any other area in the state of California and for each resident, approximately 9.4 pounds of diesel particulate matter is emitted locally each year, compared with an average of 1.3 pounds per resident for Alameda County and the state of California more generally (Iton 2007). The Alameda County Department of Public Health estimates that due to the concentrations of diesel particulate air pollution in the neighborhood, West Oakland residents have a lifetime cancer risk of 1,201 per million (or 12 per 10,000), while the US EPA acceptable threshold is 1 per million (Iton 2007). While air pollution was the most obvious target, the collaborative identified seventeen issues that community members hypothesized were contributing to poor health, ranging from air pollution and toxic contamination to gentrification and a lack of political power (Gordon 2007). The group noted that neighborhood-scale data about these issues did not exist, and according to local activist Margaret Gordon (2007), the lack of locally specific information, "made it harder for us to make the case to public agencies and others that there was a serious problem here, that the issues were all related, and that agencies at many levels needed to take action now."

The WOEIP selected six major indicator categories to measure and track: air quality and health, the physical environment, toxics, transportation, civic engagement, and gentrification and displacement (Pacific Institute 2002:10–11). Within each of these six categories a number of indicators were selected where data were easily available and local residents could gather, analyze, and monitor ongoing progress. A major aim of the project was to avoid selecting indicators that would leave the group dependent on outside technical assistance (Gordon 2007). The end result was not only a list of indicators and accompanying data but a process that hypothesized links between community health, economic opportunities, housing, and political power. According to organizer Margaret Gordon:

What we have done is show that measuring and addressing "environmental" inequalities in this place can't be done without also understanding related issues of housing and displacement, economic development opportunities, and community power. For our community, environmental indicators are about overall community well-being, not just diesel air pollution. (Gordon, quoted in CEHTP 2006)

The work of the WOEIP has begun to slowly reap rewards. For example, a West Oakland Project Area Committee (WOPAC) was created to advise the city's Planning Department and city council on redevelopment activities throughout the neighborhood (WOPAC 2006). The Region IX office of the US EPA approached the WOEIP, and after a year of meetings to develop a collaborative agreement and set of principles, the two are partnering to reduce truck traffic pollution, launch a healthy homes project, identify Brownfield sites for remediation, and engage in health impact assessments of development projects (US EPA 2006). Local activist Margaret Gordon was appointed to the Port Commission in 2007, which is drafting the Port of Oakland's Maritime Air Quality Improvement Plan (Port of Oakland 2007).

The WOEIP suggests that experiments in measurement and monitoring, when associated with political coalitions, have the potential to tie together innovations in the production of knowledge and the ordering of political activity. The WOEIP rejected the notion that the community should adopt a set of standard indicators or replicate the "best practices" from other localities. Instead, the WOEIP work acted as a "technology of visibility and accountability," since their indicators and monitoring aimed to make visible community values while at the same time acting to hold government and the private sector accountable. The WOEIP not only measured community environmental health hazards in new ways, but the Port of Oakland and the US EPA regional office took the claims of the group so seriously that they developed new practices to assess their work (in the case of the Oakland port) and partner with the organization to develop new intervention programs (in the case of the EPA). In these ways innovations in measurement and monitoring can and do contribute to transformations within both governance and government.

The work of the WOEIP also highlights that co-producing science for health equity requires incorporating local knowledge into measurement, assessment, and monitoring. Local knowledge includes the experiences and narratives shared by populations living with persistent hazardous exposures, chronic diseases, and social marginalization, and it is a valuable form of "expertise" that can temper increasingly specialized and exclusionary forms of knowledge-production used in the health sciences. Local knowledge can improve scientific analyses, the relevance of health promoting interventions, and the democratic character of public decisions (Corburn 2005).

## From Physical Determinism to a Relational View of Places

The histories of the fields of planning and public health are littered with the notion that rational physical and urban designs can change social conditions, particularly for the poor. This view has haunted planning from the turn of the twentieth century's City Beautiful ideal to twenty-first century movements for New Urbanism, Smart Growth, and designing for Active Living.[24] Research aiming to link the built environment and human health often characterizes places as only the sum total of what is designed and constructed, from streetscapes and highways to houses, businesses, schools, and parks. Yet, as is highlighted in the historical review above, a range of forces beyond physical design, from institutional and cultural commitments to economic and social policies, shape how a place functions and which populations have opportunities to engage in healthy activities. Research into the relationships between the built environment and health has tended to avoid or overlook the interactions and relations among the physical, social, political, economic, and meaning-making that combine to make a space in the universe a place (Cummins et al. 2007).

## A Relational View of Place

As an alternative to the static, fixed variable view of place offered by much neighborhood effects and built-environment and health research, the relational view of place is understood as having physical and social characteristics that are given meaning through the interactions among the people living in a place. A space becomes a place as meanings are assigned through social relations, and these social meanings, in turn, act to reshape places (Lefebvre 1991). However, the relational interplay between place characteristics and meaning-making is always contingent and contested, such as when new groups with new cultural orientations move into a place. Meanings are also essential for "making sense" of evidence and act as a form of evidence in themselves. As Peter Marris (1996:31) has noted, the "conflict between incompatible meanings cannot be resolved simply by producing evidence, not because evidence is irrelevant, but because its relevance can only be determined by the meanings themselves." The relational view of place is crucial for moving toward healthy city planning because social processes, such as power, inequality, and collective action, are often revealed through the construction and reconstruction of the material forms and social meanings of places (Emirbayer 1997; Escobar 2001).

The meanings and interactions in urban places are crucial for understanding how place shapes human well-being. For example, a "sense of place" might invoke feelings of inclusion and connections with others while a "lack of place" might induce loneliness and depression (Jackson 1984).[25] The qualities and meanings of place can also influence our performance, behaviors, and opportunity structures (Hayden 1997). Cities and metropolitan regions more generally are not shaped by faceless forces of natural succession and competition. People and organized groups or coalitions actively accomplish places, and the process is rarely the same from here to there. There are real winners and losers in the political struggles of place making, and static definitions of physical and social variables rarely capture this dynamic of place making.

In the new politics of healthy city planning, a relational view of place will demand multidimensional research and analysis that combines multiple ways of characterizing and understanding places, including resident narratives, systematic observation, and quantitative and qualitative measures of the location and spatial accessibility of resources. A relational view of place has crucial differences with the built environment and health view of place that influence both research and practice. For example, the relational view of place does not commit a priori to use existing geographic or administrative boundaries for measurement: it aims to include measures of social distance and social networks, not just physical distance, and it aims to explore longitudinal, not just cross-sectional, population characteristics. Importantly for policy making, a relational view of place considers the culturally specific meanings assigned to health promoting interventions and aims to address existing power inequities within the institutions that shape places, not just the distribution and number of health promoting resources in a specific place (table 4.3).

## From the City as Laboratory to Embracing a Population Health View

As germ theory, bacteriology and the biomedical model took hold in public health in the early part of the twentieth century, a new urban health science emerged—*the city as a laboratory*. The laboratory view of the city aligned urban policies to reflect legitimacy in laboratory settings where findings could be applied anywhere and to all population groups because, in part, the lab was a placeless, restricted, and controlled environment where

**Table 4.3**

Built environment versus relational view of place

|  | Built environment | Relational view of place |
| --- | --- | --- |
| Geography | Boundaries at specific scale (i.e., census tract) | No a priori defined scales |
| Distance | Fixed and physical | Physical and social; network distance |
| Populations | Static in time/space; cross-sectional differences between | Contingent and mobile; longitudinal differences within and between |
| Health-promoting resources | Physical and social in specific locations; culturally neutral | Physical and social plus culturally specific meanings assigned to them |
| Political power | Not explicitly addressed | Relations among populations in place and held by institutions that shape places |

mechanization and standardization created distance between the researcher and researched. Universal, nonspecific interventions, such as chemical treatment of drinking water and childhood immunizations administered by centralized and specialized bureaucracies, reflected the kinds of urban health interventions of the laboratory view of the city. The laboratory view also provided a political justification for state intervention into the economy and private life, as policies were justified as being more or less free of the vicissitudes and promiscuities of the "outside."

The laboratory view tended to search for the *one big cause* or explanation for differences in health outcomes across urban population (Rosen 1993). Today, a version of the laboratory view is perpetuated by genetic research that promises to find the "single cause" of health differences, for instance, between whites and African-Americans (Pearce et al. 2004; Keller 2000). Yet genetic differences among population groups have not only lacked for evidence, but the mapping of the human genome has confirmed that there is no genetic basis for health differences among ethnic groups (Goodman 2000). *The New England Journal of Medicine* declared in 2003 that racial categories do not act as a useful categorization of genetic information about the response to drugs, diagnoses, or causes of disease (Cooper et al. 2003). Importantly, the Institute of Medicine has documented that in the same health care setting, racial and ethnic minorities routinely receive less medication and fewer preventative interventions, including life-saving surgeries, than whites regardless of income (IOM 2003).

A field site view of the city differs from the laboratory view in that empirical observations allow investigators to examine reality before it has been made artifactual via laboratory interventions. In the field site view of the city, professionals and urban folk often act as surveyors, ethnographers, and analysts while developing a keen personal sensitivity to the uniquely revealing features of their particular place. Fieldwork often involves immersion in a site for a long period of time and developing embodied ways of feeling, seeing, and understanding—that become analogues to the cold precise instruments of the lab. When the field site view dominated city planning and public health, research and practice tended to address the interactions among social, political, economic, and biologic forces that seemed to be impacting the health of the least-well-off urban populations. For example, the field site view was the dominant "science of the city" during the American Sanitary and Progressive eras, and local institutions such as settlement houses and neighborhood health centers helped craft locally relevant and context-sensitive policy responses. Yet "the field" can carry with it a romanticized view of an unadulterated reality and that "fieldwork" reveals things about a place that cannot be understood or replicated anywhere else.

### Population Health: Combining the Laboratory and Field Site Views of Urban Health

The new politics of healthy city planning will require practitioners to embrace a population health perspective where research and interventions build on qualities from both the field site and laboratory view of cities. Importantly, planning with a population health perspective demands that practice move beyond a biomedical—where genetics and individual biology and behaviors are the focus—and a built environment—where exposures to the physical environment is the focus—approach to health and instead incorporate a social epidemiological approach. A social epidemiologic approach to urban well-being emphasizes that health equity is the result of the interactions of biology, environmental, socioeconomic and political forces, and the objective of research and action is to improve the well-being of all social groups but pay particular attention to reducing inequities in health among population groups (Young 2006).

The population health approach is grounded in the idea that the most substantial reductions in morbidity and mortality are a function of changes in social, economic, and physical conditions, not medical technologies (McKeown 1976). This differs from a biomedical view of health where the *compositional* characteristics of people—a combination of biology, genetics, and individual lifestyles—combine to explain health disparities (Mishler 1981). The biomedical model asks "why did this individual get this disease at this time," in seeking the *causes of cases* by trying to isolate individual susceptibility. According to this view, what matters most for determining health is an individual's lifestyle and how this acts as a risk factor (i.e., smoking) to induce disease, not the context within which a person lives or works. The strength of this model is its emphasis on individual risk factors, but its weakness is an inability to explain different distributions of disease across populations and geographic areas. In population health the central question is, what explains the *distribution* of disease and well-being across populations and what drives current and changing patterns of inequalities in well-being across population groups? By emphasizing distribution as distinct from *causation*, population health interrogates how social, political, and economic forces, from racism, to economic policies, to neighborhood environments, together shape which groups get sick, die earlier, and suffer unnecessarily.

The population health perspective emphasizes that health inequities mirror inequities in the distribution of social and economic resources across places, such as urban neighborhoods (Marmot and Wilkinson 2003). Health disparities result when groups with more material resources avoid risks or minimize the consequences of disease once it occurs, while those with fewer resources can do neither. Material resources also shape health behaviors because they influence whether groups know about, have access to, can afford, and are supported in their efforts to engage in health enhancing behaviors. According to Link and Phalen (2000), a vicious cycle of material inequality drives disparities in health; economic resources structure educational attainment, which in turn can force poorly educated populations to take hazardous, low-wage jobs, requiring these groups to spend more time at work to earn a living wage, increasing hazardous exposures and decreasing time spent in family and/or community social support networks.

## Merging the Laboratory and Field Site: Biologic Embodiment

Bringing the laboratory and field site views together is essential for helping planners understand the policy implications of embodiment hypotheses, or the ways that the human body biologically incorporates the material and social world in which we live, from in utero to death (Krieger 2001:694). The embodiment hypothesis suggests that the characteristics of places and political institutions (e.g., income distribution; racism; absence of supermarkets, libraries, or health centers; homelessness response plans; policing strategies; and immigration policies) can be *pathogenic exposures* as much as biologic agents. One embodiment hypothesis that highlights the importance of both laboratory and field site knowledge suggests that the persistent and chronic stress of racism, social stigmatization, poverty, job loss, threats of eviction, poor housing quality, chronic neighborhood violence, and toxic environmental exposures (e.g., lead paint and air pollution) produce a "weathering" effect on the body that denigrates the immune, metabolic, and cardiovascular systems, fueling the development or progression of infectious and chronic disease (Geronimus 1994, 2000).[26] The weathering hypothesis posits that people of color experience early health deterioration because, relative to whites, they have much greater and more frequent experiences with social and economic adversity, including coping with acute and chronic stressors. The idea suggests that while the body's ability to respond to acute stress (the "fight or flight" response) is protective in certain threatening situations, in high, chronic-stress environments these mechanisms can be detrimental for well-being. Geronimus and Thompson (2004:257–58) suggest that under chronic stress:

[T]he physiologic systems activated by stress (the allostatic systems) can damage the body. Allostatic systems enable people to respond to changing physical states and to cope with ambient stressors such as noise and crowding, as well as extremes of temperature, hunger, danger, or infection.... Long periods of overexposure result in "allostatic load," which can cause wear and tear on the cardiovascular, metabolic, and immune systems.

The weathering idea suggests that stressors over the life course wear out the body's ability to cope with or manage the harmful impacts of stress, leading to cardiovascular disease, obesity, diabetes, increased susceptibility to infection, and accelerated aging and premature death for people of color.

The embodiment hypothesis is important for pursuing healthy and equitable city planning because it combines insights from the relational understanding of places with a population health view that well-being is more than individual biology and behaviors. Embodiment also emphasizes that the cumulative impacts of social experience are not neatly confined to one or just several specific disease outcomes. Finally, the embodiment idea brings together the laboratory view of the city by acknowledging the importance of biologic processes without equating "biologic" with "innate" and the field-site views of the city, by emphasizing that both physical and social contexts influence health outcomes while avoiding social determinism. As Krieger (2005:353) emphatically states:

[E]mbodiment reminds us that a person is not one day African-American, another day born low birth weight, another day raised in a home bearing remnants of lead paint, another day subjected to racial discrimination at work (and in a job that does not provide health insurance), and still another day living in a racially segregated neighborhood without a supermarket but with many fast food restaurants. The body does not neatly partition these experiences—all of which may serve to increase risk of uncontrolled hypertension, and some of which may likewise lead to comorbidity, for example, diabetes, thereby further worsening health status.

The new politics of healthy city planning, organized around the notion of embodiment, focuses practice on changing the societal conditions that seem to adversely shape the expression of biologic traits, population distributions of disease, and social inequalities in health.

### From Professionalization and Specialization to Regional Coalition Building

As chapter 2 emphasized, increased specialization and professionalization in each field disconnected the once common knowledge base and practices of planning and public health. Professionalization also helped create specialized bureaucracies, increased disciplinary boundaries, and a need for a new elite corps of technocrats with distinct disciplinary training. Professionalization, specialization, and bureaucratic fragmentation all combined to disconnect the fields from their urban and social justice roots. This fragmentation plagues not only municipalities but entire metropolitan regions where hundreds—if not thousands—of local governments and special-purpose districts compete for tax revenues and state resources in a zero-sum game that undermines regional cooperation and equity (Dreier et al. 2004; Katz 2007). The new politics of healthy city planning must address fragmentation across the entire metropolitan region to avoid the overlap, duplication, lack of coordination, and wasting of resources in the delivery of essential services and governance more generally.

A regional approach to healthy planning is necessary because localities may be too parochial while federal policies may ignore the critical, place-based role that metropolitan clusters of firms, arts, culture, and civic groups play in addressing the needs and interrelationships of both distressed inner-city neighborhoods and aging suburbs (Pastor et al. 2007). Regional coalitions can bring together disparate interests and organizations and overcome the isolationist and often discriminatory agendas of not-in-my-backyard (NIMBY) groups. As Gerald Frug notes in his book *City Making: Building Communities without Building Walls*:

The suspicion and fear that infest our metropolitan areas threaten to generate a self-reinforcing cycle of alienation: the more people withdraw from each other, the higher percentage of strangers that cause them anxiety, thereby producing further withdrawal. (Frug 1999:80)

Frug argues that fewer meaningful interactions between residents and decision makers from different backgrounds within a metropolitan region can limit idea sharing and social learning, two essential components of policy innovation.

Thus effective regional coalitions must be attentive to local institutions, or the ways actors and organizations construct their ways of thinking and acting. Institutions are not necessarily the formal structures or procedures of public institutions, as in the traditional public administration view, but rather an established way of addressing certain social issues, such as norms of practice that become "taken for granted" and accepted over time (Healey 1999). Institutional practices often emerge in organizations and coalition building where local and regional values and knowledge are negotiated. As Healey notes:

Ways of seeing and knowing the world, and ways of acting in it, are understood, in an institutionalist perspective, as constituted in social relations with others, and, through these relations, as embedded in particular social contexts. Through the particular geographies and histories of these contexts, attitudes and values are framed. It is in *these relational contexts* that frames of reference and systems of meaning evolve. (Healey 1999:113; emphasis added)

Thus the success of healthy city planning will depend, in part, on the organizing of new cross-disciplinary and cross-sector coalitions that aim to build new institutions.

One example of a regional coalition that has reshaped institutional practice around health equity is the *Ditching Dirty Diesel Campaign*,[27] formed in 2004 in the San Francisco Bay Area (Pacific Institute 2006). This coalition brought together activists from low-income communities of color across the Bay Area and decided to target the Bay Area Air Quality Management District—the regional air pollution regulatory body (Prakash 2007). The coalition began by documenting asthma rates and diesel truck pollution in neighborhoods across the region and used this information to start local campaigns to stop truck idling. Local anti–truck idling campaigns grew into a regional organizing campaign targeting port areas across the Bay Area and were soon joined by communities near ports around the state of California, such as Long Beach and Los Angeles (Pacific Institute 2006).

The regional and statewide collaborations began to reframe their work as not just about local air quality but about how freight and the global movement of goods more generally places disproportionate burdens on the populations benefiting the least from the global economy (Pacific Institute 2006). The campaign did this by linking freight traffic with environmental health burdens. For example, the Ditching Dirty Diesel Collaborative report entitled, *Paying with Our Health: The Real Cost of Freight Transport in California*, highlighted that the California Air Resources Board (CARB) estimated that freight transport contributes to 2,400 premature deaths, 2,830 hospitalizations, 360,000 missed workdays, and over 1 million missed school days due to respiratory illnesses such as asthma, almost all of which burden low-income communities of color (Pacific Institute 2006:3).

The Ditching Dirty Diesel Collaborative has also joined with similar coalitions in cities across the United States to form a national movement for environmental health reform in and around port communities. The national partnership, called the Coalition for Clean and Safe Ports (CCSP), includes labor, environmental, and community activists organizing around many of the country's major container ports, such as Los Angeles, Long Beach, Miami, Oakland, New York–New Jersey, and Seattle. The CCSP advocates for port-management entities, most of which are quasi-public agencies, to use their clout as landlords to set standards for the trucking and shipping companies, including the hiring of drivers as employees[28] and requiring the large shipping companies, like Wal-Mart and Target, to purchase cleaner-fuel trucks to limit the pollution-induced health harms afflicting drivers and port communities (White 2008).

Another example of a metropolitan coalition that has reframed planning and public health practice is the Figueroa Corridor Coalition, a group of community-based organizations in Los Angeles. This coalition successfully negotiated a community benefit agreement (CBA) with the Los Angeles Arena Land Company, a private developer, over the Staples Center Phase

II project in downtown Los Angeles (Goodno 2004). The CBA is a legally binding agreement guaranteeing that the developer include affordable housing and public amenities such as new parks and that the new commercial establishments hire local residents at a living wage (Gross et al. 2002). Reminiscent of struggles for early twentieth-century workplace and neighborhood improvements, both the Ditching Dirty Diesel and Figueroa Corridor Coalition have partnered with organized labor unions to ensure that economic and social opportunities are linked to physical planning.

Another example of a regional coalition that is aiming to break down institutional and bureaucratic fragmentation and specialization is the Bay Area Regional Health Inequities Initiative (BARHII), one of the only metropolitan-scale coalitions focused on health equity in the nation (Prentice 2007). BARHII is a partner organization of the nonprofit Public Health Institute; it has brought together the region's public health and planning departments along with community-based organizations to build a regional strategy to promote health equity. The regional coalition, recognizing the importance of linking their work to others across the United States, has also partnered with the National Association of County and City Health Officials (NACCHO). One of four BARHII work groups is focused on the "built environment," and the mission of this group is to move practice in this area away from the categorical approach that focuses on such issues as food access and health or design and physical activity, and instead focus on redesigning public health and planning practices to address health disparities (Prentice 2007).

This chapter has offered a set of practice frames for promoting a new politics of healthy and equitable city planning. The next three chapters explore experiments in healthy city planning from the San Francisco Bay Area, and especially how each engages with these political frames and attempt to move policy making *Toward the Healthy City*.

# 5 Reframing Environmental Health Practice

Look around this place. We've got trucks, smoke stacks and toxic military land that no one wants. We ain't got one of those big supermarkets like ya'll got in the suburbs. We eat a lot of cheap meals. I go to Safeway and see what's on sale. . . . Even if I did have money to buy good food like at them health food places, I don't have time or the energy to make it. . . . You know it's tough to work 12 to 13 hours a day and try to juggle everything else. Even gettin' to the Safeway takes me an hour or more dependin' on when MUNI comes, if it ever decides to come! I got that corner store, but it ain't got nothin' fresh or organic in there. I can't even go there much because it ain't safe, ya know? Dealers hangin' out front hassling people. Once the guns come out at night, forget about getting' some food around here.
—29 year old African-American resident of the Bayview–Hunters Point neighborhood in San Francisco[29]

## Environmental Health, Planning, and Social Justice

The quote above is from a life-long resident of the Bayview–Hunters Point (BVHP) neighborhood in San Francisco. Historically an industrial neighborhood adjacent to the Port of San Francisco, BVHP bears the legacy of decades of toxic emissions from a large naval ship building and repair facility. The environmental hazards in the neighborhood range from toxic waste in the soil left by industrial uses to air pollution from power plants to noise and truck traffic from adjacent highways and industries. The neighborhood houses 187 leaking underground fuel tanks (LUFTs), 124 hazardous waste handlers regulated by the EPA, and four times as many air pollution dischargers and five times as many facilities storing hazardous materials than any other neighborhood in San Francisco (EPA 2005).

The neighborhood is also burdened, like other postindustrial urban areas, by the overlapping legacies of toxic pollution, unemployment, deteriorating infrastructure, and displacement of a once vibrant and cohesive cultural community. When the US Navy began operating the shipyard in Bayview at the onset of World War II, thousands of well-paying jobs were created. In 1944 several federal housing projects were built in Hunters Point, called "war houses," where close to half of the African-American shipyard workers lived (Broussard 1993). These projects, while originally built as temporary worker housing, remain today. The African-American population in BVHP burgeoned in the pre-and postwar years, eventually creating San Francisco's largest majority African-American neighborhood. The naval shipyard closed in 1974, and massive layoffs followed. By 1994 the entire area was shutdown, but toxic contamination, widespread unemployment, and deteriorating infrastructure, including the "temporary" public housing, remained. The shipyard that once served as a source of income was designated a toxic Superfund site by the EPA and, along with other smaller industrial facilities, left the soil, water, and air within and around BVHP as some of the most polluted in San Francisco (SFDPH 2006). Unemployment and the rising cost of living in San Francisco throughout the early 1990s forced many African-American families to leave the neighborhood, and those that stayed behind lived in one of the city's most impoverished and segregated communities.

By the early 1990s BVHP (zip code 94124) remained San Francisco's largest African-American neighborhood and one of the city's poorest and least healthy communities (BHSF 2004; Katz 2006). Today over half of the residents own their own homes. Over 48 percent of BVHP residents are African-American, 20 percent live below the poverty line, and 13 percent are unemployed. The community has the highest hospitalizations rates out of all San Francisco neighborhoods for adult and pediatric asthma, adult diabetes, chronic obstructive pulmonary disease (COPD), and congestive heart failure (BHSF 2004).

In the early 1980s residents living in public housing on Evans Avenue in Bayview, across the street from a Pacific Gas and Electric power plant, began organizing to get the facility to clean up its emissions and to shut it down (Fulbright 2006). Activists also pressured the federal, state, and local government to clean up the derelict Navy yard site. On January 22, 1992, the EPA signed a Federal Facilities Agreement with the Navy and the state of California to better coordinate the environmental investigation and cleanup of the Navy yard site in BVHP. In 1993, plans for transferring the shipyard to the city of San Francisco began under the federal Base Closure Act (Katz 2006). However, concerns over the environmental health impacts of the Navy yard, abandoned toxic sites, and the power plant

**Chapter 5**

continued, and community residents suspected that local pollution was contributing to their health problems and keeping many stuck in a cycle of dependency due to chronic illnesses (Huntersview Tenants Association and Greenaction 2004). Residents raised local and national claims of environmental injustice, and challenged government agencies to demostrate that local pollution was not contributing to their poor health.

## Building a Foundation for Healthy City Planning

This chapter highlights how community claims for environmental justice (EJ) helped redefine environmental health, transformed agency practices toward health equity, and built the foundation for healthy city planning in San Francisco and the Bay Area more generally. Residents in Bayview–Hunters Point (BVHP) organized for environmental justice in the early 1990s and one of their demands was for the San Francisco Department of Public Health (SFDPH) to demonstrate whether or not the community's health was being compromised by exposure to local hazards. Pressured, in part, by federal and state commitments to environmental justice and a desire to address health disparities in this and other San Francisco neighborhoods, the SFDPH, including its Chronic Disease and Environmental Health Section, initiated a partnership with EJ activists in the neighborhood. The collaborative was unique because it began by asking community members, through a comprehensive neighborhood survey and focus group meetings, to define their priority environmental health issues. While the SFDPH suspected that the priority issues for the community would be air pollution and toxics from neighboring facilities, the community survey and dialogues returned a different result: community members stated that crime, unemployment, access to healthy food, and housing conditions were their priority "environmental" concerns.

While many environmental health agencies might have reacted to these findings by stating that these were not issues under their jurisdiction or that they didn't have the "expertise" to address issues of crime, housing quality, food access, and so forth, the San Francisco Department of Public Health took another approach. The agency aimed to find a way to use the findings as an opportunity to re-define its environmental health mandate, to engage with non–health specific policies and agencies, and to design new processes for evaluating the social determinants of health. The agency eventually created a new program focused on addressing health inequities through research and advocacy on urban policy and planning issues, called the Program on Health, Equity and Sustainability (PHES) (www.sfphes.org).

This chapter explores why and how the shift to health equity and planning issues occurred within the SFDPH and the implications for moving toward healthy city planning in public agencies and community-based organizations more generally. Community demands for environmental justice, national and international attention to the social determinants of health, leadership within the SFDPH, and the agency's commitment to experimentation, all contributed to the reframing of environmental health in San Francisco. Ultimately, as this chapter shows, redefining environmental health to embrace the social determinants of health equity is a prerequisite for healthy and equitable city planning.

## Environmental Justice Stimulates New Government–Community Relations

By 1994 environmental justice activists in BVHP were pressuring the SFDPH to address their concerns and the Environmental Health Section began a dialogue with community members. At these meetings community residents expressed a belief that high rates of cancer in the neighborhood were due to the presence of polluting industries (Huntersview Tenants Association 2004). By this time in 1994, environmental justice had gained a high profile in the federal government, with the EPA's 1992 Environmental Equity Report and the environmental justice Executive Order 12898 issued by President Clinton in the same year. California was a focal point for community struggles for environmental justice in the 1990s, and these struggles forced environmental and public health agencies to engage in the issue. For example, a Latino community group called *El Pueblo para el Aire y Agua Limpio* (People for Clean Air and Water) in Kettleman City, California, filed a lawsuit under the California Environmental Quality Act (CEQA) claiming that a proposed incinerator project had failed to analyze the project's impact on air quality and agriculture in the San Joaquin Valley. The lawsuit forced the California Environmental Protection Agency to clarify its stance on environmental justice and how permitting processes would meaningfully include low-income populations and communities of color in environmental review processes (Cole 1994).

In San Francisco, the Department of Public Health began meeting monthly with Bayview EJ activists and other researchers to discuss options for studying environmental health in the neighborhood. One of the first tasks for the SFDPH was to map all the hazardous waste sites in the neighborhood, and at the request of community members, the agency gathered disease surveillance data on common cancers. The cancer data showed an unusually high number of cases of breast cancer among young African-American females. While agency researchers considered the breast cancer findings speculative, the study seemed to validate longstanding community beliefs that pollution was linked to local health problems (Rojas 1997). Activists used these early studies to support their call for a moratorium on new power plants in the neighborhood and the DPH publicly supported the community campaign, noting that their initial findings showed that BVHP residents bore a disproportionate burden of environmental exposures and some diseases (Rojas 1997). By successfully engaging the agency in the study of environmental health, the community's concerns were given legitimacy and contributed to increased political attention to the clean-up plan for the Navy shipyard (Bhatia 2003).

The agency's responsiveness to community concerns and public support of their power plant campaign acted to build trust and furthered collaborative efforts between EJ activists and the SFDPH. The community collaboration with the SFDPH contributed to a follow-up cancer study performed by the California Department of Health that did not find any significantly elevated rates of cancer for men or women of any age in BVHP (Glaser et al. 1998). Despite the uncertain findings the SFDPH and community members agreed to form a community coalition that would help direct research efforts toward community-defined needs (Bhatia 2003).

In addition to cancer, community members were concerned about elevated asthma rates and the SFDPH received a grant from the EPA to explore the environmental triggers of asthma in BVHP. As part of this research project, Health Department inspectors visited public housing in BVHP and documented many unhealthy conditions in homes that were likely triggering asthma, from mold and moisture to peeling lead paint. As the inspector's findings were shared at community meetings, residents told the SFDPH that they were often reluctant to share information about housing conditions to their landlords or the city housing authority due to fear of eviction and the lack of affordable housing alternatives in the region (Bhatia 2007). What began as a relatively conventional environmental epidemiological investigation into air pollution, cancer, and asthma in BVHP shifted to a discussion about land use, housing quality, and regional housing affordability. As part of this discursive shift in what "counted" as an environmental health issue, the SFDPH adopted a policy position that the BVHP community was already adversely burdened and that no additional exposures to any hazards were acceptable, even if the pollution–disease linkage could not be made using existing epidemiologic methods (Bhatia 2007). One of the first actions the group took to put this policy position into action was to form a community–academic–government coalition that would craft a hazard reduction and elimination strategy for BVHP.

## Community Environmental Health Survey

By 1999 the health agency's collaboration with BVHP activists had formed into a coalition called the Health and Environmental Assessment Task Force (HEAP). The task force, with the assistance of the SFDPH and University of California, San Francisco, crafted a household and individual survey in order to identify priority environmental and health issues for community members. The household survey was completed by 249 households and 171 individuals. A range of demographic, housing, environmental, and health data were collected. One finding was that 35 percent of respondents were always or frequently worried about their ability to pay for basic household expenses, such as rent, food, and clothes (BVHP HEAP 2001:15). The survey also revealed that crime and safety, addiction, and unemployment were greater priority issues for the community than environmental pollution (figure 5.1).

To the surprise of the agency, the survey found that only 14 percent of residents prioritized chemical contamination and pollution. The survey results were discussed at a community forum, called Landscape of Our Dreams: A Community Dialogue, where residents gave additional details about their priorities. Many residents noted that corner food markets were the only locations for residents to buy food and that these stores were seen as unsafe because they were also the locations of illicit drug sales and violence. In addition, according to community members, the corner stores sold high-priced, poor-quality foods.

According to Rajiv Bhatia, director of Environmental and Occupational Health at the SFDPH, the collaboration with the community helped make visible to the agency that local EJ claims were more than just the desire for less pollution but rather a series of interrelated demands for economic justice, safe and affordable housing, access to healthy and affordable food, and concerns about neighborhood safety and violence (Bhatia 2003). The broad view of environmental health articulated by BVHP residents reflected core social determinants of health and challenged the agency to devise a

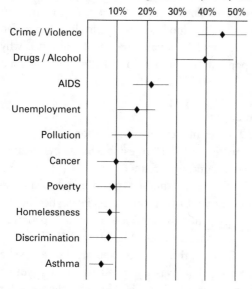

Percentage of respondents stating this was a priority issue

**Figure 5.1**
Community survey results of Bayview Health and Environmental Task Force
Source: Bayview–Hunter's Point Health and Environmental Assessment Project
(2001:11)

strategy to engage with non–health specific city policies and programs to promote community well-being.

## Emergence of a Food Systems Program

Food and health were issues that the Health Department engaged with, but only through their nutrition and restaurant inspection programs. Planning for better community access to quality food and preventing community violence were not seen as environmental health issues that were part of the agency's work (Bhatia 2003). Yet the Environmental Health Section recognized that community food security was a core issue of health equity recognized by the World Health Organization and anti-hunger advocates around the world (Wilkinson and Marmot 2003). In response to findings from the community survey, the SFDPH Environmental Health Section, with the support of the HEAP, initiated a series of projects under the broad umbrella of a food systems program. Grant financing, from the US Department of Agriculture and the San Francisco Foundation Community Initiatives program, enabled the agency to be more experimental and creative within the food systems program and add additional staff that their municipal budget would not have allowed (Bhatia 2003). A primary aim of the project was to improve healthy food access in Bayview while also addressing the broader citywide and regional forces that influence why some neighborhoods and population groups have better healthy food access than other places?

**Community Food Security in Bayview**
In the spring of 2001 the Environmental Health Section of the DPH expanded the scope of their activities in BVHP by establishing new partnerships with the San Francisco League of Urban Gardeners (SLUG) and Literacy for Environmental Justice (LEJ), another community-based organization focused on empowering youth to promote social justice in the community. Together the groups aimed to increase youth participation in addressing the community's food access issues. According to Paula Jones, a project coordinator for SLUG at the time, the collaborative developed a new Healthy Food Access Survey that was intended to provide young people from the neighborhood a way to identify additional barriers for healthy food access and work to devise solutions (Jones 2006). The questionnaire asked about where residents purchased or accessed food, what barriers existed for buying fresh foods, and what additional resources might help residents purchase fruits and vegetables?

Seventeen young people were trained by the DPH to administer the survey and the group collected responses from more than 280 individuals in the neighborhood. Survey locations included grocery stores, churches, community colleges, a post office, and a fast food restaurant. The collaborative analyzed the survey data and created a list of recommendations to improve food access in Bayview. One key survey finding was that while corner stores were the primary food shopping destination for residents, these stores only devoted an average of 2 percent of their shelf space to fresh food (SFDPH 2001).

Four specific strategies were identified from the surveys and focus-group discussions that followed to promote food security in BVHP. First, the collaborative would work to identify ways to attract a new grocery store or supermarket to the area. Second, the group would create a new neighborhood farmers market. A third strategy was to devise a plan to encourage corner stores to offer better quality fresh food on their shelves, and the fourth strategy was to identify healthy fast food retailers. The collaborative also determined that before new and improved food access could be achieved in the neighborhood, access to healthy food for Bayview residents meant traveling outside the neighborhood. The group met with the municipal transit agency to discuss how existing bus routes could be altered to link Bayview residents directly to supermarkets in adjacent neighborhoods. After a series of discussions the transit agency agreed to establish a special shuttle bus service between BVHP and numerous grocery stores across San Francisco's southeastern neighborhoods and terminating at the city's Civic Center Farmers Market.

Another project that emerged out of the collaboration with HEAP, the SFDPH, and LEJ focused on providing incentives for corner stores in Bayview to stock more healthy foods on their shelves. This project, called the Good Neighbor Program, aimed to encourage corners stores to devote at least 10 percent of their inventory to fresh produce, an additional 10 to 20 percent of inventory to other healthy foods, get them to accept food stamps, and limit their promotion of tobacco and alcohol (Bolen 2003). The program's incentives included providing stores that comply with the criteria energy efficiency upgrades, such as new refrigeration units, professional marketing assistance, and grants to make initial purchases of healthy foods. After three years of the program, sales of produce in BVHP corner stores increased by 15 percent (Duggan 2004).

## A Market in the Bayview

A third project to increase food access in BVHP initiated by the DPH and the community partners started a new farmers market in the neighborhood and worked to ensure that food stamps could be used at existing farmers markets throughout the city. As food stamps shifted to using electronic swipe cards, many farmers markets and small merchants did not have the machinery to use these cards. One result was that populations on public assistance were excluded from accessing the fresh produce and other food products available at farmers markets (Food Trust 2004).

With financial assistance from the Columbia Foundation, the DPH worked with four of the largest farmers markets in the city to identify and overcome barriers for merchants to accept food stamps as electronic benefit transfers (EBT) (SFFS 2004). The issue reached the highest levels of the SFDPH, when Director Mitchell Katz contacted David Frieders, the director of San Francisco's Department of Consumer Assurance, asking that the consumer agency finance a program for farmers markets to accept electronic food stamps (Ona 2005). Residents in Bayview expressed an interest in purchasing food at the Alemany Farmers Market, the closest market to their community and operated by the City's Department of Consumer Assurance. The DPH director wrote:

We [DPH] have been approached by a number of community based organizations and San Francisco residents voicing concerns about the market's limited accessibility to recipients of food assistance programs—especially residents that rely on food stamps, the WIC Farmers Market Nutrition Program (FMNP) and the Senior FMNP. As I understand this issue, food stamp recipients need a way to use electronic benefits at the Alemany Farmers market. . . . In addition, Alemany Farmers Market needs to find a way to accept and redeem WIC FMNP coupons. . . . In the city and county of San Francisco redemption rates for these coupons is significantly lower in the southern part of the city. . . . As I'm sure you're aware, there is a growing movement in the city and county of San Francisco to improve access to affordable and nutritious food for all residents. In the long run, greater access to the fresh produce available in farmers markets can reduce the adverse health impacts of food related disease and illness. Since the Alemany Market is the farmers market most accessible to several of San Francisco's low income neighborhoods, ensuring access to this market for food assistance recipients would promote public health.

After continued lobbying and support from local elected officials, the new operator of the Alemany market, the Department of Administrative Services, agreed to work with the DPH to ensure the market accepted all forms of food assistance (SFFS 2004).

### Social Justice through Food Systems

In addition to addressing neighborhood-scale food access, the DPH built on what they learned from working with Bayview activists to start the San Francisco Food System (SFFS), a project designed to address issues of food system planning and human health with community organizations, businesses, and other city agencies (SFFS 2004). Taking a systems approach to food was a significant departure from the nutrition and food inspection work of the Environmental Health Section of the SFDPH. Until the creation of the SFFS, the DPH focused either on the consumption or consumer side of food, by ensuring safety of retail food and providing direct nutritional services through its Women Infants and Children (WIC) program or through nutritional health education of the department's Nutritional Services Section. The SFFS approach aimed to go beyond the production of food, such as encouraging urban agricultural through community gardens, and couple social service programs aimed at addressing urban hunger with land use issues that helped create "food deserts," or urban neighborhoods that lack access to healthy and nutritious food (Jones 2006; Morland et al. 2001). According to Fernando Ona, former project director of the SF Food Systems project, the program aimed to develop an approach to food systems research and action that:

captured the full spectrum of issues under the food system, including ecological and agricultural impacts, public subsidies for certain farming practices, nutrition and human health, and social and cultural relationships different population groups have to food, and how all these are shaped by and shape the growing, harvesting, processing, packaging, transporting, marketing, consuming and disposing of food. (Ona 2005)

According to Ona, the SF Food Systems project was also a way to challenge the lack of attention to racism and white privilege in most food and urban agriculture movements:

We recognized when creating this program that in order to really speak to the issues raised by folks in communities like Bayview, we needed to make this a multi-racial multi-ethnic program. Food co-ops, health food stores, "buy organic and local" campaigns can be elitist practices often associated with white privilege. Most of the folks and organizations working in food systems are well meaning and entirely white, and often fail to recognize how their whiteness and privilege shapes the way people of color do or do not engage in well-meaning healthy food work. At the same time, much of this work aims to really transform inequities in society, from land use and ownership to distribution of healthy food to worker rights, health and safety. We wanted to design a program that, from the outset, engaged with the privilege in food movements while capitalizing on its energy for social change.

In order to accomplish these goals, the SF Food System project organized its work around a set of guiding principles. First, the project was focused on addressing the immediate needs of low-income people. Building on the anti-hunger movement, the SFFS project aimed to meet the food needs of low-income communities, but not just through food distribution. Meeting these needs would include developing new programs in job training, business skill development, urban greening, farmland preservation, and community revitalization and redevelopment. Their anti-hunger work also included a discussion of land ownership and control, in both agricultural areas and cities, and how this can shape the availability of food in low-income and people of color communities (Ona 2005).

A second principle of the SFFS project was to focus on specific neighborhoods while linking their needs to regional, state and international agricultural policies. The driving idea was that a community should have access to a range of food resources necessary to meet the needs of its population, but these choices are influenced by forces outside the community. Local food self-reliance might include supermarkets, farmers' markets, gardens, transportation to food outside the neighborhood, community-based food processing ventures, and urban farms, while related regional, state, and international issues might include agricultural subsidies, institutional food purchasing contracts, and trade agreements (SFFS 2004). The objective was to explicitly link the "local to the global." According to Ona (2005):

We recognized that food is at once a very personal and intimate thing while at the same time part of a political system that can at times unite and at others further stratify society. Few other systems touch people's daily lives in such an intimate way and offer an opportunity to exert larger political influence.

Ongoing community involvement, like the partnership between the SFDPH and activists in BVHP, was viewed as an essential part of making the program serve the local and global dimensions of the food system in San Francisco.

Building on the commitment to community involvement, the SF Food Systems project established a participatory governance structure called the San Francisco Food Alliance. The Alliance is a membership-based governing unit of the food systems project and consists of public and private sector volunteers. The Alliance has a range of working groups[30] that helped publish San Francisco's first Collaborative Food System Assessment (SFFS 2005).

**Institutionalizing Environmental Health Equity**

The establishment of the food systems project as a formal project of the Environmental Health Section of SFDPH represented a significant institutional change. According to Kami Pothukuchi and Jerome Kaufman (1999, 2000), municipal agencies do not generally promote food systems projects with an emphasis on social justice or food security; they instead opt to focus on more limited goals, such as improving the number and location of food services, community gardens, or farmers markets. These authors note that "food justice" projects are more commonly located in community-based or nongovernmental organizations, not municipal government.

Yet, what additional forces contributed to the municipal public health agency institutionalizing the new approach to environmental health? The institutionalization of health equity and a commitment to addressing the social determinants of health was part of a more general shift within the SFDPH. The agency began to make a series of changes—even before the food systems work—to their surveillance and data-analysis practices that also reflected their new commitment to engage in the non–health specific forces that shape health inequities.

## Health Equity and the Living Wage Ordinance

One example of the shift within the SFDPH to engage in issues outside traditional public health to promote health equity was the agency's assessment of a proposed living wage ordinance. In 1999 San Francisco's Board of Supervisors began debating a living wage ordinance for the city that required a minimum wage of $11 per hour for city contract workers. Since the living wage proposal was controversial, the city established an inter-agency task force to oversee an economic analysis of the proposal. The commissioned study examined the likely changes in wages across various sectors of the economy, the public and private monetary costs of the ordinance and potential labor market effects from a living wage ordinance (Katz and Bhatia 2001). After reviewing a draft of this study, epidemiologists within the SFDPH noticed that there was no mention of the health benefits from such a legislative proposal (Bhatia 2003). At the request of a city legislator, the SFDPH produced an analysis using estimates of income's effects on premature mortality, preventable hospitalizations, and emergency room visits. The SFDPH study stated that "modest gains" in income from a living wage law would generate substantial health benefits for both full- and part-time workers, including reductions in premature mortality, overall health status, depression, and sick days (Bhatia and Katz 2001:1400). The DPH also showed that the educational attainment of children of workers and the risk of premarital childbirth among offspring would also be improved from the living wage ordinance.

The living wage law eventually passed in San Francisco. While the influence of the DPH analyses on legislators is uncertain, according to Mitch Katz, director of the SFDPH, the exercise had a deep and sustaining impact on the agency (Katz 2006). The health impact assessment of an economic policy opened up a new venue for research, analyses and policy within the city health department, namely working to address social inequalities outside of the traditional domains of public health. The policy analysis also revealed to the agency that having the internal capacity to reframe policy and municipal actions as public health and equity issues required integrating this commitment across departments and programs (Katz 2006).

## An Agency's Commitment to the Social Determinants of Health

As part of its annual reporting requirements, the SFDPH issues a statistical analysis of the health status of city residents. These reports are a traditional function of many public health agencies. In San Francisco the public health agency's Population Health and Prevention Division publishes the annual *San Francisco: Overview of Health* report. The annual report is intended "to contribute to the best evidence on health conditions and needs in San Francisco and focus intervention strategies" (http://www.dph.sf.ca.us/reports/HlthAssess.htm).

Between 2000 and 2002, the same years of the BVHP collaborative and the living wage analyses, a significant change in the reporting of these health data occurred within the SFDPH. More specifically, the agency seemed to shift its focus from an emphasis on individual behaviors and lifestyles, or a biomedical model of disease, to a social epidemiologic orientation. This change was reflected in the explicit hypotheses the agency used to explain health inequities and contributed to a shift in health promotion strategies advocated by the SFDPH.

In the 2000 Health Status Report, the SFDPH emphasized that "our health is largely a product of who we are and how we live" (SFDPH 2000:26). The report highlighted that each year the report is altered to "enhance our understanding of the health of" San Franciscans, and "because social conditions and personal health behaviors have a significant effect on health, this year's report has been expanded to include additional statistics on social issues such as poverty and unemployment, behaviors such as exercise (physical inactivity and overweight), and health risks such as high blood pressure" (SFDPH 2000:1). While recognizing that social issues influence health, the emphasis was clearly on how individual risk factors and behaviors influence health outcomes.

The next year, 2001, the annual report had a distinctively different tone and orientation. In a revised and expanded introductory section, the report noted that:

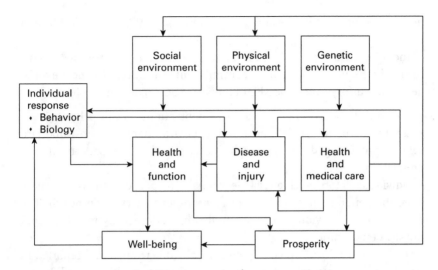

**Figure 5.2**
Field model of health developed by the San Francisco Department of Public Health
Source: San Francisco Department of Public Health (2001:1)

[The department] continues to expand our information about the major conditions that contribute to the patterns of health, illness and injury in San Francisco. Furthermore, we have tried to present data that will be useful for thinking about prevention activities: by showing disparities across groups, determinants of ill health, trends over time, comparisons to state or national levels or national standards, or by choosing measures of premature death or disability. (SFDPH 2001:1)

The explicit recognition of health disparities across different social groups frames the 2001 report. A mention of individual risk factors, the previous year's focus, was absent in the 2001 report. In addition a new model of the determinants of health was presented in the 2001 report, called the "field model of health" (figure 5.2) (SFDPH 2001:1). The "field" was a reference to "ecologic" approaches in epidemiology that aim to account for the environmental contexts where morbidity and mortality occur. A view of urban health through the "field site" view is also rooted in historical models of how to generate accurate "truths" about urban life and, as noted in chapter 2, is often juxtaposed with a laboratory view of the city (Gieryn 2006).

Importantly, in the DPH's field model, social and physical environments are at the top of the model and appear to exert as much influence on well-being as, for example, genetic factors. This model is similar to others that aim to address the social determinants of health and explicitly address health inequities (Whitehead and Dahlgren 1991; Wilkinson and Marmot 2003).

Included in the 2001 SFDPH annual report was a list of statements further highlighting the agency's commitment to health equity and the social determinants of health. The SFDPH report (2001:2) notes the following:

- The contribution of medical care to a population's health is limited.
- Conditions of the social and physical environment play an important role in producing different health, disease, and injury patterns in our population.
- Individual factors, such as risk decisions or response to stress, can moderate the general effects of broader environmental factors on health. The occurrence of individual factors can also be patterned by the social and physical environment.
- Disease and injury, which can be clinically determined and reported in health systems data, are not quite the same thing as health and well-being, which is based on how people experience their own conditions and function with them.
- To change a population's health profile, we have to consider possible changes in their physical and social environment and in the factors influencing behavior, and not just at health care. Indeed, since many health care interventions occur late in sometimes long sequences of events leading to diseases or injuries, in many cases earlier interventions would be more effective or more cost-effective at reducing the ultimate burden of disease.

The physical and social qualities of places, and how they influence human well-being, were now firmly rooted in the rhetoric of the SFDPH. The agency also emphasized the limits of a focus on health care and the need for health professionals and others to understand "how people experience" and make sense of their living and work conditions in order to most effectively promote well-being.

According to Director Katz of the DPH, the policy shift within the agency was, in part, a reflection of a growing international and national understanding in public health of the importance of the social determinants of health (Katz 2006). For example, Healthy People 2010, the US blueprint for public health action, stated that addressing health disparities and their causes was the second of the top two priorities of the Department of Health and Human Services (http://www.healthypeople.gov). By 2003 data reporting within the SFDPH had changed to monitor a range of social determinants of health and the agency was beginning to reorganize its units to fulfill this changing view of its core functions.[31] The San Francisco Health Commission also weighed in on the subject and requested that the DPH develop a prevention framework for the city. A Prevention Planning Team and a DPH-wide Prevention Workgroup were established, consisting of fifteen public health sectors, their directors, and additional staff representatives. Sections ranged from the AIDS Office to Environmental Health to Maternal and Childhood Health to Dental and Primary Care (SFDPH 2004e).

The Workgroup was charged with reviewing evidence and identifying "priority prevention issues and to develop the best strategy for allocating limited public health resources to reduce the burden of the leading health problems in San Francisco" (SFDPH 2004e:2). At the request of the DPH director, the group reviewed the WHO publication *The Solid Facts: The Social Determinants of Health* and a range of studies documenting the determinants of health for urban populations (Katz 2006). The group was also required to explore how social and economic policies might promote health. The work group reached a consensus that four social determinants acted as the primary drivers of health disparities in San Francisco and would constitute the foundation of their recommendations for health promotion and prevention policies. The four priority social determinants included (1) low socioeconomic status, (2) social isolation/connectedness, (3) institutional racism, and (4) transportation (SFDPH 2004e:4). Building on these four priority areas, the SFDPH team devised the "Prevention Strategic Plan, 2004–2008, Five-Year Plan," which included ten policy goals (table 5.1) reflecting the Department's commitment to advocate for public action that was consistent with its "field model" of health (SFDPH 2004e:7–8).

These policy goals reflected the SFDPH's commitment to and explicit recognition of how non–health specific urban policy can act to prevent illness, disease, and death. Combined with their endorsement of the "field model," the prevention framework further institutionalized a social determinants of health mission within the agency and set a framework for engaging with non–health specific policies and agencies across city government (Katz 2006).

While the policy recommendations and data collection orientation taken by the SFDPH seemed like a logical extension of a growing international consensus on the determinants of well-being, the agency's social and health equity commitments are far from the norm. For example, the New York City Department of Health and Mental Hygiene launched a new health promotion and prevention program the same year as the SFDPH

**Table 5.1**
San Francisco Department of Public Health, Prevention Strategic Plans of 2004 to 2008

---

Objective 1.3(a) Advocate for public policies that improve health status, such as:
- Livable wages
- Employment development/full employment
- Results based employment training
- Adequate supply of quality child care
- Improved quality and quantity of housing
- Ensuring the social safety net
- Improved public transportation
- Increased public participation in political and social organizations
- Improved availability of respite services
- Equal and fair education policies.

---

Source: SFDPH (2004e:7–8).

Strategic Plan. New York City's program, entitled Take Care New York, is described as "a policy for a healthier New York City" and offers a "comprehensive health policy that sets an agenda of ten key areas for intervention" that would be measured over four years (NYCDOHMH 2004). The New York prevention program (figure 5.3) defines the priority actions, health responsibility, and important interventions with a focus on individuals and clinicians, as opposed to the social focus taken by the SFDPH. In short, Take Care New York perpetuates a biomedical view of health promotion while the SFDPH Strategic Prevention Plan embodies a population health approach. In fact the NYC DOHMH Commissioner, Thomas J. Friedan, emphasized in launching the program that the policy's "success depends greatly on the power of the clinical setting and on the influence of physicians and other providers such as yourself" (NYCDOHMH 2004:1). While San Francisco's policies are focused on public policies that might change the material, physical, and social environments where people live and work, NYC's policies are geared almost exclusively toward individual behavioral change and clinical interventions.

## The Program on Health, Equity, and Sustainability

By formally embracing an ecologic and social orientation to well-being, the SFDPH created an organizational culture that encouraged innovation and a commitment to health equity. The Environmental Health Section of the

# City Health Information

**June 2004**     The New York City Department of Health and Mental Hygiene    **Vol. 23(3):11-18**

## 10 STEPS to a LONGER and HEALTHIER LIFE
### More Information for Providers

TAKE
CARE
NEW YORK

**1. HAVE A REGULAR DOCTOR OR OTHER HEALTH CARE PROVIDER**

- Information on public insurance programs: www.nyc.gov/html/doh/html/hca/plus2.shtml

**2. BE TOBACCO-FREE**

- Treating nicotine addiction: www.nyc.gov/ html/doh/downloads/pdf/chi/chi21-6.pdf

**3. KEEP YOUR HEART HEALTHY**

- Clinical guidelines for blood pressure control: www.nhlbi.nih.gov/guidelines/hypertension/ index.htm
- Clinical guidelines for cholesterol control: www.nhlbi.nih.gov/guidelines/cholesterol/index.htm
- Clinical guidelines for diabetes: www.nyc.gov/ html/doh/downloads/pdf/chi/chi22-3.pdf

**4. KNOW YOUR HIV STATUS**

- The Department's public STD clinics: www.nyc.gov/html/doh/html/std/std2.shtml
- A list of syringe exchange programs: www.harmreduction.org/resources/usnep/ newyork/hours.html

**5. GET HELP FOR DEPRESSION**

- 9-item, self-administered PHQ-9 screen for depression: www.depression-primarycare.org/ clinicians/toolkits/materials/forms/phq9/ questionnaire
- A clinical guide for the recognition and treatment of depression: www.nyc.gov/html/ doh/downloads/pdf/chi/chi23-1.pdf

**6. LIVE FREE OF DEPENDENCE ON ALCOHOL AND DRUGS**

- Brief counseling for alcohol dependence: www.niaaa.nih.gov/publications/aa43.htm

- Becoming a certified buprenorphine provider: http://buprenorphine.samhsa.gov/bwns/ waiver_qualifications.html
- Alcoholics Anonymous: www.nyintergroup.org

**7. GET CHECKED FOR CANCER**

- Colon cancer screening: www.nyc.gov/html/ doh/html/cancer/cancercolon_actionkit.shtml
- Cervical cancer screening: www.ahcpr.gov/ clinic/uspstf/uspscerv.htm
- Mammography screening: www.ahcpr.gov/clinic/uspstf/uspsbrca.htm

**8. GET THE IMMUNIZATIONS YOU NEED**

- Immunization information for providers: www.nyc.gov/html/doh/html/imm/immpinfo.shtml

**9. MAKE YOUR HOME SAFE AND HEALTHY**

**Domestic Violence**

- Recognizing and treating victims of domestic violence (brief guidelines from the American Medical Association): www.opdv.state.ny.us/ health_humsvc/health/deskref.html

**Lead Poisoning**

- Legally mandated childhood blood lead screening, risk assessment, and risk reduction education: www.nyc.gov/html/doh/downloads/pdf/chi/chi23-5.pdf

**10. HAVE A HEALTHY BABY**

- Folic acid: www.cdc.gov/doc.do/id/0900f3ec800523d6
- Contraception, including emergency contraception: www.nyc.gov/html/doh/html/ms/ms6.shtml

## Figure 5.3
New York City's health promotion strategy initiated in 2004
Source: http://www.nyc.gov/html/doh/html/tcny/index.shtml

DPH took this as an opportunity to create a new program aimed at improving population health by addressing the environmental, social and economic conditions under which San Franciscans live and work. Before 2001 the EHS of the SFDPH functioned as a typical environmental health bureaucracy conducting mandated enforcement of environmental and sanitary regulations through surveillance and sanctions. The EHS analyzed and regulated chemical use and disposal, enforced violations of regulatory standards, and relied on quantitative tools, such as risk assessment, to evaluate whether a single hazard resulting from a single pollution source was likely to have deleterious effects on humans. However, the EHS did include individual staff focused on researching health inequities, and this unit investigated such issues as the health impacts of a living wage policy and the health equity impacts of a food systems program. According to Rajiv Bhatia, this research group soon recognized that their work often included building collaborations with others organizations across the city and investigating non–health specific policies and programs.

Recognizing that their health equity work extended beyond research, the EHS organized a formal process to develop a new program to coordinate and manage this diverse work. The EHS director launched a visioning and values-setting process among staff that expressed an interest in the social determinants of health. These staff members participated in a number of retreats and internal dialogues where a mission statement and project list were collaboratively developed for a new group, entitled the Program on Health, Equity, and Sustainability (PHES, www.sfphes.org).

The PHES aimed to embody calls by the World Health Organization and the US Institute of Medicine for environmental health practice to work across a range of social, built environment, and other sectors to improve health. For example, the World Health Organization noted:

In its broadest sense, environmental health comprises those aspects of human health, disease, and injury that are determined or influenced by factors in the environment. This includes not only the study of the direct pathological effects of various chemical, physical, and biological agents, but also the effects on health of the broad physical and social environment, which includes housing, urban development, land use, and transportation, industry, and agriculture. (WHO 1989)

A similar charge was issued by an Institute of Medicine report in 2001 entitled *Rebuilding the Unity of Health and the Environment: A New Vision of Environmental Health for the 21st Century*. This report called on environmental health leaders to work with policy makers, other health professionals, industries, and the public to expand and enhance the vision of environmental health in the twenty-first century. More specifically, the report stated:

New approaches toward building environments that actively improve health will be required, including strategies to deal with waste, unhealthy buildings, urban congestion, suburban sprawl, poor housing, poor nutrition, and environment related stress.

Again, international and national evidence combined with local political commitments to encourage the Environmental Health Section within the SFDPH to create the PHES.

The mission, guiding principles, and core values of the PHES offer insights into the specific kinds of practices necessary for linking environmental health with other sectors of urban policy making to promote health equity. The mission of the PHES includes a commitment to collaborative work and valuing multiple forms of environmental health expertise and practices such as "initiating and facilitating dialogue and collaboration among public agencies and community organizations, expanding public understanding of the relationships between the natural, built, and social environments and human health, and developing and evaluating new methods for interdisciplinary and inclusive involvement in public policy" (SFDPH 2005).

In addition to the food systems project and commitment to working in BVHP, the PHES included specific projects on day laborers, children's health, transportation, and community planning. The approach to each project included specific commitments to five components of health equity: public access and accountability, healthful environments, equity, sustainability, and interconnectedness and meaningful participation. For example, the *public access and accountability* statement under the community planning project of the PHES stated that "the process of urban development may be contentious and inaccessible to those without financial and political resources. Communities most impacted by public and private development decisions must have access to those processes to maintain and improve their quality of life." The *healthful environment* commitment stated that "a healthy 'built environment' creates opportunities for healthy living. Good land use patterns, neighborhood design and transportation systems are key to advancing public health goals." And the agency's commitment to *equity* stated that "the process of development favors some communities in San Francisco over others. The goal of our work is to provide equal opportunities for different groups to democratically participate in developing and advancing a 'Healthy City Vision.'" Ultimately the *sustainability* goal of the community planning project is to "develop recommendations that protect and advance the quality of life of diverse city communities and achieve environmental, political, economic, and social sustainability" (see the sidebar below).

---

**San Francisco Department of Public Health, Program on Health Equity and Sustainability Mission**

The Program on Health, Equity, and Sustainability supports San Franciscans working together to advance urban health and social and environmental justice through ongoing integration of local government and community efforts and through valuing the needs, experiences, and knowledge of diverse San Francisco residents. We accomplish this by:

- Initiating and facilitating dialogue and collaboration among public agencies and community organizations
- Expanding public understanding of the relationships between the natural, built, and social environments and human health
- Supporting local participation in public policy making
- Conducting and supporting local and regional research
- Developing and evaluating new methods for interdisciplinary and inclusive involvement in public policy
- Documenting and communicating our strategies

In our vision of San Francisco, communities are engaged in democracy and committed to equality and diversity. We believe this will create and maintain sustainable and healthy places for all San Franciscans to live, work, learn, and play.

**Guiding Principles and Core Values**
**Healthful Environments**  Healthy people reflect healthful environments. Following the 1986 WHO Charter on Health Promotion, we define the basic conditions and resources needed for health to be peace, shelter, education, food, income, stable ecosystems, sustainable resources, social justice, and equity.
**Equity**  A fair distribution of economic, political, social, and natural resources and opportunities improves individual livelihood and the overall health of society.

---

The creation of the PHES was aided by a commitment by the agency's director, Mitch Katz, to address issues across traditional public health boundaries and to hire new staff and allow time for existing staff to explicitly engage with issues of health equity. The PHES also benefited from the agency's organizational management strategy that allowed staff to experiment and learn about new analytic techniques and topics and make decisions about their unit's priorities, program development, and implementation strategies. According to EHS Director Bhatia, the combination of emerging knowledge about the social determinants of health and an organizational culture that rewarded experimentation and valued commitments to social justice, coupled with fairly flexible staff performance measures, all contributed to the successful launch of the PHES (Bhatia 2007).

As a program with multiple overlapping projects, the PHES has initiated a new orientation to environmental health within the SFDPH and San Francisco more generally. The food systems and urban health and place work, among other programs, of the PHES have created new networks of organizations and government agencies and involved individuals that previously did not consider themselves part of the work of environmental health. The expansion of the environmental health network was made possible, in part, through the SFDPH's commitment to partnering with community-based organizations and members of the public that have often been systematically ignored by government institutions, including public health. Creating a specific institutional home for health equity and the social determinants of health has allowed the Environmental Health Section of the SFDPH to seek external funding for their projects, which allows them to experiment with new, often controversial projects (Bhatia 2005). Taken together, these elements began to set the stage for healthy city planning in San Francisco and the Bay Area more generally.

## Building a New Foundation of Environmental Health Planning

This chapter has explored how a municipal health department responded to issues of health inequity and community demands for social justice. As noted in earlier chapters, reconnecting city planning and public health to promote urban health equity will require changes to existing *formal institutions*—such as organizational structure, issue definitions/jurisdictions, interagency collaborations and reporting requirements—and *informal institutional practices*—such as public participation processes, norms of generating evidence and expertise, and practices aimed at public accountability. The examples in this chapter have highlighted that even governmental agencies with strict mandates can and do change. While overcoming bureaucratic inertia may seem insurmountable in some locations—and San Francisco politics may be more anomalous than other places—this case illustrates that a set of overlapping forces helped redefine environmental health and provided the impetus for healthy city planning (table 5.2).

The first contributor to change in this case was the organizing and claims making of the environmental justice movement. The EJ movement has had a profound effect on environmentalism and on environmental health by redefining the "who, what, and where"—or the hazardous living conditions the poor and people of color face in their communities—that constitutes environmental health (Di Chiro 1996). Environmental justice has also asserted a central role for community perspectives and expertise, grassroots leadership, and collaborative sciences that have helped redefine environmental health more generally (Frumkin 2005; Wing 2005).

A second factor that contributed to the transformation of the work of the SFDPH was an emerging consensus within the field that the biomedical focus on health behaviors and health care was not addressing health disparities. From the World Health Organization to the US Institute of Medicine, researchers and practitioners in the field of environmental health increasingly recognized that an exclusive focus on toxins without also considering the socioeconomic context where people were exposed was an

**Table 5.2**
Transforming environmental health for healthy city planning

| Characteristic | Conventional environmental health | Healthy city planning |
|---|---|---|
| Definition of environmental health | • Direct pathological effects of various chemical, physical, and biological agents | • Social determinants and contexts<br>• Including indirect influences on well being of housing, transportation, buildings, land uses, food access, economic resources, and social exclusion |
| Typical agency practices | • Regulation, enforcement of standards, and monitoring of ambient environment | • Commitment to address health inequities through health promotion strategies<br>• Review non–health specific urban policies<br>• Collaborate with community organizations and others to address inequities |
| Credible evidence base | • Quantitative measurement, modeling, and risk assessment | • Quantitative and qualitative data<br>• Community-based participatory research |
| Experts | • Professional scientists, especially toxicologists | • Professionals and lay people<br>• Range of disciplines |
| Approaches to uncertainty | • Gather additional data<br>• Use safety factors in models<br>• More detailed studies | • Experimental interventions adjusted as new information emerges |
| Public involvement | • Legally required hearings | • Collaborative research and agenda setting<br>• Advisory committees<br>• Voluntary councils comprised of public and private agents |
| Implementation objectives | • Meet regulatory standards | • Adjusted for specific conditions of places and population groups<br>• Include participatory monitoring to make adjustments if not improving well-being<br>• Multiple scales from neighborhood to international |

insufficient approach for environmental science. The leadership of both the director of the health agency and of the environmental health unit was instrumental in finding ways to apply the new view of environmental health to agency practices. Thus bureaucratic change occurred through pressure from above and below.

A third set of factors that help explain the reframing of environmental health in San Francisco include engaging with new, sometimes experimental methods of building the scientific evidence base to promote health equity. The SFDPH's willingness to experiment with health analyses of the living wage ordinance—the first such analysis in the United States—was a significant risk but also an opportunity to display the relevance of health analyses to non–health specific urban policies (Bhatia 2005). Linking environmental justice to housing and food systems also demanded new data-gathering processes and partnerships that expanded the work of the agency.

Another factor that helped shift the definitions and practices of environmental health planning was the creation of publicly transparent and accountable oversight committees for the new projects. Instead of taking on each of the new projects as part of their exclusive domain, the SFDPH created interdisciplinary advisory committees that set agendas, organized research and data analyses, published reports, and performed outreach and interventions. In most cases such as the food systems project, SFDPH staff helped these groups secure their own funding so that they could make some decisions independent of municipal funding. The SFDPH provided trainings and a forum for community members to take leadership roles and build capacity within specific communities—from food justice advocates in Bayview to day laborers and community health workers. This shifted the notion of public accountability and trust, since these new environmental health projects were not seen as controlled exclusively by the health agency. By bringing marginalized population groups and issues into public view, valuing their expertise, and giving them a prominent seat at the table for shaping research and action, the SFDPH not only changed the way specific program activities were managed but also began to change the ways socially disadvantaged groups engaged with processes of urban governance.

# 6  Healthy Urban Development

In the summer of 2003 a redevelopment proposal for the Trinity Plaza apartment complex became the centerpiece of long-standing battles between developers and community groups in San Francisco over affordable housing and land use planning more generally. Trinity Plaza, a rent-controlled building in the Mid-Market Street area near downtown, was slated to be demolished and replaced with market rate condominiums. Existing tenants would be evicted and the developer had no plan for re-housing the low-income families. Activists from the Mission District, already mobilized around preventing building demolitions, gentrification and preserving affordable housing, joined groups in the neighboring South of Market area (SoMa) to stop the project.

The Trinity Plaza project was particularly controversial because it was the first proposed major demolition of rent-controlled housing in San Francisco. Before the Trinity Plaza proposal, hundreds of market-rate housing units had been built in the SoMa and Mission District neighborhoods of San Francisco. The market rate housing boom catered to young, mostly high-tech workers who worked from home or commuted to Silicon Valley. The new housing had also reduced the proportion of affordable housing in the city and increased incentives for landlords to evict existing tenants and charge higher rents. What was unique and very new for this project was that the city's Department of Public Health had decided, at the urging of housing activists and residents, to enter the labyrinth of land use planning and weigh in on the controversial project. The San Francisco Department of Public Health's (SFDPH) Program on Health, Equity, and Sustainability (PHES) worked with residents to analyze the likely human health impacts from the Trinity Plaza development proposal. The PHES analysis, submitted as a comment letter on the adequacy of the scope of a planned environmental impact report required under the California Environmental Quality Act (CEQA), offered a qualitative analysis of the likely health impacts from direct and indirect residential displacement that would occur from the Trinity Plaza project. The city's Planning Department had determined that the project was likely to have "no significant" impacts on housing and local populations, and the DPH analysis presented a conundrum for the Planning Department; they had never before been asked to consider the kinds of human health impacts of residential displacement in the environmental review process, but they were required, by law, to respond to the evidence and arguments being put forward by the Health Department.

What followed were a series of meetings between the agencies, community activists, and the developer. The DPH argued that their analytic report—called a health impact assessment (HIA)—ought to be considered in this project and that CEQA required the planning agency to consider the broad determinants of health. The city's Planning Department, reluctant to add another layer of complexity to the already cumbersome environmental review process, balked at the idea of including health analyses in the review process. Meanwhile community opposition to the project grew and, now armed with health data, activists also pressured the Planning Department to reconsider its ruling. The Planning Department eventually revised its determination on the scope of the EIR to require the analysis of "Displacement of the tenants and its potential significant impact" and to require analysis of a no-displacement project alternative. The Trinity Plaza developer submitted a revised project plan and environmental impact report, recognizing community demands for preserving affordable housing and the Health Department's analysis of displacement. In the revised project plan the developer agreed to set aside 12 percent of the project for below-market rate housing and would permit all current occupants of Trinity Plaza to keep their homes at their current rents. The DPH had entered the world of urban development and staked-out a new space for human health.

**Toward Healthy Urban Development**

Why did the Health Department agree to analyze the Trinity Plaza project? How did the agency select health impact assessment as the method and how were the analyses performed? How were the findings injected into the typically rigid environmental impact assessment process? How did the

Planning and Health Departments reconcile their different interpretations of significant impact for the Trinity Plaza project? How was the community-based struggle for affordable housing impacted by the introduction of health arguments?

This chapter addresses these and other questions by highlighting how affordable housing conflicts—a perpetual concern in San Francisco (Brazil 1998) and many other American cities—often act as the entry-point for developing new tools and practices for more healthy and equitable city planning. I will highlight how struggles over housing affordability and quality can address immediate and vital physical, economic, and social determinants of health, open up analyses and decisions to address human health issues across the broader "residential environment," and offer a strategic entry point for renegotiating relationships between community groups and governments as well as between different government agencies. As this chapter shows, housing and health is just one planning issue, but can be crucial for opening-up political processes, discourses, and analytic practices to a much broader and comprehensive debate and analysis of the impacts of urban development on population health. This chapter explores the specific practices, tools, and processes for incorporating the social determinants of health into urban development decisions. More specifically, I highlight how the SFDPH Program on Health, Equity, and Sustainability (PHES) introduced the practice of health impact assessment into the land use and development planning process. By exploring how the PHES aimed to introduce the broad determinants of health into development decision making, this chapter explores the political challenges of establishing new interagency partnerships for healthy urban policy making. The chapter also reveals how the PHES approach to health impact assessment built new capacity for research, analysis and decision making within non–health focused community-based organizations—including those working on issues of affordable housing, environmental justice, and community economic development. The construction of interagency partnerships along with new community-based expertise and organizing around the health impacts of development decisions combined to generate some of San Francisco's first experiments in healthy city planning.

## Urban Development and the Local Impacts of Global Change

The Trinity Plaza redevelopment project stimulated worry and outrage in the community after the developer, Angelo Sangiacamo, announced that he was planning to demolish the current building and construct a high-rise, market-rate housing complex in its place. The existing building, a seven-story former hotel converted into 360 rent-controlled housing units in the early 1980s, was to be replaced with three to five 12- to 24-story towers containing approximately 1,700 new market-rate housing units. Existing tenants protested the project from its outset and the struggle between existing residents and the developer became a symbol for community control over land use decisions and against the forces of a rapidly globalizing high-tech economy.

During the high-tech boom of the 1990s and into the twenty-first century, activists in the neighborhoods surrounding Trinity Plaza, namely the SoMa and Mission District, organized to stop what they viewed as "gentrifying development" (Shaw 2007). The dotcom high-tech boom brought an influx of capital and new residents to San Francisco (Epstein 1999). Silicon Valley, less than 60 miles to the south of downtown San Francisco, had grown into one of the world's leading high-technology industry spatial clusters and a site of great wealth. Between 1992 and 2000 Silicon Valley industries created over 275,000 new jobs, many of which were highly paid professional and managerial jobs (Silicon Valley Network 2000). Many of these jobs were for young computer and technology workers. Yet land use restrictions in the cities and towns in Silicon Valley, such as Palo Alto and Mountain View, California, made new housing construction difficult and a time-consuming process (Urban Habitat 1999). The young high-tech workers flocked to the vibrant life of San Francisco and found cheap land in the formerly industrial Mission District and SoMa, which was also close to the 101 Freeway that was a direct route to Silicon Valley (Borsook 1999). San Francisco became a "bedroom community" for Silicon Valley high-tech workers (Solnit 2000).

Developers rapidly converted industrial buildings to live-work lofts and landlords began evicting existing residents to capitalize on the new housing demand (Lempinen 1998). Between 1997 and 2000 tens of buildings were demolished while others were often illegally converted to live-work lofts (MAC 2004). Many existing residents in the Mission District and SoMa were low-income immigrants, and the threat of their eviction helped organize a group of social service, housing, and economic justice organizations into the Mission Anti-displacement Coalition or MAC (http://mac-sf.org). Some of the founding members of the MAC included tenant organizing groups such as Mission Agenda and St. Peters Housing Committee, community development corporations such as the Mission Housing Development Corporation (MHDC) and the Mission Economic Development

Association (MEDA), and an environmental and economic justice group, People Organizing to Demand Environmental and Economic Rights (PODER).

The MAC organized protests and chained themselves to buildings to gain media attention that might help pressure the city to stop approving new construction projects (Wetzel 2000). The Coalition successfully lobbied San Francisco's Board of Supervisors to legislate a temporary ordinance banning building demolitions. The Trinity Plaza project was slated to begin just as the temporary ban was set to expire. Many activists viewed the approval of the Trinity Plaza project as evidence of the city's disregard for low-income residents and communities of color (Grande 2005).

During one public meeting with the city's planning commission in March 2003, community members testified about the likely community impacts from the Trinity Plaza project. Eric Quezada, from the MAC, noted that Trinity Plaza was "a critical site because of everything that's come before it." Marcela Azucar, a local resident, stated that the Trinity Plaza project might force families into homelessness and that without affordable housing, residents will be forced out of the neighborhood, where "you can't go to the corner stores like Casa Lucas and get things from your country and you know that you belong." Nick Pagoulatos, of St. Peter's Housing Committee, stated:

You have families with two or three kids living in a 10 by 10 room with a shared bathroom and no cooking facilities. . . . Now, the solution, of course, is to build more affordable housing, and that's why everybody from the community is here right now. Because this is a serious community need, it's not a desire that's going to bring more money into the pockets of these residents, it's a matter of life and death.

Activists argued that the city's much-prized diversity, its ability to be a sanctuary for refugees fleeing Central American death squads or queer kids fleeing Bible Belt prejudice, as a locale for artistic experimentation and political activism, was predicated on its relative affordability—which was now being threatened and in many cases destroyed (Shaw 2007). The MAC organized over 500 residents to attend a public meeting with the Planning Department demanding that some action be taken to slow development and give the community more control over land use changes. The Planning Department's director at the time, Gerald Green, refused to take any action. The MAC decided to initiate their own planning process with residents, eventually drafting what came to be called The People's Plan.

## The People's Plan
The MAC drafted the People's Plan for Jobs, Housing and Community, after months of community workshops and visioning processes with over one thousand residents (MAC 2005). The People's Plan prioritized retaining existing and building new affordable family housing, preserving light industrial and manufacturing jobs, and increasing community oversight over land use decisions. The MAC helped organize over 600 people to attend a series of community meetings in 2002 to come up with a neighborhood-designed development blueprint for the Mission District. The Plan was, in part, a reaction to the lack of attention given to the area by the city's Planning Department, particularly a failure to update the zoning code to allow for more community-centered development. The Planning Department had promised to rezone the Mission and surrounding areas to make redevelopment priorities more clear, but the city's plan had not been issued by the time the People's Plan was released. The MAC released the Plan to the city, stating:

Today we are reclaiming our community to preserve affordable housing, community serving businesses and improve living conditions for the neighborhood's diverse community: working class people, Latino families, immigrants, seniors and youth. We come together to envision and ensure community development based on equity, justice, and democratic participation. (MAC 2005:2)

The MAC presented its People's Plan to the San Francisco Planning Commission, Department of Planning, and Board of Supervisors. However, city agencies were reluctant to consider the recommendations of the People's Plan in the upcoming rezoning process that the Planning Department was scheduled to begin (Grande 2005).

## Experimenting with Health Impact Assessment
While activists were drafting their own land use plans in response to the rapid development changes in some neighborhoods, the SFDPH was also seeking ways to engage with the land use changes in San Francisco from a health equity perspective. The agency sought to build on its partnership with Bayview–Hunters Point environmental justice activists and partner with other community-based organizations. The Environmental Health

Section of the DPH, aiming to implement the goals of the Program on Health, Equity, and Sustainability (PHES),[32] sought a process for learning about the concerns of community members while also applying new knowledge about the social determinants of health to land use decisions (Bhatia 2005).

After exploring the literature and emerging practice of health impact assessment (HIA) in Europe, Canada, and Australia, the SFDPH decided to design and offer workshops on the practice with community-based organizations. According to Rajiv Bhatia, director of Environmental and Occupational Health for the SFDPH, the workshops were designed as an effort to build relationships with community-based groups, much like the agency had done with Bayview activists and to "learn-HIA-by-doing it." As Bhatia recalled, the initial HIA workshops were learning experiences for the agency and community groups:

We were interested in how this new tool, health impact assessment, might help promote a more holistic vision of health in communities, but we weren't really sure how that would work. We gathered some background material on the practice from health agencies in other places, like the UK and Australia, and designed a very loose workshop. The agenda was intended to let community groups define the issues that were important to them and we would help them think about the positive and negative health impacts attached to their issues. The hope was to move from knowledge building to action. (Bhatia 2005)

More specifically, the DPH borrowed workshop ideas and structure from the growing literature on HIA in Europe and within the World Health Organization (Ison 2000; Scott-Samuel 1996; Scott-Samuel et al. 1998; WHO 1999). The DPH also reviewed participatory processes within environmental and social impact assessment in the US (NOAA 1994). Drawing from these materials, the DPH designed two-hour workshops that would begin with a group brainstorming session where participants would first be asked to describe their vision of a healthy, sustainable, and equitable society. They would then be asked to describe how the vision related to specific concerns in their community and then to select one pressing issue to work on as a group. Participants would then be asked to identify what population groups were impacted by their priority issue, the likely impacts on the broader community, and information gaps and uncertainties surrounding their issue. The second half of the workshop would walk the group through analyses and move toward identifying a range of action items to address the issue. The workshop would close with the development of a plan to communicate the learning and action items to the wider community and a plan to implement and monitor proposed actions. While occurring in an abbreviated format, the workshops reflected the typical steps in the emerging practice of health impact assessment.

## Health and Environmental Impact Assessment

Health impact assessment (HIA) is an evolving practice, used by health and environmental planners in Europe, Canada, and Australia to evaluate the social, economic, and environmental effects of plans, projects, and programs for the purpose of promoting population health (Kemm et al. 2004). HIA developed from a concern that non–health specific public policies and plans were having a negative impact on human health and exacerbating health inequities and that these impacts were not being adequately captured and analyzed in environmental or social impact assessments (Kemm and Parry 2004; Scott-Samuel 1996). One strand of HIA emerged in 1983 after the World Health Organization (WHO) published procedures for analyzing the positive health impacts of water and sanitation projects in developing countries (Birley 1995). In Canada, another strand of HIA emerged in the 1980s analyzing the positive and negative human health impacts of non–health-related public policies, and a national heath guide for environmental assessment was created (Milio 1986). In the United Kingdom, the Manchester airport's second runway project in the early 1990s stimulated a series of efforts aimed at capturing the social and human health impacts of projects, with the Merseyside Guidelines for Health Impact Assessment setting early precedent (Scott-Samuel et al. 1998). The United Kingdom has committed to HIA as one of its principal strategies for addressing health inequalities (Acheson 1998).

HIA practitioners have defined the practice as a combination of procedures, methods, and tools by which a policy, program or project may be judged as to its potential positive or negative effects on the health of a population (Lehto and Ritsatakis 1999). There is no common set of methods or approach for analyzing these impacts, but the typical HIA follows a screening, scoping, analysis, and mitigation development process commonly used in impact assessment. In addition the practice of HIA is often used to extend the environmental impact assessment process, especially of development projects, to include analyses of health equity (Quigley et al. 2006).[33] Yet the scope and aims of HIA remain open to interpretation

**Table 6.1**
Some definitions of health impact assessment

---

- The prospective estimation of potential impacts of a proposed policy or program on a population's health, or any combination of procedures or methods by which a proposed policy or program may be judged as to the effects it may have on the health of a population (Kemm, Parry, and Palmer 2004).
- The estimation of the effects of a specified action on the health of a defined population (Scott-Samuel 1998).
- A combination of procedures or methods that enable a judgment to be made on the effect(s)positive or negative of policies, programs, or other developments on the health of a population or on parts of the population where inequalities in health are concerned (Kemm 1999).
- A combination of procedures, methods, and tools by which a policy, program, or project may be judged as to its potential effects on the health of a population, and the distribution of those effects within the population (WHO 1999).
- A methodology that aims to identify, predict, and evaluate the likely changes in health risk, both positive and negative (single or collective), of a policy, program, plan, or development action on a defined population (BMA 1999).
- Health impact assessment is a formal, systematic analysis to prospectively assess the potential health impacts of proposed projects, programs, and policies and communicate this information to policy makers and stakeholders (Cole et al. 2004:1154).
- Health impact assessment is a process through which evidence (of different kinds), interests, values, and meanings are brought into dialogue among relevant stakeholders (politicians, professionals, and citizens) in order to imaginatively understand and anticipate the effects of change on health and health inequalities in a given population (Williams 2007).

---

and definitions of the practice can differ from a desktop analytic process using secondary data sources intended to document impacts to a participatory process that collects new data and aims to transform social inequalities that adversely impact human well-being (table 6.1).

Since HIA is still emerging and there is no one common approach, evaluating the efficacy of HIA is difficult. However, a review of eighty-eight HIAs performed between 1996 and 2004, in Europe, Asia, Africa, and North America, varying in scale from the local to supranational, found that HIAs successfully influenced policy when key decision makers were involved in the design and conduct of analyses, an institutional commitment to HIA existed, and the policy process included a statutory framework for HIA (Davenport et al. 2005).

## Comparing HIA and EIA in the United States

While widely practiced in Canada, Europe, and Australia, the use of HIA in the United States is new and largely untested, particularly in community planning (Cole et al. 2005; Dannenberg et al. 2006). The National Environmental Policy Act (NEPA) of 1969 was intended to capture human health under its environmental impact assessment process and the law stated that its intention is to prevent damage "to the environment and biosphere and stimulate the health and welfare of man" (Sec. 2, 42 USC § 4321). The California Environmental Quality Act (CEQA) mandates that the EIA process analyze "environmental effects of a project [that] will cause substantial adverse effects on human beings, either directly or indirectly" (California Code of Regulations §15065). While NEPA requires agencies to consider and disclose environmental impacts, CEQA contains a mandate that public agencies refrain from approving projects with significant environmental impacts when feasible alternatives or mitigation measures might lessen or avoid those impacts (CEQA 1998). However, NEPA and CEQA both require a determination over whether a proposed action may *potentially* impact the quality of the human environment, give broad latitude to agencies to determine thresholds of "significance," and mandate that analyses include direct, indirect and cumulative impacts.

Importantly, the analytic *content* of HIA can differ significantly from that of EIA, as the former aims to evaluate how changes to the natural and built environments, social and cultural relations, and socioeconomic conditions may enhance or harm the health of populations using both quantitative and qualitative data (Kemm 2005). A crucial difference between HIA and EIA in the United States is that the former does not have statutory authority or legal standing, unless the HIA is integrated into an environmental impact statement. Because of the lack of statutory backing, health analyses performed outside of the formal EIA process may not be considered as seriously by decision makers as analyses within EIA. A key challenge for environmental planners is determining the benefits and potential limitations of integrating HIA into existing environmental review requirements (table 6.2).

While including at least some components of an HIA within formal environmental assessments may ensure the findings have greater legal standing, drawbacks to subsuming HIA within EIA also exist. For instance, an EIA tends to occur after proponents have made key project design decisions and secured political support, making it unlikely that findings from health analyses conducted within this process will have any significant

**Table 6.2**

Comparing health and environmental impact assessment in the United States

| Characteristic | EIA | HIA |
| --- | --- | --- |
| Authority | • Legal under NEPA and most states' "little NEPAs" | • None outside EIA<br>• Public health considered as part of EIA |
| Timing of analyses | • After key project decisions are made | • Flexible, most often prospective, but can be retrospective<br>• Can also analyze existing policies on human health |
| Focus of analysis | • Projects, plans, policies, or programs<br>• Misses "as-of-right" development | • No limits on scope of analyses<br>• Often non–health specific plans and policies |
| Methodology | • Linear screening, scoping, drafting, commenting, and reporting | • Can follow same linear process as EIA<br>• Also flexibility with methods and data inputs |
| Health analyses | • Health, if analyzed at all, limited to direct physical hazards<br>• Oriented to meet existing regulatory standards and/or risk assessment process | • Indirect impacts on well-being<br>• Social determinants of health and health equity<br>• Not limited to specific outcomes, risk factors, or regulations |
| Public involvement | • Comment periods after analyses<br>• Public hearings | • Flexibility allows for range of participatory processes early in policy process<br>• Local knowledge considered important form of evidence |
| Outputs | • Discovery and disclosure of impacts<br>• Rarely develops alternatives or monitoring | • Social learning<br>• Networks of previously unconnected, non–health-focused actors and organizations to public health<br>• Positive and negative impacts on well-being<br>• Suggestions for policy change to mitigate adverse impacts<br>• Often includes indicators to track progress |

influence. However, HIAs performed outside of EIA can occur at any stage in the policy and design process and potentially early enough to shape project alternatives (Kemm 2005). In addition most NEPA and state environmental analyses are triggered only when federal or state funding is involved, thereby missing many "as-of-right" neighborhood-scale development projects that can have a significant impact on the health of local populations. In contrast, an HIA can be applied to a range of projects and policies at various scales. When HIA is performed outside of the legal shadow of NEPA, analysts may be more inclined to use interdisciplinary and experimental methods to consider the range of social and economic impacts that are regularly ignored in EIA (or relegated to separate social impact analysis processes). For example, HIAs in Europe have tended to not only analyze impacts but simultaneously use health as an organizing principle to integrate behavioral, social, economic, and environmental considerations into more inclusive public decision making (London Health Observatory 2002; Williams 2007).

Finally, while NEPA contains a legal requirement for community participation, such as regular public hearings and comment periods, participation is often modeled around a decide–announce–defend model where expert agencies and their consultants generate analyses, announce findings in a draft document, and defend their analytic choices in the face of oral and written comment periods (Petts 1999). Impact assessment processes not burdened by EIA's legal precedents mandating strict procedural steps can choose to employ more inclusive and deliberative participatory planning methods as shown in table 6.2 (Karkkainen 2002). While these choices and opportunities exist in theory, there is little empirical work testing the potential of HIA in US planning practice (Cole et al. 2004).

### From Health Impact Assessment Workshops to Project Analysis

The health impact assessment workshops organized by the PHES included a range of community members and groups from across the city. In one workshop, high school students chose to evaluate the impacts of a new farmers market while at another, representatives from a number of community-based organizations assessed a city policy proposal that would provide rent subsidies to immigrants denied public housing supports under the federal Quality Housing Work Responsibility Act. During one workshop, members of PODER approached the SFDPH to ask if conducting a health impact assessment of their People's Plan might help increase the report's standing with city officials and whether the city health agency would help them conduct the health impact assessment (Grande 2005)? Seeking to deepen its work to promote health equity, HIA, and community planning, the SFDPH began an extended dialogue with the MAC in November 2002 to discuss the nature of the partnership and the scope of a potential assessment (Bhatia 2005).

MAC expressed a strong interest in retaining ownership and control of the research process and requested SFDPH play the role of technical support. To help generate mutual understanding of the content of a potential HIA, SFDPH facilitated a public, community-visioning session with MAC organizational leaders to identify health objectives and issue linkages between the land use priorities they identified in the People's Plan and relevant public health evidence. Knowledge and data gaps were identified, and the DPH agreed to provide further training in research methods, such as in-depth interviewing, to help the MAC gather new information. The agency also agreed to gather existing data that could be included along with resident's knowledge in a future health analysis of the People's Plan. A data book, co-authored by the SFDPH and PODER, was compiled for the process and noted:

The San Francisco Department of Public Health Occupational and Environmental Health Section's Program on Health, Equity, and Sustainability (PHES) is working together with neighborhood residents on institutionalizing a public health role in urban planning to build healthier communities through the application of research, policy analysis, technical support and by convening and participation in collaboratives. These efforts aim to make transparent the health impacts of land use projects and policy making, and to promote opportunities for community involvement in these decision-making processes. This data book is intended to serve as a tool to share health information with residents, and for residents to share with the Public Health Department and other public and private organizations information on the assets and strengths of their communities that should be considered during the assessment and planning phases of city re-zoning proposals. (SFDPH 2004d)

While the HIA partnership between the MAC and DPH was proceeding, the city was approving real estate development projects that were at odds with the social justice objectives of the People's Plan. The MAC struggled to maintain the capacity to simultaneously engage in new health impacts research and organize community opposition to development projects that they felt were threatening to community well-being. The South of Market Community Action Network (SOMCAN) requested that the MAC join them to stop the Trinity Plaza project. The MAC agreed to help SOMCAN, and together with the DPH, they organized focus groups with Trinity Plaza residents to discuss and document likely displacement-related stressors. The focus groups revealed the specific fears among residents from displacement, such as the stress on their families and familiar routines, and offered invaluable local knowledge into the likely adverse health impacts of the Trinity Plaza project (Bhatia 2006). The discussions during these focus groups of housing–displacement–health issues also contributed to the decision by the PHES to document the health impacts of housing policies and decisions more generally.

**Housing, Residential Environments, and Health**
Researchers within the SFDPH explored the literature on community health and housing in fields such as public health, sociology, environmental psychology, and social medicine. They gathered their findings into a report that noted the strong evidence linking the cost of housing, homelessness, residential displacement, and the quality of the residential environment to human health (Fullilove and Fullilove 2000; Hood 2005; Krieger and Higgins 2002). The DPH decided to focus their report on the indirect health impacts of unaffordable housing and involuntary displacement since these were often overlooked aspects of the environmental review process (Bhatia 2005).

The DPH report highlighted that inadequate and unaffordable housing can force residents into crowded or substandard structures, increasing the likelihood of respiratory infections and ear infections and health-damaging environmental exposures such as mold (a known asthma trigger), moisture, cold, and toxic lead paint (Krieger and Higgins 2002). Substandard housing also contributes to an increase in pest infestations, causing many residents to apply toxic insecticides and rodenticides that can retard fetal growth and contribute to low birth weights (Perera et al. 2006). Housing insecurity, such as the threat of eviction or rising price of rent, contributes to health-damaging stress on individuals and families (Sharfstein et al. 2001). The loss of housing can result in homelessness, which is also known to contribute to psychosocial stress that is associated with greater incidence of influenza, heart disease, and diabetes (Thomson et al. 2001). Homeless shelters can expose residents to violence, increase the spread of infectious diseases, such as tuberculosis, and contribute to the development of risky behaviors and academic delay in children (Freudenberg et al. 2006; Zima et al. 1999). Direct and indirect displacement often severs health-supporting social and family ties that can promote health, for example, by providing emotional and material support. Social and family support can buffer health-damaging stress by reducing feelings of isolation. Conversely, having a consistent home can increases one's feeling of safety, control, and stability (Fullilove and Fullilove 2000).

The report also emphasized the regional health impacts from unaffordable housing in a city. For example, the DPH noted evidence suggesting that when housing in cities becomes unaffordable for average wage earners, they are often forced to move outside of cities, compromising their access to urban jobs, commercial, and social services. When workers live farther away from job centers, the region suffers by losing valuable open space and natural resources that can improve human health, such as flood-controlling and pollution-filtering wetlands, while increasing activities that contribute to pollution, such as vehicular air pollution. Unaffordable housing can also force low- and moderate-income residents to work multiple jobs to make ends meet. The high cost of rent can force families to trade off paying rent for other basic goods, such as food. High housing costs act as a disincentive for new businesses to locate in an area because workers may not be able to afford to live nearby.

As Mindy Fullilove, a professor of psychiatry and urban health at Columbia Univeristy's Mailman School of Public Health has noted, while health departments and others have studied the adverse impacts of individual housing characteristics and dynamics on human health, the synergistic and cascading impacts on well-being from housing and neighborhood instability are not well studied:

What we [researchers and activists] don't have as good a handle on is what happens to a child's health, and the well-being of the entire community, after an eviction because the landlord saw an opportunity to triple the rent? The chain of events this displacement triggers can be extremely detrimental to physical and mental health; time in a shelter or crowed living with friends or family, kids moving to different schools or missing lots of school days, family stress that can trigger domestic violence or increase drinking and smoking, re-settlement in a highly impoverished neighborhood farther away, increasing economic and racial residential segregation. It goes on and on, but planners are not attempting to capture these cascading events when they talk about the impact of development on communities of color. (Fullilove 2006)

In an attempt to offer a more holistic analytic framework for analyzing the human health impacts of unaffordable housing, the SFDPH issued their report on the indirect impacts of unaffordable housing and displacement and included a model for how housing provides a set of basic human needs. Instead of limiting their work to the physical, direct health impacts of qualities of the built structure, the agency framed their work around how adequate housing and residential environments fulfill basic human needs and offered a framework emphasizing that housing ought to be analyzed for how it does or doesn't contribute to the basic conditions needed for well-being (Figure 6.1). This positive vision of housing and health acted as the framework by which the agency, at the request of MAC and others, assessed the Trinity Plaza redevelopment proposal (Bhatia 2005).

### Assessing the Health impacts of the Trinity Plaza Project

Combining evidence gathered from focus group discussions with residents about the stressors of displacement and their review of the literature linking residential environments to human health, the SFDPH analyzed the Trinity Plaza development project. The MAC informed the DPH that the California Environmental Quality Act required analyses of human health impacts within the environmental impact assessment process and that these analyses were missing from the environmental impact report for the Trinity Plaza project. According to Rajiv Bhatia of the DPH, the Health Department had been unaware of the responsibilities for health impacts analysis under CEQA and the information provided by the MAC offered the agency new insights into its possible role in development decisions:

MAC provided SFDPH with legal language from CEQA illustrating requirements for health analyses. The implications of this language—that CEQA required study of health effects related to environmental change—had not been reflected in the statements and positions of the Planning Department to SFDPH in the past. It changed the way we looked at CEQA.

Armed with data and awareness of the statutory requirement for human health analyses within CEQA, the SFDPH issued a letter to the Planning Department noting that the proposed project would likely result in adverse human health and environmental impacts, largely from the displacement of low-income residents (SFDPH 2003a). The DPH letter noted that the likely health impacts from the Trinity Plaza project ought to be, but currently were not, considered by the planning agency as part of their environmental review under the CEQA. The SFDPH letter detailed that the development project would displace people resulting in "adverse health effects on human beings due to the loss of affordable housing, inadequate

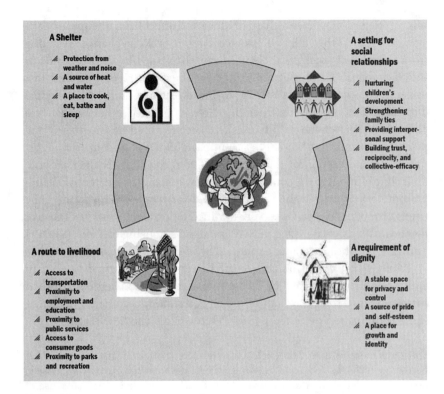

**A Shelter**

⚖ Protection from weather and noise
⚖ A source of heat and water
⚖ A place to cook, eat, bathe and sleep

**A setting for social relationships**

⚖ Nurturing children's development
⚖ Strengthening family ties
⚖ Providing interpersonal support
⚖ Building trust, reciprocity, and collective-efficacy

**A route to livelihood**

⚖ Access to transportation
⚖ Proximity to employment and education
⚖ Proximity to public services
⚖ Access to consumer goods
⚖ Proximity to parks and recreation

**A requirement of dignity**

⚖ A stable space for privacy and control
⚖ A source of pride and self-esteem
⚖ A place for growth and identity

**Figure 6.1**
Residential environment and health framework developed by San Francisco Department of Public Health
Source: San Francisco Department of Public Health (2004c)

housing, or displacement; conflict with land use planning and policy including fair-share housing goals, affordable housing goals, transit first policy, and family housing goals" and contribute to "potential environmental justice impacts" (SFDPH 2003a:1).

The health agency made their case by first weighing-in on and interpreting the "significant impact" clause of the California environmental review statue. The SFDPH noted that the California statue required a determination of "significant impact" when the environmental impact assessment process noted "any direct or indirect adverse effect on humans." According to the SFDPH, the statue also required that "a social or economic change related to a physical change should be considered in determining whether the physical change is significant" (§15382) and that an "EIR [Environmental

Impact Report] may trace a chain of cause and effect from a proposed decision on a project through anticipated economic or social changes resulting from the project to physical changes caused in turn by the economic or social changes" (California CCR §15131). The SFDPH emphasized that under their interpretation of CEQA, the direct and indirect residential displacement from the destruction of rent-controlled housing that was planned as part of the Trinity Plaza project required an analysis of the potentially significant human health impacts (SFDPH 2003a).

In a second section of the comment letter, the SFDPH detailed both their commitment to the construction of new housing as a potential health-promoting activity and the legislated need for new housing to meet the needs of moderate-, low-, and very low-income residents, not just those of higher incomes, as reflected in San Francisco's housing element (SFDPH 2003a:2). The health agency continued by noting that few existing tenants at Trinity Plaza would be able to afford rents in the new development and residents would likely be forced into accepting housing beyond their means, be forced to move out of the city or region, become homeless, or some combination of all these (SFDPH 2003a:2). The SFDPH noted:

Spending more of their household income on rent often means doing without necessities such as food and clothing. Accepting substandard or overcrowded housing conditions affects health conditions such as asthma, personal sense of control, level of stress and children's school performance. People unable to afford housing also work extra hours or at multiple jobs at the expense of personal well-being and family relationships. Displacement results in the loss of supportive family and community relationships. . . . Frequent family relocation leads to children's grade repetitions, school suspensions, and emotional and behavioral problems. Homelessness is the most severe consequence of unaffordable housing and results in exposure to the elements, disease susceptibility, a decrease in self-esteem, a loss of a sense of control and an ability to care for oneself, and social stigma. (SFDPH 2003a:3)

After reviewing how the Trinity project may conflict with affordable and family-oriented housing commitments the city had already made, the SFDPH also suggested that the Trinity Plaza project likely violated commitments to environmental justice. The SFDPH noted that the California Assembly Bill 1553 required that the principles of environmental justice be incorporated into state guidelines for local general plans and that the 2003 draft General Plan Guidelines include mixed-income housing development as a component of its environmental justice strategy. The agency's letter noted that "an environmental justice analysis of this project would focus on the potential for disproportionate impacts to low-income and minority populations both living in the current units as well as in the surrounding neighborhood" (SFDPH 2003a:3). In an effort to be proactive, the SFDPH concluded their letter by suggesting a suite of analytic methods for further assessing the likely health impacts from the Trinity Plaza project and that the agency was eager to work with the Planning Department to identify mitigation strategies so that the Trinity Plaza project could go ahead without harming human health (SFDPH 2003a:4).

## Health Assessment and the Politics of Planning Practice

The SFDPH made a strategic decision to offer a formal comment letter on the environmental impact assessment of the Trinity Plaza project since, by law, these letters are part of the permanent public record and required the Planning Department to respond to all submitted comments in writing. According to Amit Ghosh, a senior official in the San Francisco Planning Department:

The DPH weighed in on the project and forced our hand; we weren't prepared to respond nor had we considered health concerns in prior EIRs. They [DPH] might have been more effective by working with us before issuing a public letter. It wasn't the way I would have done it.

After reviewing the evidence offered by the DPH, the Planning Department acknowledged that the California Environmental Quality Act did require project proponents to assess any likely health impact resulting from the demolition of housing. However, the Planning Department, particularly Paul Maltzer, the director of Environmental Review, challenged the DPH to provide proven quantitative assessment methods for performing health analyses of displacement (Chion 2005).

The request for quantitative and proven methodologies by the Planning Department was part of a more general challenge by the agency questioning whether human health impacts, especially those associated with social, economic, and political determinants of health, ought to be part of the CEQA process. Until the Trinity case human health impact analyses outside of those from physical and chemical hazards were not a component of environmental reviews in San Francisco. According to Rajiv Bhatia of the DPH, the health agency suggested to the Planning Department that guidance documents under CEQA gave local agencies considerable latitude to develop specific "objectives, criteria, and procedures for the evaluation of projects" and that California law allowed for determinations of significant impact to be made using "qualitative or quantitative data that reference health goals, service capacity standards, ecological tolerance standards, a city's general plan, or any other standard based on environmental quality" (CEQA 1998). In fact, several California cities had explicitly recognized the loss of affordable housing as a potential significant impact in their local guidelines for CEQA analysis.

Instead of using this project to try and resolve these questions, the Planning Department approached the developer and requested that they conduct an analysis of residential displacement and its potential adverse impacts on health along with an analysis of an alternative project without displacement in a revised environmental review. The Planning Department acknowledged that when a project had the potential to result in direct residential displacement a more in-depth environmental impact statement was often required (Selna 2007). The change in the Planning Department's position gave activists and an elected official, Supervisor Chris Daly, new evidence to support their request that the Trinity Plaza project include more below-market rate units and preserve the homes of existing tenants (Carroll 2006). Facing rising financial costs due to project delays, the developer modified the final project and never completed the health analysis of displacement. The modified project would still demolish the existing building, but all existing tenants were given guarantees that they could remain in the new building in rent-controlled units. Moreover the developer agreed to add a new playground and community center in the revised project (Goodyear 2005).

Inserting health arguments into the review of the Trinity Plaza project began to change the ways in which planning related to public health. First, the Health Department opened up the question of what counts as a "significant impact" in the environmental review process, and successfully made the case that direct and indirect residential displacement was one of these impacts. The SFDPH broke the public health agency's historical silence over environmental planning and land use issues by developing internal research capacity and offering evidence even in the face of an obstinate planning bureaucracy. While expressing some reluctance to acknowledge many of the health impacts noted by residents and the DPH, the Planning Department was forced, for the first time, to consider how it would approach health equity claims in development projects, particularly those raised within the environmental review process (Chion 2005). While the planning agency did not take any actions to investigate or promote health in the Trinity case, they acknowledged for the first time that health analyses could improve development project outcomes. As important, the health analyses provided new evidence for community groups advocating for more equitable development.

### Large-Scale Urban Development and Health: The Rincon Hill Area Plan

Soon after the Trinity case, the Planning Department approached the SFDPH and asked them to review and comment on the community and human health impacts of a proposed condominium development plan in the Rincon Hill area south of downtown. A major part of the Rincon Hill Plan was the development of the Spear and Folsom Towers, which consisted of 1,600 residential units in two 35-story and two 40-story buildings on an underutilized parcel of land. The Planning Department asked the DPH to comment at a public hearing about the project, specifically on the social value of affordable housing and public infrastructure benefits, in part because the planning commission was considering including a public benefits package as part of the EIR approval (Bhatia 2005).

The Rincon Hill Plan was designed as the largest development project in San Francisco. It was part of the city Planning Department's strategy to make the downtown area a new residential destination and take advantage of underutilized waterfront property (figure 6.2). According to the draft impact assessment performed by the project proponent, the Rincon Hill Plan would increase the population in the South of Market area by 7,300 to 8,800 people. However, the Planning Department was concerned that the developer had not included an adequate amount of new public infrastructure to support these new residents, including schools, parks, and transit improvements (Exline 2006). Senior management at the Planning Department asked the SFDPH to develop an analysis similar to the one for Trinity Plaza and comment at a public hearing on the potential public health impacts from the Rincon Hill Plan.

The DPH agreed to testify at the hearing and produced two comment letters, one in 2003 and a follow-up in 2004, to the Planning Department summarizing possible project impacts with supporting evidence from the health literature. The DPH analyses focused on the fact that the relatively high price of the new condominiums meant that they would only be affordable to a limited number of existing downtown employees and that affordable housing requirements would be met through construction of affordable

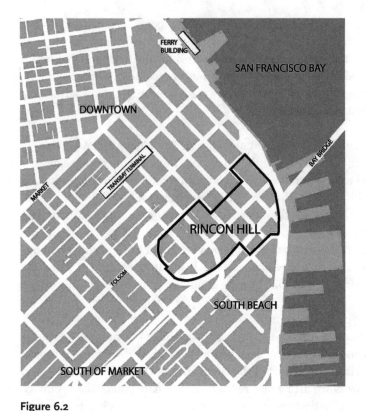

**Figure 6.2**
Boundaries of Rincon Hill area
Source: San Francisco Planning Department, www.sfgov.org/site/planning_index
.asp?id=25076

units off site, in neighborhoods with existing concentrations of poverty and public housing. In this case the DPH highlighted the likely health impacts of unaffordable housing and residential segregation.

In their review letters the DPH noted that the developer's Draft Environmental Impact Report (DEIR) stated that some new jobs generated by the project "would be filled by individuals who already live and work in the city, those who live in the city but who were previously not employed, those who live in the surrounding communities, or by those unable to afford to reside in the city." The DPH questioned whether the retail and office jobs proposed as part of the Rincon Hill Plan would pay enough for employees at the lower end of the income distribution, such as cashiers, waiters, and sales people, to afford the new market rate housing (SFDPH 2004b). The health agency noted that the DEIR listed the price of a market rate housing unit in a Rincon Hill project as $625,000, and according to their analyses this would require a household income of approximately $157,000 in order to purchase one unit (SFDPH 2004b:5).

The SFDPH emphasized that significant adverse impacts can result from indirect pathways, including those mediated or modified by social and economic forces. The DPH noted in its letter that "an EIR (Environmental Impact Report) may trace a chain of cause effect from a proposed decision on a project through anticipated economic or social changes resulting from the project to physical changes caused by the economic or social changes." Of more immediate concern for the DPH was that the Rincon Hill project was likely to exacerbate the jobs–housing "spatial mismatch," or the notion that the incomes offered by existing downtown jobs were insufficient to afford a home in the new Rincon Area development. The agency referenced the State of California General Plan's environmental justice and sustainability section to support their position that the jobs–housing mismatch ought to be part of the EIR, stating:

The 2003 State of California General Plan Guidelines similarly emphasizes the need to carefully match employment potential, housing demand by income level and type, and new housing production. If housing affordability is not consistent with distribution of current and expected income levels in mixed use neighborhoods, the expected environmental benefits of transit-oriented mixed use development and the social benefits of mixed-income integrated neighborhoods will not occur. (SFDPH 2003b:6)

The DPH requested that the Rincon Hill project's environmental impact report estimate what proportion of new residents would likely work in the downtown area and what proportion of current or future downtown employees would be able to afford to live in the proposed development. The environmental and human health impacts from the spatial "mismatch" between jobs and housing would be felt by the entire region according to the DPH analysis. The agency noted that since the Rincon Hill project could potentially increase trips by automobiles into the downtown area, the expected health benefits of the project, such as increased opportunities for walking, pedestrian activity, and fewer local automobile trips, might be outweighed by the air pollution from the increase in regional vehicle trips (SFDPH 2003).

Finally, the DPH analysis highlighted that the developer planned to meet their housing affordability requirement (12 percent of total units by San

**Table 6.3**
SFDPH summary of health impacts of the Rincon Hill Plan

| Elements of healthy cities | Rincon Hill Plan | Effects on regional population health | Effects on vulnerable population health |
|---|---|---|---|
| Goods and services: access to food, retail goods, transit, child care, and health facilities | 65,000 sq. ft. retail /office space<br>Access to regional transit nodes<br>Adjacent to downtown | Beneficial | Uncertain |
| Housing adequacy: affordable, adequate, and stable housing | 5,500 new units at $625,000 estimated base price<br>900 new affordable units likely in low-income neighborhoods | Less than Desirable | Adverse |
| Healthy economy: diverse and integrated businesses providing meaningful, safe, and living wage jobs | 65,000 sq. ft. retail and office space<br>Job-growth occupations with low-moderate wages | Uncertain | Uncertain |
| Public infrastructure: access to high-quality roadways, sidewalks schools, libraries, parks, and recreational facilities | Existing adjacent transit corridors<br>New "living streets" designs<br>New park, but overall deficient open space<br>No site for neighborhood school | Mixed beneficial and adverse | Uncertain |
| Safety and security: protection from crime, physical injury, and physical hazards | Potential new vehicle—pedestrian conflicts | Mixed beneficial and adverse | Uncertain |
| Social cohesion: cohesive and supportive relationships among friends, neighbors, and co-workers. | Community center site proposed | Uncertain | Uncertain |
| Social equity: economic and ethnic diversity and an equitable distribution of public resources and opportunities | Housing affordability excludes low-income households participation | Adverse | N/A |
| Environmental stewardship: sustainable use and management of environmental resources | Increased housing adjacent to downtown<br>Housing costs exceed employee capacity | Mixed beneficial and adverse | N/A |

Source: SFDPH (2004b:1).

Francisco law) by building these units in a low-income neighborhood miles away from the proposed project. This was likely to exacerbate residential segregation by race and class in the city. By building low-income units in areas with existing public housing, the Rincon Hill project would likely exacerbate residential segregation and further concentrate poverty, dynamics that adversely impact health and perpetuate health inequities (SFDPH 2004b). The SFDPH provided a summary table of the likely adverse impacts from the proposed Rincon Hill project on both population health and specifically on vulnerable populations (table 6.3).

## Health Assessment and Community Power

The SFDPH's analyses of the Rincon Hill Plan did not persuade the planning commission to amend the environmental review and the development plan was approved. However, the DPH's research findings were shared with concerned community-based organizations and members of the city's Board of Supervisors. A group of supervisors, led by Chris Daly, used some of the DPH's analyses on displacement and residential segregation to demand that the developer increase the proportion of below market rate units in the Rincon Hill project to 17.5 from 12 percent and construct all the below-market-rate housing either on site or within the local planning district (Brahinsky 2005). In addition the South of Market Community Action Network (SOMCAN), the group that had worked with the MAC to oppose the Trinity Plaza project, used the SFDPH health impact assessment to also challenge the Rincon Hill Plan.

SOMCAN pressed the city's supervisors and Planning Department to respond to the local community's needs and the adverse impacts from the Rincon Hill Plan. The organization emphasized that the Planning Department had defined "planning areas" in SoMa in such a way that it caused neighborhood residents to compete against one another for community benefits and limited their ability to craft a community planning vision for the entire SoMa. The group noted that even though the South of Market area was relatively small compared to other city-defined neighborhoods, the Planning Department had divided SoMa into thirteen separate planning districts (figure 6.3). According to Chris Durazo (2005), an organizer with SOMCAN:

[Dividing up SoMa into so many planning districts] sent a clear message from the city that redeveloping the area was going to take a "subdivide and conquer" approach, pitting neighbor against neighbor and historical allies against one another. The impacts of this strategy were clear; the boundaries of the EIR were just the little redevelopment area, not the entire neighborhood or, better yet, the Eastern Neighborhoods of the city. The reality was that there were at least 60 different projects being proposed or under construction in SoMa at the time. By placing their reviews in these tiny, artificially defined "development areas," the Planning Department could expedite review and approval and not "see" the cumulative impacts all these projects were having on our once vibrant cultural community.[34]

The SoMa was the landing point for many Filipino immigrants arriving into San Francisco and home to its "Manilatown." However, urban renewal programs that had destroyed much of San Francisco's Fillmore District threatened nearby Manilatown buildings (Broussard 1993). In the 1970s the city, developers, and Filipinos engaged in a struggle to preserve the International Hotel (the "I-Hotel")—a building that housed many seasonal Asian laborers, particularly Filipino and Chinese men[35] and many elderly (Salomon 1998). The grassroots movement led by Asian-Americans to save the I-Hotel is viewed by some historians as one of the most important chapters in the history of Asian-American housing advocacy in the United States (Solomon 1998). The struggle lasted until 1979, when activists were forcibly removed and the building was razed.

SOMCAN argued to the city that the Rincon Hill project was likely to exacerbate gentrification pressures in the area and strain existing infrastructure. SOMCAN defined gentrification as:

The process by which poor and working-class residents, usually communities of color, are displaced from neighborhoods by rising costs and other forces directly related to an influx of new, wealthier, and often white residents. These forces include both market forces and public policies which may deliberately or inadvertently make a neighborhood more attractive or accessible to a high-income population. (SOMCAN 2004:4)

During a public hearing about the Rincon Hill project, SOMCAN offered data suggesting that the project would also severely strain essential infrastructure across SoMa, such as open space and elementary schools. Using a map developed by the SFDPH showing the existing open space and primary schools in the neighborhood (figure 6.4), SOMCAN argued that the Rincon Hill project needed to account for how they would mitigate the impact of hundreds of new families on existing parks and schools. In addition, using data provided by the SFDPH, SOMCAN argued that the lack of open space and recreation areas for children would adversely

**Figure 6.3**
South of Market planning and redevelopment areas
Source: South of Market Community Action Network (2006)

impact community health by increasing pedestrian injuries and school overcrowding. According to SOMCAN director April Veneracion (2005):

The map was a powerful image showing how inadequate amenities are for folks in SoMa. While it wasn't our entire platform, it was symbolic of existing neglect and the incoherence of analyzing the thirteen districts separately. The map also helped show that health impacts from a lack of parks and community infrastructure was going to impact children the most. These data, along with the health-based affordable housing arguments, helped us justify new demands on the project, specifically a development impact fee to fund community benefits.

## A Development Impact Fee and Community Benefit Agreement

SOMCAN called for a development impact fee that would require the Rincon Hill project proponents to provide resources to the community that could be used for new infrastructure. After months of negotiations among

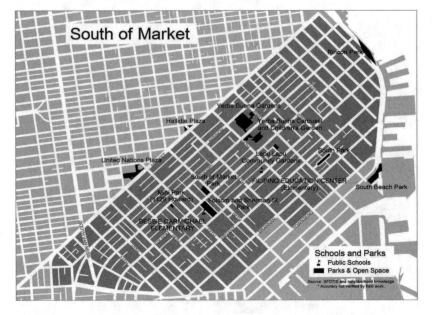

**Figure 6.4**
South of Market area, parks and schools
Source: South of Market Community Action Network (2006)

activists, the developer and city supervisors, particularly Chris Daly, the Planning Commission drafted City Ordinance 217-05, on August 9, 2005, calling for the project to include affordable housing on site, increase the percentage of affordable housing and create a development impact fee of $25 per square foot. The impact fee was a notable accomplishment in itself, but the amount was also notable because it exceeded the amount of a possible impact fee suggested by private consultants hired by the mayor's office and the city's Planning Department by $10 to $15 per square foot. In exchange for paying the development impact fee, the developer would be granted a "zoning bonus," or be allowed to build the proposed buildings higher than the current zoning allowed. A portion of the fee was specifically designated for the construction of affordable housing. In sum, the city expected to generate approximately $50 million for a SoMa Community Stabilization Fund (Goodyear 2005).

While development impact fees are not a unique tool in planning, using public health arguments to justify and support an impact fee was new.

Importantly, SOMCAN convinced the city's supervisors that the impact fee should be managed by a newly created SoMa Community Advisory Committee. The Committee would have representatives from the mayor's Office of Community Development and seven members elected from the neighborhood and approved by a vote of the full Board of Supervisors (SFMOCD 2005). The developer, eager to move forward on the project, agreed to the impact fee and project changes requested by community members (Vega 2005).

However, San Francisco's Mayor Gavin Newsom called the agreement "the worst type of strong-armed 'alderman-style' tactics" and that such behavior was "simply unacceptable" (Vega 2005). In an August 11, 2005, editorial in the *San Francisco Chronicle*, entitled "Shakedown at City Hall," the newspaper lambasted the agreement, noting:

[Supervisor] Daly has strong-armed developers hoping to build a half-dozen giant condo towers in his South of Market district to put up $68 million for affordable housing, a noble if pertinacious goal. . . . But along with his colleagues, Daly managed to pry from the developers an additional $34 million for a "nonprofit community fund" that will be overseen by a group handpicked by him and his fellow board members to do with as they please. . . . Deals of this dubiousness usually happen behind closed doors. The outrage is that no one at City Hall is stepping forth to stop it. (SF Chronicle 2005)

Yet the city's Planning Department lauded the agreement as "a return to thoughtful and deliberate urban planning in San Francisco," noting that hundreds of citizens had attended public workshops to craft the initial plan and the final agreement was the result of a multi-party, public negotiation among city officials, the mayor's office, Supervisor Daly, and a host of community-based organizations (Macris 2006). Despite his apparent opposition, the mayor signed the ordinance into law on August 19, 2005.

By March 2008 the members of the Community Stabilization Fund's Advisory Committee[36] had drafted a set of overarching goals that focused on strengthening community cohesion, supporting economic and work-force development for low-income residents and businesses that serve the SoMa community, increasing access to affordable housing opportunities for existing residents of SoMa, and improving the neighborhood's infrastructure and environment (http://www.sfgov.org/site/mocd_index .asp?id=44635). The group had also agreed that core strategies to achieve these goals would be to leverage their funds by investing in endowments, purchasing land, developing a SoMa community land trust, identifying and engaging other grantors who could match their funds, and strengthening the capacity of existing community organizations. The Community Advisory Committee was managing about $5 million, and finalizing criteria for soliciting small grants from community organizations that wanted to initiate community improvement projects. The group was also developing an investment strategy to ensure the long-term fiscal viability of their planning efforts and considering establishing an emergency fund for displaced residents.

Since the Community Stabilization Fund needed to wait for the impact fee monies until after buildings were completed, no funds could be secured until nearly two years after the group was approved. However, the advisory committee spent its first two years clarifying governance issues with community members and the mayor's office. For example, the committee has redefined the benefit area as the entire SoMa community, not just the Rincon Hill development area, and according to Jazzie Collins, co-chair of the Community Advisory Committee, the first two years of meetings discussed community needs and provided a new forum for residents, local businesses, youth, and elderly to shape the initial spending priorities of the Stabilization Fund (Collins 2007). The mayor's Office of Community Development has also recognized the explicit social justice agenda for the Stabilization Fund, noting:

[M]onies deposited in the Fund shall be used to address the impacts of destabilization on residents and businesses in SOMA including assistance for affordable housing and community asset building, small business assistance, development of new affordable homes for low-income households, rental subsidies for low-income households, down payment assistance for home ownership for low-income households, eviction prevention, employment development and capacity building for SOMA residents, job growth and job placement, small business assistance, leadership development, community cohesion, civic participation, community-based programs and economic development. (SFMOCD 2005)

In the Rincon Hill planning process, the Planning Department recognized early on that additional public benefits beyond what the developer was offering would be necessary for the surrounding neighborhood. However, the Planning Department did not have the upper level political support for making these demands. Community advocacy combined with evidence gathered by the local public health agency to provide the political momentum that ultimately secured tangible public benefits from the planning process.

## Toward Healthy Urban Development

This chapter has highlighted some of the ways public health and planning practices might come together to promote health equity. More specifically, the environmental impact assessment process offered a venue for the health department and community-based organizations to weigh into the planning process with human health analyses. The Trinity Plaza and Rincon Hill cases suggest that health analyses are crucial, but insufficient, for ensuring urban development promotes health equity. Community organizing and involvement, especially from groups not traditionally focused on health such as housing and environmental justice groups, proved crucial for creating the political pressure on agencies to act and for offering important local knowledge about likely adverse health impacts from development plans.

A key lesson from these cases for the politics of healthy and equitable city planning is that strong social movements that can build new networks across sectors—such as housing, parks and recreation, and economic development—and with health and planning agencies are an essential aspect of healthy city planning. The MAC used their organizing base and the knowledge and expertise within their coalition, such as informing the DPH about the legal requirement for health analyses within CEQA, that combined to provide the political pressure that convinced the public health agency to analyze and weigh in on new development projects. Thus community groups acted as advocacy coalitions that helped co-produce innovations in the production of new knowledge and the re-ordering of political activity (Sabatier and Jenkins-Smith 1993; Jasanoff 2004).

### Reflection in Action
At the same time that community coalitions were advocating for change within municipal governance, the community groups themselves were faced with changing their own organizations. By engaging in health impact assessment work, SOMCAN was forced to participate in unfamiliar territory and faced the prospect of potentially alienating some of their members. Both the MAC and SOMCAN built their power base through community organizing and developing a broad membership base, which is often made easier by targeting one actor or institution such as an unscrupulous developer, slumlord, or obstinate planning agency (Bobo et al. 1996; Shaw 1996). The decision to participate in health impact assessments forced the coalitions to reflect on their own organizing strategies and how to negotiate

with developers, city agencies, and elected officials for land use changes and community health improvements. Oscar Grande, an organizer with PODER and MAC, reflected on these dynamics:

Moving from organizing to drafting the People's Plan and working with the DPH on the health assessment challenged us to combine base-building strategies with research and analysis, things we hadn't focused on too much in past campaigns. We didn't want to lose member commitment and enthusiasm by engaging them too much in the complexities and uncertainties of health research. At the same time we saw health as a resource for our movement and as one more, but not the only, strategy to promote social justice.

April Veneracion, executive director of SOMCAN, expressed a similar challenge when reflecting on the role of health assessments in their work to promote equitable development:

We were skeptical that the health assessments would change the Planning Department or projects. At the same time the health evidence helped expand our platform and turned affordable housing and employment justice issues into community health issues. Before the DPH reports we had never really thought about our work as community health promotion. But we took a strategic approach and used the DPH assessment selectively, like showing how Rincon [Hill area plan] was going to place a huge burden on existing parks and schools.

This comment not only highlights how the health analyses influenced the coalition's affordable housing organizing but also how the analyses helped the community group become a new advocate for health equity. A crucial aspect of healthy city planning is that civic organizations and the private sector—not just government agencies—that do not currently see themselves as contributing to health promotion and equity begin to recast their work as part of a new movement for promoting community well-being.

**Learning by Doing**
The approach to health analysis used by the SFDPH also offers insights for the more general practice of healthy city planning. The DPH applied HIA broadly, not relying on one specific methodology, and combined secondary health and land use data with the local knowledge of residents facing eviction and living in impacted communities. Additionally the DPH revealed that even within the legal and procedural constraints of California's Environmental Quality Act, analyses of the direct and indirect

social determinants of health are not only possible, but can force project proponents (and lead agencies) to consider impacts on existing vulnerable populations. The DPH was also committed to public disclosure even as they experimented with new and uncertain health analyses of development projects. This transparency improved the legitimacy of the health analyses in the eyes of skeptical publics and public agencies. Yet, as these cases revealed, the road to healthy urban development decisions was slow and steady; the DPH learned from community members, performed their own research, conducted collaborative trainings/dialogues on the social determinants of health, commented at hearings, wrote comment letters, and built strategic alliances with community-based organizations and city agencies along the way. While this approach did not always directly change decision making, it did help build new knowledge and the capacity to use health evidence within community coalitions and legislators, both of which altered development in ways that are likely to improve community health.

In order to build stronger relationships with the Planning Department, the SFDPH might have offered joint trainings with planners in HIA. This way planners might have had more background about the relationships between development and human health before being confronted with making a contentious public decision, such as in the Trinity Plaza example. The Community Stabilization Fund reflected an attempt to build a new, democratically accountable institution that could promote health equity, but it may be too early to tell if this new institution will achieve its goals. Ultimately the collaborations between community groups and the SFDPH suggest that learning by doing is essential for promoting healthy and equitable urban development.

# 7 Health Impact Assessment[37]

In November 2002 community members and city officials met in San Francisco's Mission District to discuss how the Health Department might support the Mission Anti-displacement Coalition's (MAC) "People's Plan." The People's Plan was a land use, zoning, and community development plan drafted by the MAC and endorsed by thousands of local residents. The document proposed, among other things, zoning and land use changes that would promote the development of more affordable housing, preserve industrial sector jobs, and stop the demolition of existing buildings. At the same time, the city's Planning Department announced that they were set to launch a planning process aimed at developing new zoning controls for the Mission and the surrounding Eastern Neighborhoods of San Francisco. At a meeting with the city agencies, representatives from the MAC—already aware that the health department was interested in using the practice of health impact assessment (HIA) to address health inequities in urban policy and planning—asked the agency to help them review the likely health impacts of the goals and objectives of their People's Plan. Having spent years organizing the community to draft the People's Plan, the MAC was interested in demonstrating the value of their vision but reluctant to lead a health impact assessment—which they had never done before—without the assistance and experience of the San Francisco Department of Public Health (Grande 2005).

The Health Department agreed to work with the community coalition to explore the process and content of a community-based health impact assessment. By March 2003 the SFDPH helped facilitate a community meeting that was considered the first meeting of the Mission Neighborhood Community Impact Assessment process (Bhatia 2005). During the meeting the DPH asked residents to envision the elements that make their

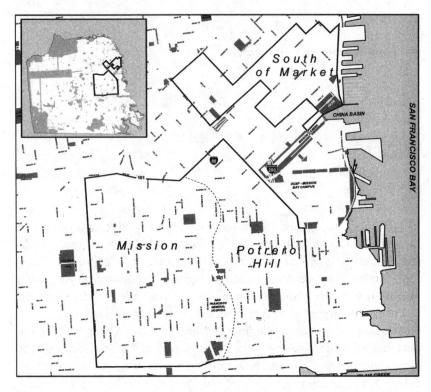

**Figure 7.1**
Eastern Neighborhoods of San Francisco
Source: San Francisco Department of Planning (2003)

community "healthy," and much of the discussion focused on affordable housing. Regular meetings between the MAC and the DPH continued, and discussions shifted from envisioning the healthy neighborhood to building an evidence base. Community residents also requested that the assessment consider how neighborhood changes were influenced by regional dynamics, like the high-tech economy. As the MAC and the DPH discussed the agenda and process for conducting a broader health impact assessment, the city's Planning Department released a new rezoning plan for the city's Eastern Neighborhoods, which include the Mission District, Showplace Square–Potrero Hill, and South of Market areas (figure 7.1). The Planning Department also announced that they were preparing both an environmental and social impact assessment of the rezoning plans and that these assessments would be done independently using experienced consultants.

The MAC and DPH agreed that they should meet with the Planning Department to explore adding health analyses into the environmental or social impact assessments.

## Merging Participatory Planning with Health Impact Assessment

This chapter highlights the planning process and outcomes of the Eastern Neighborhoods Community Health Impact Assessment (ENCHIA)—the process that emerged in response to the Planning Department's rezoning plan. During the ENCHIA, community groups and city agencies collaborated in a participatory planning process that built new working relationships, gathered new evidence to assess the health impacts of planning proposals, and generated a new analytic process, called the Healthy Development Measurement Tool (HDMT), that could be applied to future urban planning and policy decisions. Over twenty-five different interest groups participated in the ENCHIA and met monthly for close to two years. Through a consensus-based collaborative process, the ENCHIA produced a vision of the healthy city, established objectives and indicators necessary to implement and measure progress toward this vision, and gathered and mapped data to populate these indicators. The group also analyzed over thirty non–health specific policies that might promote the healthy city vision. Ultimately the ENCHIA would have a significant influence on planning decisions not just in San Francisco but also on healthy planning and health equity coalition building across the entire Bay Area. This chapter examines the political factors that contributed to the local and regional success of the ENCHIA and the implications for designing planning processes that promote healthy and equitable urban governance.

## Framing Healthy City Planning

The MAC and the DPH met again with the Planning Department in January 2004 to discuss how the assessments of the Eastern Neighborhoods rezoning plans might include human health. Miriam Chion, a senior planner with the San Francisco Planning Department at the time, suggested that the health impact assessment process that the MAC and DPH had already started ought to be expanded to include the rezoning plan. Rajiv Bhatia, Director of Environmental and Occupational Health at the San Francisco Department of Public Health, recalled that in the meeting Paul Maltzer, director of environmental review for the Planning Department, acknowledged that public health was already part of the environmental assessment process but rejected the idea of broadening the scope of analyses to include such social determinants of health as housing affordability, displacement, and social cohesion in the Environmental Impact Report (EIR). Maltzer was also candid about the obstacles to broadening the scope of the California Environmental Quality Act (CEQA), including the need for objective, replicable analyses and the likelihood of political and even legal pressures to constrain CEQA analyses. Maltzer also expressed his personal belief that the environmental review process was not the right venue for addressing community needs and he refused to initiate any changes unless directed to do so by city leaders (Bhatia 2005). However, Maltzer did offer his support for an HIA in parallel to the required environmental review process. With the Planning Department refusing to include the social determinants of health in the pending environmental review process, the MAC looked to the DPH to take the lead. MAC leaders requested that the health impact assessment of the People's Plan be expanded to include the Eastern Neighborhoods rezoning plan and the DPH agreed to work with the group. The Planning Department agreed to participate in the health impact assessment process, but made no commitments to incorporate its findings into either the environmental or social impact assessment.

## Deliberative Democracy and Health Impact Assessment

As the MAC and SFDPH began organizing the new health impact assessment, both groups recognized that they needed a strategy to identify and recruit new participants from beyond the Mission District. The SFDPH recognized that they must serve broad city interests and remain unbiased to any political constituency while being an advocate for health needs throughout the assessment process. An added challenge was that this new HIA would likely need to propose healthy land use and policy changes, since the final rezoning plan had not been released. According to Rajiv Bhatia, the political controversies that already surrounded the HIA meant that its legitimacy was likely to rest as much in the process and representativeness of participants as in its proposals and recommended outcomes (Bhatia 2006).

The DPH also aimed to design a process that embodied the values of the World Health Organization's consensus statement on HIA, commonly called the Gothenburg Statement, which emphasized democratic participa-

> **WHO Principles for Health Impact Assessment**
>
> **Democracy**   The right of people to participate in the formulation and deci-
> sions of proposals that affect their life, both directly and through elected
> decision makers. A distinction should be made between those who take risks
> voluntarily and those who are exposed to risks involuntarily.
>
> **Equity**   The desire to reduce inequity that results from avoidable differences
> in the health determinants and/or health status within and between different
> population groups. In adhering to this value, the HIA [health impact assess-
> ment] should consider the distribution of health impacts across the popula-
> tion, paying specific attention to vulnerable groups and recommend ways to
> improve the proposed development for affected groups.
>
> **Sustainable development**   Development meets the needs of the present gen-
> eration without compromising the ability of future generations to meet their
> own needs. Good health is the basis of resilience in the human communities
> that support development.
>
> **Ethical use of evidence**   Transparent and rigorous processes are used to
> synthesize and interpret the evidence: that the best available evidence from
> different disciplines and methodologies is utilized, that all evidence is valued,
> and that recommendations are developed impartially.
>
> **Comprehensive approach to health**   Physical, mental and social well-being
> is determined by a broad range of factors from all sectors of society.
>
> Source: Quigley et al. (2006:3).

tion, equity, and transparency in the analytic process (Quigley et al. 2006:3),
as noted in the sidebar above. In order to do this, the SFDPH researched
models of participatory HIA, such as the Merseyside Model for Health
Impact Assessment, and public processes used to address controversial
science policy issues, such as the Danish Consensus Conferences and
Science Shops used in Europe (Fischer et al. 2004; Scott-Samuel et al.
2001; Wachelder 2003). The SFDPH also understood that the process did
not have to be constrained by established impact assessment practice or
procedural rules, and it was specifically motivated to achieve a high level
of power for participants by facilitating their ownership and oversight in
the design and outcomes of the HIA. Building on international models of
participation and HIA, the SFDPH and the MAC drafted a set of guiding
principles for designing their health impact assessment that included:

• evaluating social and economic effects not considered in environmental
impact assessment,

- using a broad definition of health to consider the comprehensive effects of planning,
- creating meaningful participation opportunities for socially marginalized stakeholders,
- allowing participating stakeholders to have power in determining the scope of the assessment,
- valuing community experience as evidence,
- providing scientific methods and data as a response to questions emerging from the process, and
- applying deliberative and consensus-building methods in decision making. (SFDPH 2007a)

The SFDPH also recognized that they needed to build support within their own agency as well as other city agencies for a participatory HIA (Farhang 2006). Staff from the environmental health unit began meeting with other units across the health agency, explaining their objectives for the HIA and seeking expert input. The SFDPH also aimed to build support for the process outside of city government. The agency met with over forty interest groups and private organizations from across the Bay Area that might participant in the assessment. These meetings helped the DPH learn about concerns that different interest groups had with the proposed rezoning plan and other issues that the agency wasn't aware of but could impact the quality of life in the Eastern Neighborhoods (Farhang 2006).[38] Combining aspects of participatory science–policy processes, consensus building and knowledge gleaned from the informational meetings, the DPH and MAC designed a process called the Eastern Neighborhoods Community Health Impact Assessment (ENCHIA) and collaboratively drafted a new set of goals and objectives (table 7.1) and process map outlining the stages of a proposed eighteen-month public process (figure 7.2).

### The Eastern Neighborhoods Community Health Impact Assessment
On November 17, 2004, over twenty-five different nonprofit and private sector organizations and four public agencies in addition to the Departments of Planning and Public Health, joined the Community Council of the ENCHIA and attended the first meeting.[39] The meeting focused on stakeholders getting to know one another, a review of how a consensus-building process works, and a group visioning exercise where participants brainstormed about the elements of a healthy neighborhood. The early

**Table 7.1**
ENCHIA goals and objectives

---

- Identify and analyze the likely impacts of land use plans and zoning controls on health determinants, including housing, jobs, and public infrastructure
- Provide recommendations for land use policies and zoning controls that promote community priorities
- Demonstrate the feasibility of health impact assessment methods
- Promote meaningful public involvement in land use policy making by making explicit competing interests and facilitating consensus
- Develop capacity for inter-agency working relationships

---

Source: SFDPH (2007a:9–10).

objectives for the HIA process were to have group discussions about the elements of a healthy place, how land use does or does not influence these elements, and how the rezoning proposals might influence these elements in a positive or negative way? Meeting agendas, summaries, presentations, and a range of supporting documentation were regularly posted and available to the public on the project website (www.sfdph.org/phes/enchia.htm).

Another early objective was distinguishing for participants how the HIA process was going to be *different* from other assessment processes of the Eastern Neighborhoods rezoning plans. Many participants asked at early meetings, "how is this process different from the environmental and social impact assessments" and "who would be accountable to its findings?" A matrix was developed by the DPH comparing the ENCHIA process with the proposed environmental and social impact assessment processes (table 7.2). The categories the DPH selected reflect, in part, their view of what makes HIA important and different as a public knowledge generating process. For example, the DPH emphasized each process's institutional setting, analytic scope, orientation toward evidence gathering and research methods, roles for the public and nonexperts, use of evidence, and public accountability of both procedures and outcomes.

The first meetings of the ENCHIA were spent in small and large groups building a vision of the "healthy city." Substantive work of participants during early ENCHIA meetings focused on deliberating over and working toward consensus on the elements of a "healthy place." Discussions ranged from the physical characteristics of places to social relationships to measurable health outcomes. One ENCHIA participant described the healthy city

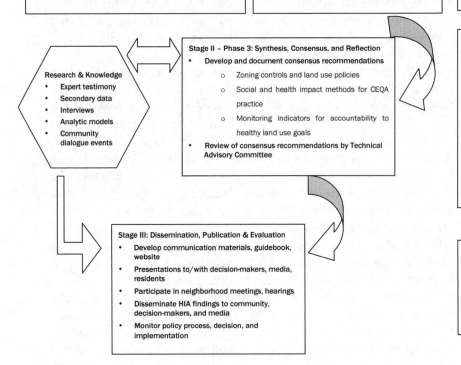

Stage I: Gain Commitments and Develop Organization and Structure
- Interviews with community residents and stakeholders to preliminarily define health impact assessment (HIA) objectives and purpose
- Secure funding and staff resources
- Establish planning committee
- Establish technical advisory committee
- Planning committee selects agencies, organizations, and residents for Stakeholder Council
- Convene Community Council; establish decision-making structure

Stage II – Phase 1: Create collective vision, prioritizing potential impacts of concern and identify assessment knowledge needs
- Introduce 10 elements of healthy land use
- Relate to participant experiences and organizational missions
- Dynamics of land use and demographics in project area
- Translate elements into specific objectives
- Identify land use policies and zoning in effect;

Stage II – Phase 2: Predictions, Challenges, and Model Strategies
- Make prediction of zoning plans and policies to achieve healthy land use goals
- Identify conflicts among objectives and among stakeholders
- Identify political financial and policy barriers
- Identify feasible model strategies to address barriers and healthy development goals

Research & Knowledge
- Expert testimony
- Secondary data
- Interviews
- Analytic models
- Community dialogue events

Stage II – Phase 3: Synthesis, Consensus, and Reflection
- Develop and document consensus recommendations
  o Zoning controls and land use policies
  o Social and health impact methods for CEQA practice
  o Monitoring indicators for accountability to healthy land use goals
- Review of consensus recommendations by Technical Advisory Committee

Stage III: Dissemination, Publication & Evaluation
- Develop communication materials, guidebook, website
- Presentations to/with decision-makers, media, residents
- Participate in neighborhood meetings, hearings
- Disseminate HIA findings to community, decision-makers, and media
- Monitor policy process, decision, and implementation

March to August 2004

September to November 2004

December 2004 to February 2006

April to June 2006

**Figure 7.2**
Eastern Neighborhood Community Health Impact Assessment (ENCHIA) process map

**Figure 7.3**
Rendering of the healthy city, Eastern Neighborhood Community Health Impact
Assessment (ENCHIA)

as a place "where you feel good about living, raising your family, spending
leisure time . . . you know, where you, your kids and your mother-in-law
would like to live." Others suggested a healthy place was more tangible: "A
healthy place is one that helps people recover when they are down, and not
just those living there, but visitors too." Still other participants emphasized
ongoing learning, adaptation and change: "The measure of healthy place
is if people and institutions can learn about what is not working and are
committed to fixing it." As part of the discussions the group drafted pic-
tures to help map some of the more tangible characteristics of a healthy
place (figure 7.3). A set of common elements for the healthy city began to
emerge and facilitators from the SFDPH organized these to include basic
living conditions, a secure livelihood (e.g., a "healthy paycheck"), social
interaction in public places, diverse political representation, and living
near extended families. Six specific elements were formulated into a
Healthy City Vision (table 7.3) and the group decided to use these to frame
their future work. The Healthy City Vision included the following categories: environmental stewardship, safety and security, public infrastructure,

**Table 7.2**
Comparison of environmental, social, and health impact assessment processes by San Francisco Department of Public Health

| Components | CEQA environmental impact assessment (Planning Department) |
|---|---|
| Objectives | To identify significant adverse effects of environmental changes; identify and ensure mitigation; identify and evaluate project alternatives with regards to environmental effects |
| Institutional setting | Legally required by California law prior to project or plan approval |
| Scope | Focus is on potentially adverse changes in the physical environment. Scope of the analysis is constrained by procedural requirements and past practice. Eastern Neighborhood EIR proposed analysis includes: (1) Transportation, including a description of existing conditions and estimates of new vehicle, transit trip generation (2) Air quality, including evaluation of the consistency between the plans and regional air quality plans (3) Noise, including evaluation of noise impacts on residential uses (4) Cultural resources, including impacts on landmarks and historical districts (5) Visual quality and shadow (6) Hydrology and water quality, including storm water outfalls (7) Hazardous materials, including an evaluation of permitted and expected hazardous materials uses (8) Land use, including environmental effects from the displacement of businesses (9) Employment, population, and housing |
| Research methods | Checklists; secondary data analysis, quantitative modeling; expert predictions. Will also include some area specific primary data collection and analysis (e.g., traffic counts for transportation analysis) |
| Role(s) of the public | Public has opportunities to comment verbally and in writing at specific stages in the assessment process, including public scoping meetings at the start of the environmental review process and comment on the Draft EIR; final EIR must include responses to all comments on the Draft EIR |
| Role of experts and evidence | Experts and consultants do discipline specific research and provide analysis and interpretation |

| Socioeconomic analysis (Planning Department) | HIA of Eastern Neighborhoods rezoning (SFDPH) |
| --- | --- |
| To identify, predict, and document the socio-economic changes related or influenced by the proposed zoning alternatives | To identify the impacts of proposed rezoning policy on people and communities; to make recommendation for zoning controls, specific plans, and related changes in transportation and public infrastructure in order to protect and promote public health; to increase awareness of urban planning—public health relationships; to test a model practice that may provide lessons for community planning, public involvement, and EIA practice |
| Discretionary analysis requested by Planning Commission based on public interest | Discretionary analysis based on public and Planning Commission interest; convened by public agency (SFDPH) |
| Focus on indirect economic, fiscal, and demographic effects of planning; relation of these effects to human health is indirect (e.g., job loss) and scope is determined by Planning staff and constrained by available methods and financial resources | Focus on social, economic, environmental determinants of human health; impacts of concern determined by stakeholder Council originally selected by project planning team. Analyses include: (1) Housing design and location and indoor/outdoor air quality (2) Vehicle volumes and pedestrian injuries (3) Public transit access and health care utilization (4) Housing adequacy and social cohesion (5) Parks and physical activity (6) Natural spaces and recovery form illness (7) Neighborhood schools and student achievement (8) Building design and violence (9) Social segregation and premature mortality (10) Access to food resources and healthy nutrition (11) Access to child care and child development |
| Primary and secondary data analysis; limited qualitative methods and focus groups | Literature review; secondary data analysis; quantitative analysis and forecasting; qualitative methods; group deliberative processes; policy analysis; consensus building methods |
| HIA stakeholders will be tapped to participate in focus groups | Stakeholder Council is established with representatives of public agencies, for-profit and nonprofit organizations; lay residents are also actively recruited and trained for participation on the Council; affected populations may be sampled as respondents for surveys and focus groups; Council also may hold public hearings |
| Consultants conduct research and analysis and provide interpretation in partnership with Planning staff | Process primarily values experiences of Community Council members as expertise; project staff conducts research and collects data/evidence for Council to review; where necessary the process uses disciplinary and content experts to respond to stakeholder questions |

**Table 7.3**
Elements of a healthy city, ENCHIA process

---

**Environmental stewardship** (1) Clean air and water, (2) renewable and local energy sources, (3) sustainable and green infrastructure, (4) healthy habitats, and (5) sustainable agriculture

**Sustainable and safe transportation** (1) Multiple transportation options, (2) affordable and accessible public transit, (3) safer streets and sidewalks, and (4) fewer cars on roads

**Public safety** (1) Safe and walkable streets and sidewalks, (2) clean and accessible public spaces, and (3) the absence of crime and violence

**Public infrastructure/access to goods and services** (1) Quality schools and child care, (2) safe parks, playgrounds, and sports/recreation areas, (3) neighborhood commercial districts to meet daily needs, (4) active street life and uses, (5) healthy and affordable foods, (6) community services and resources for youth and seniors, (7) space for community leisure activities, and (8) disability access

**Adequate and healthy housing** (1) Affordable, (2) safe from physical hazards, (3) stable and secure, (4) diverse in terms of type and size, (5) located in mixed-income and mixed-race communities of friends and neighbors, and (6) located in close proximity to access to jobs, education, goods, and services

**Healthy economy** (1) Jobs that are safe, pay living wages, and provide insurance and other benefits, (2) diverse employment opportunities for residents and individuals with a range of education, languages, and skill levels, (3) locally owned businesses, (4) a local economy where money is flowing through the neighborhood, and (5) economy does not harm the natural environment

**Community participation** (1) Active engagement of community members affected by proposed development, (2) community involvement in proposal visioning/planning, allocation of responsibility, appraisal/data collection, decision making, monitoring, and evaluation, (3) opportunities for public comment on proposal, (4) open and transparent discussion about trade-offs, and (5) accountability and compliance of specific projects with general plans

---

Source: SFDPH (2007a).

access to goods and services, adequate and healthy housing, and healthy economy (SFDPH 2007a:38).[40]

By starting with a discussion of a vision for a healthy community, rather than a narrow focus on problems and failures, the ENCHIA process aimed to understand, describe and explain the strengths and assets of the area, its population groups, and existing institutions—the very things that give life and meaning to a place. The ENCHIA process also emphasized that every neighborhood and population group are continually searching for ways to function better and improve survival, often in the face of dire circumstances, and learning from these strategies could benefit the HIA process.

## Debating Objectives for Healthy Policy Making

Once the Council created the Healthy City Vision, the process turned to helping participants articulate Community Health Objectives for each element of the vision. Six subgroups were established to match the "healthy city elements," and these groups worked to draft specific health objectives for each element. For instance, a specific objective developed for the healthy city element of "access to goods and services" was "to assure affordable and high-quality child care for all neighborhoods." One objective from the "healthy economy" subgroup was to "increase jobs that provide healthy, safe, and meaningful work." During this process participants noted that it was not clear how some objectives could be achieved by land use and zoning changes alone. For example, one participant asked: "How can zoning for a retail use influence the kinds of products offered in the store or the way they treat their workers?" The process of trying to attach objectives to the healthy city vision began to highlight to participants the strengths and limits of HIA (SFDPH 2007a:41–42).

During the process of assigning specific objectives to elements of the healthy city vision, participants noted that many were linked to one another and could sometimes be in conflict. For example, some participants highlighted that policies that encouraged economically and racially diverse neighborhoods might exacerbate gentrification in existing places. Others noted that requiring "green buildings" could increase the cost of housing construction, and adding more park space might increase property values in an area but also contribute to residential displacement. The complexities and potential conflicts of objectives were recorded and ENCHIA participants increasingly wanted to attach "hard" data to their newly drafted objectives.

### Engaging with Structural Inequalities

ENCHIA participants also debated whether acknowledging conflicts among objectives was enough or whether the ENCHIA ought to take a position on certain objectives. Group members disagreed over which way to proceed and discussions often highlighted the competing interests represented in the process. Consider this exchange among Council members:

**Participant 1:**  What many of the objectives focus on are economics and acquiring more income for health, but what about racism that limits choices even when you have money?

**Participant 2:**   Yeah, I mean, race and class can't be separated, but what I think we are doing is trying to be practical here about what it takes to lead a healthy life, right?

**Participant 1:**   But what you are assuming is that there is a level playing field; that if I get affordable housing, I'll be healthier. But for blacks, Latinos, Asians, people of color, discrimination and racism almost always gets in the way. I'm asking where does white privilege and oppression fit into our objectives?

**Participant 2:**   Of course racism exists, and we want to address it, but that is a value. The objectives are practical ways to address discrimination.

**Participant 1:**   Look, take the objective of increasing bicycling. By increasing bike lanes, you create more safe opportunities to bike. Seems good. But what this ignores is who is riding bikes, why and where are they going? Latinos use bikes more in this city than anyone else, for work and deliveries, not exercise or leisure. So when we ignore discussing the assumptions behind these objectives and who they are intended for, that ignores that we live in a racialized society.

This exchange was one of many discussions over how and if the ENCHIA process was going to make racism a focus of the assessment process. Some participants wanted race and racism, and the health evidence of racial inequities, to act as the central focus of the ENCHIA. However, others wanted to stick to more "tangible" objectives and outcomes. Staff of the DPH facilitating the process aimed to keep racism part of the discussion, but the group did not reach a consensus that racism should act as the central focus of the assessment.

Some Council members, speaking confidentially, feared that the "focus on racism would polarize the group and contribute to participants leaving the process." Others saw the ENCHIA as an opportunity to highlight "that even progressive white-led organizations discount how powerful racism is as a motivator for social action and minimizing the importance of racism by emphasizing cross-racial unity for the sake of 'getting things done' might lead to people of color withdrawing from the process." Eventually the group reached agreement that a commitment to addressing racial privilege through dialogue and policy was necessary, but this assessment would focus on how racism might be manifested in land use issues, such as transit access, affordable housing, environmental quality, and economic opportunities.

After months of dialogue and subgroup meetings, the ENCHIA reached agreement on twenty-seven overarching Community Health Objectives that defined the healthy city vision (table 7.4). The objectives would also act to direct data gathering, the next stage in the ENCHIA process.

**Table 7.4**
Objectives of the healthy city, ENCHIA

---

**Environmental stewardship (ES)**

Objective ES.1    Decrease consumption of energy and natural resources
Objective ES.2    Restore, preserve and protect healthy natural habitats
Objective ES.3    Promote food access and sustainable urban and rural agriculture
Objective ES.4    Promote productive reuse of previously contaminated sites
Objective ES.5    Preserve clean air quality

**Sustainable transportation (ST)**

Objective ST.1    Decrease private motor vehicles trips and miles traveled
Objective ST.2    Provide affordable, safe, and sustainable transportation options
Objective ST.3    Create safe quality environments for walking and biking

**Public safety (PS)**

Objective PS.1    Improve accessibility, beauty, and cleanliness of public spaces
Objective PS.2    Maintain safe levels of community noise
Objective PS.3    Promote safe neighborhoods free of crime and violence

**Public infrastructure/access to goods and services (PI)**

Objective PI.1    Assure affordable and high-quality child care for all
                  neighborhoods
Objective PI.2    Assure accessible and high-quality educational facilities
Objective PI.3    Increase park, open space, and recreation facilities
Objective PI.4    Assure spaces for libraries, performing arts, theater, museums,
                  concerts, festivals for personal and educational fulfillment
Objective PI.5    Assure affordable and high-quality public health facilities
Objective PI.6    Assure access to daily goods and service needs, including
                  financial services and healthy foods

**Adequate and healthy housing (HH)**

Objective HH.1    Preserve and construct housing in proportion to demand with
                  regards to size, affordability, tenure, and location
Objective HH.2    Protect residents from involuntary displacement
Objective HH.3    Increase opportunities for home ownership
Objective HH.4    Increase spatial integration by ethnicity and economic class

**Healthy economy (HE)**

Objective HE.1    Increase high-quality employment opportunities for local
                  residents
Objective HE.2    Increase jobs that provide healthy, safe, and meaningful work
Objective HE.3    Increase equality in income and wealth
Objective HE.4    Increase benefits to communities impacted by development
Objective HE.5    Promote industry that benefits and protects natural resources
                  and the environment

**Community participation (CP)**

Objective CP.1    Assure equitable and democratic participation throughout the
                  planning process

---

Source: SFDPH (2007a:42–43).

### Building a New Evidence Base for Health Impact Assessment

Having worked for almost nine months debating and refining the vision and objectives of the healthy city, the group began gathering evidence to support their objectives. The SFDPH organized data available through municipal agencies and identified additional sources of relevant data, such as those gathered by nonprofit organizations. Public agencies participating in the ENCHIA, from the police department to transit agency, also provided access to data. To help narrow the data collection process, the Council agreed to try and limit "healthy place" indicators to quantitative or qualitative data that was meaningful and valid to ENCHIA participants, regularly collected, reliably measurable and/or observable, actionable, and motivated action.

Using existing data sets, SFDPH staff analyzed and mapped information at the request of ENCHIA participants and meetings were used to discuss preliminary findings. Yet conflicts often surfaced during meetings about the meaningfulness and accountability of different evidence. For instance, the San Francisco Recreation and Parks Department (SFRPD) provided information on the location of parks across the city, and these data were mapped and shown with a quarter-mile buffer around each park (SFDPH 2007a:45). The map was intended to show the number of residents that had access to a park, defined by those living within a quarter mile. Additional analyses using these data suggested that the Eastern Neighborhoods comprised 7 percent of San Francisco's land area and 11 percent of the population, but contained only 1 percent of the city's open space (57 of the 6,410 total acres respectively). During discussions of the map and these data, some participants noted that the quarter-mile distance may be irrelevant if the park was unsafe, occupied by homeless people or drug dealers, and didn't include activity spaces for all groups, such as barbeque pits and playgrounds. Others noted that using linear distance was irrelevant in San Francisco, where "a park can be 500 feet away but if it's straight up-hill to get there or on a steep grade, you may never use it." The quality of the resource and whether the data analyses reflected local context—from park user's needs to local topography—was emphasized as a necessary but often overlooked aspect of gathering evidence about healthy places.

### The Limits of Quantification and Place-Based Meanings

The discussions over data gathering and analysis also revealed to participants that not all healthy city objectives could or ought to be measured quantitatively. For example, after presenting police department crime statistics for the area around the 16th Street Bay Area Rapid Transit (BART) station in the Mission District, some group members from the Mission noted that these data misrepresented the "safety" of the area and may stigmatize the area in a way that may be counterproductive (SFDPH 2007a:46). Participants offered personal experiences and anecdotes discussing what they interpreted as "racial profiling" in the area while others suggested that safety couldn't be captured by indicators alone. One member stated: "Feeling safe is about a relationship between you and your surroundings, not counting the number of assaults, how many lights work, or the number of cops on the street. I don't mean to dismiss the statistics, but it's important that we ask who is being counted, why are people on the street, and how do the users of this space feel about safety and crime?" ENCHIA members expressed a desire to explore the social and political questions that often reside behind statistics and numbers and highlighted that quantitative information can often hide social meanings. While quantitative statistics often act as a tool of public policy by offering a semblance of rationality and objectivity to political decisions, ENCHIA participants requested that the quantitative measures be complemented with interpretative qualitative data.

## Community Health Experts: Youth, Elderly, and Workers

Aiming to more systematically capture qualitative information and narratives about health issues, the SFDPH and the ENCHIA Council decided to initiate two new research efforts. The first was a series of focus group meetings and interviews by DPH staff with community members that were not participating in the ENCHIA. The aim of this process was to capture views of the "healthy city" from the direct experiences of community residents. A second research project aimed to gather more in-depth data on the relationships between employment and well-being in San Francisco, a principal concern of ENCHIA participants. This second study would interview day laborers, domestic workers, artists, restaurant workers, and software engineers in the Eastern Neighborhoods. The community study asked participants how they would define the healthy neighborhood and how changes in their neighborhood were impacting their perception of health and safety? The labor study asked participants about their physical conditions at work, sense of job security, whether they received health insurance through work, the amount of control and participation in decision making they had over their job, and the amount of time spent at work versus with family and other activities.

The findings from these research projects were presented to the ENCHIA Council in two reports. The community assessment report was entitled, *Results from a Community Assessment of Health and Land Use* (SFDPH 2007a:app. 3) and the labor study was compiled into a report entitled, *Tales of the City's Workers: A Work and Health Survey of San Francisco's Workforce*. The qualitative data findings helped fill information gaps left by quantitative data. For example, while a citywide database tracked the changing demographics of the Eastern Neighborhoods, the community assessment included interviews and focus group discussions with seniors and revealed that many lived with a great fear of eviction and felt their mobility was increasingly constrained due to increased vehicular traffic. Young people noted that they felt constant stress from overcrowded living conditions, regular gang violence when traveling to school outside their neighborhood, and from a lack of future job opportunities in the area.

The labor study revealed that workers in San Francisco were faced with either very low-wage, indeterminate, high-stress and high-paced jobs that lacked health insurance or highly paid professional positions requiring an advanced college degree that included health benefits and a perceived sense of control. Low-skilled, well-paying jobs that included health benefits and a sense of control over decision making were almost nonexistent in San Francisco. Day laborers and domestic workers emphasized that their lives often revolved around the daily stress of finding work, overcrowded housing conditions and frequent disruptions to their family life, especially for their children. The findings from these two studies not only provided new data on populations that are often overlooked in health and planning analyses but convinced many ENCHIA participants that the process ought to analyze and make recommendations for a much broader set of urban policies for promoting health equity than just those related to land use changes in the Eastern Neighborhoods.

## Drafting Healthy Urban Policies

The process of developing objectives to define the healthy city vision and exploring the availability of data that might act as supporting evidence for the objectives increasingly convinced most ENCHIA participants that some healthy city objectives might be best achieved through legislation, rather than administrative decisions or land use plans. For example, during discussions over energy conservation and efficiency some ENCHIA participants stated that land use rules, such as "green" building requirements in the zoning code, were limited because they only applied to new construction. Other members noted that the Public Utilities Commission and energy purchasing contracts negotiated between state regulators and power generators were a better place to address energy conservation and efficiency than in land use policies. Still others noted that only federal policies were appropriate, such as energy efficiency requirements on consumer products.

These discussions highlighted that ENCHIA participants had many ideas for "healthy public policies" beyond changes to the zoning code. At the same time some city administrators began questioning whether the ENCHIA was only identifying problems and impediments to but not potential solutions for healthy urban policy (SFDPH 2007a:51). In an effort to be responsive to criticism and more solution oriented, the SFDPH built on the knowledge and ideas of ENCHIA participants and began researching possible policy solutions for implementing their healthy city objectives.

The ENCHIA meetings became a forum to vet policy proposals and explore supporting evidence. ENCHIA participants agreed that policy briefs would be drafted by the DPH and include a short background, situate the policy within the larger regulatory context, provide case studies or examples of how the policy was drafted and implemented somewhere else, and link the policy to direct and indirect influences on human health. The request not only reflected the broad scope that the group was willing to take but that they increasingly realized the limitations of health analyses and recommendations only focused on the Eastern Neighborhoods. As policy discussions moved forward, the tone of the ENCHIA process shifted from an exercise in spatial, often neighborhood scale, analysis to more general policy discourse. Over the course of three months SFDPH staff researched and drafted twenty-seven policy briefs (table 7.5).

Recognizing the difficulty of shifting the ENCHIA process from a discussion of local land use and zoning to more general policy making, participants devised a process for evaluating and debating each brief that included using small groups that reviewed policy details and then reported back to the larger group. Each small group was tasked with reviewing the evidence base used to draft each brief, evaluating the policy's relevance to San Francisco, and making a suggestion to the larger group over whether or not the policy should be endorsed by the ENCHIA. While some ENCHIA members thought the policy drafting process would allow the group to

**Table 7.5**
Policy briefs created by ENCHIA

1. Adopt Structural and Operational Requirements for Residential Hotels
2. Amend Inclusionary Housing Ordinance
3. Amend Residential Off-street Parking Requirements
4. Area-Based Congestion Pricing in the Downtown Business District
5. Charging Market Rates for On-street Parking
6. Community Benefits Districts/Business Improvement Districts
7. Community Benefits Policy/Community Impact Report
8. Community-Based Mechanisms to Reduce Air Pollution
9. Creating Special Use Districts in San Francisco's Mission District
10. Develop a Healthy Economy Element
11. Develop City-Funded Program to Aid in Providing Child Care Benefits
12. Develop Food Enterprise Zones
13. Development Impact Fees for the Eastern Neighborhoods
14. Establish Housing Development Equity Fund
15. Eviction Prevention
16. Formula Retail Use Restrictions
17. Improve the Effectiveness of Workforce Development Programs
18. Increase Collection Fees for Specialized Adult Recreation Programs
19. Increased Inclusionary Housing for Zoning Incentives
20. Mandatory Paid Sick Days
21. Master Strategy for Funding Affordable Housing Development
22. Neighborhood Schools as Centers of Community
23. Open Space Zoning Requirements
24. Promote Accessory Dwelling Units
25. Reduce Marine Vessel Air Emissions by Requiring Cruise Ships to Use Shore-side Power
26. Regulate Provision of Employee Parking Benefits
27. Strengthen First Source Hiring Program

address a broader set of issues beyond the rezoning plan, others had concerns about the documents themselves and questioned whether they included a sufficient amount of information that would allow the group to evaluate each policy?

ENCHIA meetings focused on reaching a group consensus on which policies to endorse and propose as part of promoting healthier urban policy and planning. However, some members often spent more time debating whether they were in a position to make a recommendation rather than discussing the content of the specific policy briefs. One member stated: "I need more time to evaluate the information you have here. Normally our organization would discuss the options and issues with our members before endorsing a possible legislative proposal." Another member stated: "The research behind these policies seems fine, but they are all missing a plan for getting them passed and implemented. As they stand now, I cannot see endorsing any without a more complete legislative plan." After three months of deliberations the ENCHIA Council was unable to come to any agreement over which policies, if any, to endorse. The ENCHIA process seemed to reach an impasse; frustration over the lack of agreement on the policy briefs and the role of policy in the ENCHIA process was evident in both the DPH and ENCHIA participants. Meeting attendance dropped as organizations that were recruited to work on recommendations for the Eastern Neighborhoods rezoning plan did not want to spend their time on policy discussions.

## Sustaining Participation: Moving from the Specific to General

The DPH struggled to retain interest and met again with the Planning Department to respond to some criticisms from the department's new interim director, Dean Macris. Health Department staff briefed the new director, and he commented that he thought the ENCHIA could be perceived as antagonistic to the interests of developers and viewed by many as a front for progressive movements in the city. He challenged DPH staff to prove that they had political support behind their work by asking: "Does Mitch [Katz, SFDPH director] know what he's getting into?" (Bhatia 2006). The DPH responded that they did have their director's support, and Katz (2006b) would soon thereafter note:

The ENCHIA is about supporting healthy development and preventing disease for all. It is not about more administrative burdens or another bureaucratic hurdle for private developers. The kinds of issues ENCHIA debates and the connections it makes between land use and human health are not only exciting and relatively new, but the way planning must move to create a healthy economic, social, and physical climate for all. We are committed to making planning see that this can be a win-win for them and not hinder development. I don't see us [health department] going away from this work anytime soon.

Yet the message from the Planning Department was that the ENCHIA might, at best, be duplicative of existing planning processes and, at worst, a vehicle that highlighted the failure of planning processes to consider human health and an impediment to new development where it was needed most, namely the Eastern Neighborhoods. The SFDPH realized they needed a new strategy to both retain participant interest and better engage with the Planning Department, if the process was going to continue.

After a year of meetings the ENCHIA process had produced a vision of the healthy city, selected seven elements and objectives to attach to the vision, gathered quantitative and qualitative evidence to show how each element promoted health, and drafted twenty-seven non–health specific policy briefs that could advance the vision. Still the group was in a bind; the Planning Department had still not issued the final rezoning plan and accompanying environmental and social impact assessments. All the work that the group had done was supposed to prepare them for analyzing these documents, but they did not yet exist.

After discussing disbanding and where the group might go, an idea that was mentioned throughout the process, namely developing a health and land use "scorecard" using data the group had already compiled, resurfaced during Council discussions. A scorecard, participants noted, would be a valuable health impact analysis tool for this and future decision making, and would not be contingent on the final Eastern Neighborhoods' rezoning documents. ENCHIA participants agreed to re-focus their efforts to develop this scorecard tool.

A small group of ENCHIA participants met to strategize on ways to convert all that the group had produced—the healthy city vision, associated elements, supporting data, and policy recommendations—into one screening tool. The group also focused on identifying specific land use and development policies that could promote each of the healthy city elements. With the assistance of DPH staff, ENCHIA participants gathered additional land use and health data specific to different San Francisco neighborhoods in order to help compare conditions and development options in the Eastern Neighborhoods with other parts of the city.

This work resulted in a set of healthy development targets; concrete actions that planners, developers, and/or policy makers could take that would move toward the ENCHIA's specific healthy city objectives. Instead of including one action item, ENCHIA participants suggested a range, from those that were "minimally acceptable" for promoting health, to those that were the target or "benchmark," to those that were viewed as the "maximum attainable." This way the group recognized that not all plans and development projects should be held to the same standard and "something was often better than nothing." These concrete development targets were added to the objectives and health-based evidence that the ENCHIA process had already gathered, and together these data became the basis of the group's new screening tool.

## The Healthy Development Measurement Tool

In May 2006 the group finished their first draft of the screening tool, now called the Healthy Development Measurement Tool (HDMT). The draft was reviewed in detail by ENCHIA members, and sent to over a dozen different city agencies and sixty external peer reviewers around the world. The SFDPH spent three additional months incorporating comments and suggestions from reviewers and making revisions to the HDMT. A second draft was completed and an interactive web version (thehdmt.org) was released.

The HDMT was organized based on an expanded set of healthy city elements developed through the ENCHIA process, including environmental stewardship, sustainable transportation, public safety, public infrastructure/access to goods and services, adequate and healthy housing, healthy economy and community participation. The HDMT also contained twenty-seven community health objectives that, if achieved, would result in greater and more equitable health assets and resources for San Francisco residents. Also included were measurable indicators with a health-based rationale, along with the most current "baseline data" documenting how well the city—specific population groups and different neighborhoods—was performing with respect to each indicator. A set of development targets and policy recommendations accompanied each healthy city objective. The analytic steps and content of the HDMT for one healthy city element, environmental stewardship, are shown in figure 7.4. (Farhang et al. 2008).

The objective was to allow anyone with web access the ability to understand neighborhood conditions related to health in San Francisco and to evaluate a land use plan or project against the criteria offered in the HDMT. For example, imagine you wanted to screen a proposed development in your area for whether it would assure access to daily goods and service needs, including financial services and healthy foods (healthy city, public infrastructure objective 6; see table 7.4). One measureable indicator for this objective is the proportion of households within half a mile from a full-service grocery store, and the development target for new residential development is that it has a full service grocery store within half a mile (figure 7.5). In the next step you would evaluate the baseline data for your

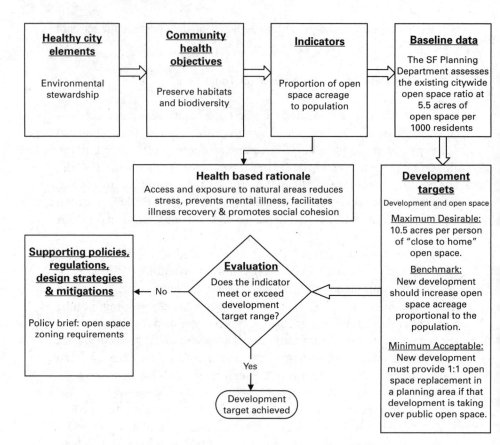

**Figure 7.4**
Environmental stewardship example of the Healthy Development Measurement
Tool (HDMT)

neighborhood, surrounding areas, and the city as a whole. These data are
included for all San Francisco neighborhoods in the HDMT. Imagine that
there are no grocery stores in your neighborhood. The third step is a close
reading and evaluation of the proposed development project and land use
plan to see if it includes, in this case, a grocery store. Let's imagine the
plan includes new housing for 8,000 new residents and calls for "new
commercial and retail space" but does not explicitly mention a grocery
store. The fourth step is to explore project alternatives or improvements to
ensure it meets the healthy development target. In this example the HDMT

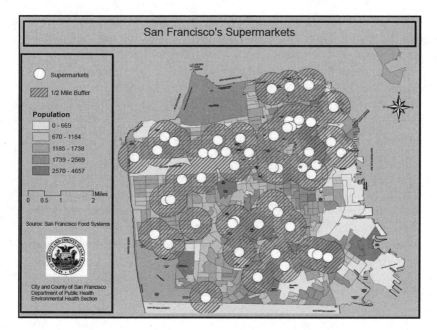

**Figure 7.5**
Supermarkets within a half mile of population density by the 2006 San Francisco census tract

recommends financial, zoning, and/or political incentives to encourage the project to designate a site for a grocery store or, if a grocery store exists off-site, a plan for improving pedestrian, bicycle, and public transit access to the existing grocery store (Farhang et al. 2008).

## ENCHIA Deliverables

The HDMT emerged as the final deliverable of the ENCHIA, but the process also produced a set of tangible outcomes. First, the healthy city vision, crated during a public deliberative process, captured specific features and the social meanings of a healthy place. The data-gathering process brought together disparate secondary data sets—including health outcomes, economic and employment statistics, land uses, social services, and transit access—in one place for the first time. The data-gathering process also facilitated spatial and comparative analyses of information that are rarely analyzed in this way, such as grocery stores, poverty, and population density across city neighborhoods. Consequently the public deliberative process allowed community members to challenge and question the local relevance of certain quantitative data, forcing the process to gather original qualitative information revealing local knowledge and understandings highlighting how local people navigate through the physical and social hazards and opportunities in their place.

The flexibility and participatory design of the ENCHIA process allowed both the SFDPH and participants to re-shape the objectives and outputs of the process along the way. In the end, the ENCHIA process achieved most of the original objectives defined by its organizers, from identifying and analyzing the likely impacts of land use plans on health determinants to offering recommendations for land use policies and zoning controls that could promote community health. The ENCHIA also demonstrated that a participatory HIA process was feasible and could provide a forum for meaningful public involvement in urban policy making, fulfilling another objective. As I highlight in more detail below, the ENCHIA also provided a space where new interagency and organizational networks could develop and be nurtured, a crucial component of moving toward healthy city planning.

## New Issue Framings through Envisioning the Healthy City

This chapter has explored the ways a participatory health impact assessment process can begin to transform urban governance through redefining problems and solutions, collaboratively gathering new evidence and generating alternatives to entrenched planning and policy-making process that often fail to consider human health.[41] One of the significant aspects of the ENCHIA, as noted above, was that participants were able to define their own vision of the healthy city and deliberate over the meanings and implications of this vision. The policy framing offered by ENCHIA participants included the broad determinants of well-being, namely economic, social, and physical characteristics of neighborhoods, the region, and beyond. As one ENCHIA participant, reflecting on the visioning process, stated:

Before this process, I thought of a healthy community as one that lacked disease, didn't have pollution, and people had access to health care. Now [after ENCHIA] I'm more aware that housing is one of the key issues and that you can't consider one thing in isolation. I mean, if you have housing but no other neighborhood life, the place won't be too healthy. If you got a job, but it don't pay enough to live in a community with your family or you got to work two jobs to make good money, this ain't a healthy place either. Measuring unemployment in that situation might make the place look pretty good, but that one measure won't show how people are really living.

Interviews with ENCHIA participants during and after the process suggest that the visioning process and resulting issue reframing also influenced the work of their organizations. According to one ENCHIA member who directs a social service delivery organization, the process opened up his organization to a reframing of their own work:

I never thought of issues like the design of street intersections, where supermarkets are located, and the mix of commercial activities as public health and equity issues, but now I do. I've been in community planning processes before, but not one that involved thinking about health in this broad a way. Our organization is now redefining what we do as promoting health, although we used to think about it as just delivering essential social services of emergency housing and job training for the chronically homeless.

Another ENCHIA member that works for a housing advocacy organization echoed similar sentiments:

Before the ENCHIA we never attempted to make community economic development and housing affordability a public health issue. Yet we always talked about our work as defending "human needs" and "basic living conditions." The ENCHIA has helped us see that we were making public health arguments all along, but just not being explicit about it. Now, by making explicit the connections of our work with health, we have not only seen that [city] supervisors and other elected officials are paying more attention, but it has also helped us expand our organizing base in the neighborhood.

The broad issue framing has also begun to influence the work within the Planning Department, reluctant for so long to acknowledge the links between human health and land use planning decisions. One planning official stated:

I think we [Planning Department] always knew land use decisions had some impact on human health, but we just didn't believe it was our role to make these explicit or find ways to incorporate them into our analyses. The ENCHIA process highlighted that the decisions we make on an everyday basis—whether they are directed at housing, transportation, environment, open space, or zoning—have some human health impacts. This insight, combined with unyielding persistence from the DPH and community groups to consider health in our plans, has begun to change the way we think about land use planning processes and who we include in analyses.

## Building New Networks

A second lesson from the ENCHIA is that new professional relationships between organizations and agencies unfamiliar with one another is crucial for building the broad knowledge base and political legitimacy necessary for healthy city planning. By bringing together stakeholders from a range of issue areas and city agencies that rarely, if ever, incorporate human health into their work, the ENCHIA facilitated the construction of new "healthy governance" networks. As one ENCHIA member stated:

I see a lot of these same people at other meetings, but now I'm more likely to go talk with them or try and work with them now that I know them better. I never knew some of these groups worked on the same issues that we do and I would have never known who to call. This process has changed this.

Other participants noted that their relationship with city government, particularly the Department of Public Health, was positively altered through the ENCHIA process. An ENCHIA participant reflected on their new relationship with the health department:

My relationships with the DPH have improved through this process. I would have never even thought of calling them about a land use issue before, but now I know how knowledgeable they are about these issues. I trust them more after the commitment they made to this process, and after getting to know them better, they [DPH] have helped us build better relationships with other city agencies.

Another ENCHIA council member echoed these sentiments and reflected on the political power that can come by aligning their planning efforts with the public health agency:

The ENCHIA process has revealed to our organization that when a public health agency says "displacement" or "this land use may cause a health problem, do something else," the government and the public are more likely to listen then when planners say the same thing. I mean when a doctor gets up and says "this plan or project may cause harm to health" who's going to argue with that? After this process we also have the health evidence to support our non–health specific plans and policies.

The ENCHIA also helped the DPH build new working relationships with organizations beyond the Planning Department. For example, the ENCHIA process introduced the DPH to the work of the San Francisco Bike Coalition and Transportation for a Livable City. After the ENCHIA concluded, these organizations approached the DPH and built a partnership to investigate ways to revise the use of vehicle level of service (LOS) analysis in project reviews. The SFDPH is helping these groups use health evidence to make the case that using automobile LOS as a performance measure leads to increased vehicle traffic and travel speeds, resulting in more air and noise pollution and jeopardizing the safety of pedestrians and bicyclists (Bhatia 2006). The SFDPH was asked to participate in the Western SoMa Citizens Planning Task Force and offer health-based technical support. The agency used the HDMT and partnered with community organizations to complete a health analysis of the Executive Park Sub Area Plan in the Visitacion Valley area of San Francisco. Also after the ENCHIA was complete, two participating organizations, SOMCAN and the Mission Economic Development Association (MEDA), applied for and received funding from The California Endowment to continue their research and activism linking land use, development, and community health issues.

### Redefining Expertise and Legitimate Evidence

The deliberative character of the ENCHIA process allowed participants to discuss the merits of different kinds of data for each element of the healthy city vision. When disagreements emerged, ENCHIA members were encouraged and allowed to offer alternative ways to evaluate the issue. The SFDPH recognized that trust in and the credibility of the ENCHIA would not rest solely in the scientific data it used but also in public accountability and transparent evidence gathering and evaluation. To increase the transparency of this process, all documents from the ENCHIA were regularly posted on the web. The public deliberations over evidence further revealed that each participant brought their own expertise to the process. The ENCHIA process straddled conventional views of expertise by simultaneously looking to disciplinary professionals for advice and valuing the knowledge of local people.

Yet the broad public involvement and multiple forms of expertise that characterized the ENCHIA also enhanced conflict and alienated some participants. One participant noted after participating in the process for a year:

The process is still amorphous to me and I'm still not sure where it is going. A few people can push the group off on tangents, and the DPH just agrees to let them all speak and offer ideas. I mean, there is objective data that we should be gathering, not people's opinions.

Other participants disagreed, and noted that the openness of the dialogue was rare for a public planning process:

I've been to many public planning meetings and most often the agencies just sit there shaking their heads and you never get the sense they are taking you seriously. In this process, when it came to talking about homelessness and living in an SRO [single-room occupancy hotel], the doctors, lawyers, and PhDs in the room don't know what I know; I've lived that kind of life and been there, know what I mean? For the first time I felt like the DPH was listening to what community people know and turning that into credible data.

Lydia Zaverukha, a participant in the ENCHIA from the San Francisco Recreation and Parks Department, stated that the participatory process "should become the model for San Francisco's city planning process." However, other ENCHIA members suggested that the process spent too much time listening to all points of view and didn't do enough to gather hard evidence that could prove certain land uses were harming community health. One ENCHIA participant noted:

We need to show the "hard data" that gentrification and displacement makes you sick, I mean diseased. Without that, I don't see this process having much of an impact, since it is already hijacked by city planning and private developers.

Despite the ENCHIA's commitment to meaningful participation and valuing a range of expertise, some controversial issues were left unresolved. For instance, the discussions over whether the process should address racism as a key determinant of health and which policy proposals the group ought to endorse were never resolved.

The participatory and transparent process the ENCHIA used to gather and evaluate a range of evidence and expertise did help the process build and maintain *public trust*. Through their participation in the ENCHIA, community-based organizations recognized that government, especially the health department, could be an ally.

### New Institutional Practices
In one of the most significant impacts of the ENCHIA on city planning in San Francisco, the Planning Department agreed after the conclusion of the process to have the DPH review three Area Plans, or neighborhood-scale land use plans, produced as part of the Eastern Neighborhoods Rezoning Plan using the HDMT. The area plans included the Eastern Neighbor-

hoods of the Mission District, East SoMa, and Showplace Square–Potrero Hill. What began as a skeptical and antagonistic Planning Department shifted to support human health analyses in land use decision making. At a meeting of Department Directors, the Health and Planning Departments mutually committed to a formal HMDT evaluation of community plans and subsequently staff met several times to collectively review the HDMT and the draft Area Plans (Farhang 2007). By December 2007 the SFDPH released their reviews of these three plans, noting the positive and negative impacts of each on community health. In a cover letter for the review Rajiv Bhatia (SFDPH 2007b) of the Health Department wrote:

Over the past year, staff from the SFDPH worked closely with staff from SF Planning to apply the HDMT to Area Plans for East SoMa, Mission and Showplace Square/Potrero Hill. During this time, SFDPH provided SF Planning with many recommendations on draft versions of the plans which have already been integrated into the current version. Following the public release of the December 1st 2007 version of the plans, SFDPH re-evaluated the three Area Plans using the HDMT and documented this "final" evaluation in a document—*Impacts on Community Health of Area Plans for the Mission, East SoMa, and Potrero Hill/Showplace Square: An Application of the Healthy Development Measurement Tool.*

By the end of 2007 the San Francisco Planning Department, local governments and organizations from across the Bay Area, and private foundations were engaging with health analyses and using the tools developed through the ENCHIA process.

## Policy Diffusion across the Metropolitan Region

As noted earlier, healthy city planning cannot be limited to one neighborhood or even within a city; it must become standard practice across entire metropolitan areas since city policies are regularly influenced by other actors within the region (Dreier et al. 2004; Katz 2007). The ENCHIA process—through its commitment to public participation, transparency, and inclusive data gathering—encouraged other local governments and community-based organizations across the Bay Area to engage with health analyses of land use and urban policy decisions.

In late 2006 the city of Richmond, California, decided to borrow from the ENCHIA, particularly the HDMT, to draft the state's first Health Policy Element as part of the city's general plan update (Johnson 2007). The

Health Element was drafted by a group of technical experts and community organization representatives, including some that participated in the ENCHIA,[42] and the SFDPH acted as a key advisor on this project. The drafting of the Health Element was coordinated by MIG, Inc., a Berkeley, California, based land use planning firm, in cooperation with the Contra Costa County Health Services Department. By August 2007 a Technical Advisory Group had adapted indicators from the HDMT for Richmond and drafted ten healthy community planning objectives (City of Richmond 2007a).

Two regional nongovernmental organizations, Urban Habitat and the Transportation and Land Use Coalition (TALC), are also building on the work of the ENCHIA to promote healthy and equitable planning. Urban Habitat, an Oakland-based group that aims to "build power in low-income communities and communities of color by combining education, advocacy, research, and coalition building," is coordinating the Richmond Equitable Development Initiative (REDI). The REDI is working to empower, inform, and share ideas with Richmond residents about land use and development issues and how these decisions can promote social justice (urbanhabitat .org/richmond). As part of this work Urban Habitat is facilitating the REDI's participation in the Richmond General Plan Update and providing help to incorporate the health equity work of groups such as the Asian Pacific Environmental Network's Laotian Organizing Project, Communities for a Better Environment, and Ma'at Youth Academy into the Health Element planning process.

## Healthy Regional Planning

TALC is helping to coordinate the Great Communities Collaborative (GCC, www.greatcommunities.org), a regional partnership of five advocacy organizations and two community foundations: the Nonprofit Housing Association of Northern California, Urban Habitat, Greenbelt Alliance, Reconnecting America, the San Francisco Foundation, and the East Bay Community Foundation. This collaborative is focused on regional growth issues, and TALC is coordinating health impact assessments of three transit-oriented development plans sponsored by the GCC in the Bay Area cities of San Leandro, Santa Rosa, and Pittsburgh. One HIA analyzed an extension of the Bay Area Rapid Transit (BART) system in Pittsburg, California, and another focuses on improving the San Pablo Avenue Corridor in El Cerrito, California.

The TALC is receiving guidance in their "healthy transit planning" from a third regional nonprofit that has benefited from the ENCHIA—Human Impact Partners (HIP). HIP was founded after the ENCHIA as a new nonprofit organization to conduct HIAs with community partners and to provide training and mentorship to community-based organizations, governments, and elected officials so that they can perform their own health impact assessments (www.humanimpact.org). Human Impact Partners and another regional organization—Communities for a Better Environment (CBE)—are collaborating with West Oakland residents to use the HDMT and health impact assessment methods more generally to screen and analyze a range of development projects in the community.

### Regional Health Equity Coalitions

Many of the organizations from the ENCHIA and those working in the region on healthy planning came together to form the Healthy Places Coalition in 2006. The Healthy Places Coalition, coordinated by the Oakland, California, based Prevention Institute, brings together over thirty different organizations interested in improving health and social justice through policy and planning changes (www.preventioninstitute.org/healthyplaces.html). In 2007 three members of the Coalition, California Pan-Ethnic Health Network, Human Impact Partners, and Latino Issues Forum, along with SFDPH, drafted and co-sponsored the California Healthy Places Act (Assembly Bill 1472). This bill proposed to prevent illness and disease, improve health, and reduce health disparities in California by, in part, requiring that a health impact assessment program for land use, transportation, and development policies, modeled largely around the ENCHIA, be established by the state's Department of Public Health by 2010. Under this bill an interagency working group would be established to develop guidelines for conducting HIAs, share information about best practices with local governments, and evaluate HIAs performed under the program.

Finally, the ENCHIA has had a significant impact on the state of California's largest health foundation, the California Endowment (TCE), and on the national research and advocacy group PolicyLink. TCE viewed the work of the ENCHIA as a way to expand its community health and health disparities work and promote the experimentation of a new practice for health promotion, namely HIA (Aranda 2008). Prior to ENCHIA, both TCE and PolicyLink were researching and supporting built-environment and health issues and exploring ways to integrate health equity into planning and land use decisions. After the ENCHIA, TCE became the primary fiscal sponsor of the health impact assessment work within community organizations in San Francisco (e.g., SOMCAN and MEDA), local government (e.g., the Richmond Health Element planning process), and nonprofit organizations across the region (e.g., HIP, Urban Habitat, TALC, and CBE). PolicyLink has supported this grant-making by acting as the fiscal agent for some grants, providing oversight and advice on design and implementation of projects, and convening meetings of Bay Area public health and urban planning professionals, researchers, and activists (Lee and Rubin 2007). A guidebook entitled, *How to Create and Implement Healthy General Plans*, was funded by TCE and drafted by the nonprofit group, Public Health Law and Policy, and the planning consulting firm, Raimi Associates (www.healthyplanning.org/toolkit_healthygp.html). Since these are relatively recent reports, their impact on future "healthy regional planning and policy making" remains uncertain. However, what is clear is that absent financial support from TCE, the diffusion across the Bay Area of ENCHIA lessons, such as innovative assessment practices, coalition building strategies, and the generation of a new healthy planning evidence base, would not have taken root in so many different organizations and institutions.

The ENCHIA offers an important model for understanding the politics of healthy city planning, from its participatory process for defining the elements of a healthy city to the evidence base and evaluation tool it offered to the new professional networks and trust in local government that it helped build. While the process set out to evaluate the human health impacts of one rezoning plan in San Francisco, the ENCHIA offered insights for building a more general practice of healthy city planning within cities and metropolitan regions everywhere.

# 8 Planning Healthy and Equitable Cities

Moving toward healthy city planning requires new political processes that re-orient and re-unite the work of public health and planning by building new institutional practices that promote social justice through new coalitions, democratic participation, and expanding existing uses of scientific evidence. Planning and public health agencies, community-based organizations, researchers, and philanthropic organizations have all initiated efforts to incorporate human health considerations into urban development, land use, and policy decisions more generally. However, only a commitment to promoting both equity and health will ensure that these efforts orient practices toward the healthy city.

The efforts described here from the San Francisco Bay Area are some of the most exciting examples of healthy and equitable urban planning in the United States, as governments and community-based coalitions have experimented with new analytic and decision-making processes, built new health equity coalitions, and reshaped long-entrenched urban governance institutions that have worked for decades to keep health and planning separate. Yet even the experimental and progressive work in the San Francisco Bay Area is limited, and many outcomes remain uncertain. It is still too early to tell if health inequities within and between neighborhoods, cities, and the region will change from the practices described here. However, the lessons from the practices described in the preceding cases suggest that any political process aiming to move toward more healthy and equitable city planning must be attentive to such governance issues as the framing of environmental health practice, the gathering of new scientific evidence, and the construction of new social and policy networks. Absent an attention to the political frames underwriting efforts to reconnect city planning and public health, these efforts will likely fail to address the pressing needs of the least well off urban populations.

## Outstanding Challenges for Healthy and Equitable City Planning

The cases offered in this book suggest the multiple political, social, economic and scientific changes that are needed to move toward more healthy and equitable city planning. Yet attention to the political forces that enable healthy and equitable city planning is no panacea; significant barriers to this practice remain unaddressed. For instance, environmental impact assessment practices remain deeply encoded in most planning institutions and resistance, similar to that expressed by the San Francisco Planning Department, is likely to be strong in many urban planning bureaucracies. Decision making in cities remains fragmented and segmented by outdated and outmoded sectoral categories. Collaborative urban administration and management and disrupting existing routines are rarely rewarded in city hall. The cases presented here recognized the difficulties for making systematic changes to planning and public health practice, as they note that many of the experiments with healthy city planning remain just that, ad hoc experiments.

City planning agencies are still "finding their way" back to health and some, like the San Francisco Planning Department, have been slow to acknowledge that human health was part of their mission all along. Another barrier for moving toward healthy city planning is that urban planners today are not educated (e.g., in graduate school) in public health methods and analyses, and few public health professional degrees offer students insights into land use planning and urban governance more generally. While some universities now offer joint masters degrees in city planning and public health,[43] the lack of training across disciplines has resulted in professionals not having a common vocabulary or a mutual understanding of each other's practice, both of which are important for effective collaborations.

The timing of planning processes also presents a barrier for healthy city development planning. Many planning reviews occur after key project decisions are made and the most comprehensive planning process that has the potential to include public health considerations, namely the environmental impact assessment process, has a set of legally mandated steps and time constraints that make creative health analyses difficult. At the same time ad hoc processes that do engage with the broad determinants of health and aim to be "out-front" of policy and planning decisions, such as the ENCHIA described in chapter 7, do not have any formal legal authority.

The powerful interests of private sector developers present one of the most significant challenges for healthy city planning that was not fully addressed in the cases presented here. Yet certainty over the timing and extent of a planning process is one of the greatest concerns for developers, since this can allow them to estimate project costs. Even small delays from a planning review can cost a large development project millions of dollars. While inserting health analyses into the planning process may add time to project reviews, it does not necessarily have to increase uncertainty. For example, the HDMT is an evaluation process that might offer developers certainty while still evaluating the broad determinants of health equity.

## Extending the Politics of Health City Planning

The cases presented here exploring the politics behind healthy planning efforts in the San Francisco Bay Area offer important insights for all cities and metropolitan regions interested in moving toward more healthy places. Recall that in order to move toward healthy city planning, epistemological and institutional changes need to occur. Public health practice needs to take a new orientation that embraces population health, and planning processes need to take a relational view of place and urban governance while simultaneously engaging with power inequities in the city.

The normative framework in this book outlined specific strategies for practicing healthy city planning at different scales, from project specific (e.g., Trinity Plaza), to neighborhood (e.g., Rincon Hill), to zoning and citywide policy (e.g., ENCHIA), and to the entire region (e.g., Ditching Dirty Diesel Campaign and TALC). The healthy planning practice framework included a precautionary and preventative approach, co-producing the science evidence base underwriting action, combining the "field site" view of the city with the laboratory view, and building new transdisciplinary collaborations and regional coalitions. In combining insights from the epistemological and normative frameworks, this chapter offers lessons for how city planners, public health professionals, policy makers, community and other nongovernmental organizations everywhere might embrace health and equitable city planning.

## Prevention and Precaution

Healthy and equitable city planning must find new ways to prevent the physical and social hazards in urban areas that are detrimental to well-being while encouraging health-promoting change. As these cases have highlighted, planners, health professionals, and community activists must work to redefine environmental health to embrace the prevention and precaution framework. Activists in Bayview–Hunters Point, SoMa, and West Oakland all placed new demands on government agencies to focus on preventing harms in ways that link the built, social, and economic environments. As Howard Frumkin (2005:A290) has noted, the environmental justice movement has and will continue to play a crucial role in reframing public health and city planning practice:

At least two paradigm shifts have revolutionized the [environmental health] field since Rachel Carson's day. One occurred when environmental health encountered civil rights, forming the environmental justice movement. We are in the midst of the second, as environmental health reunites with architecture and urban planning. . . . Each of these trends—the environmental justice movement and the focus on the built environment—has helped transform the environmental health field.

This book has shown that the environmental justice movement, its claim-making, research partnerships, and integrated policy analyses are crucial for framing healthy and equitable city planning.

A second component of the precaution and prevention frame is how it reorients practice. For example, in the Trinity and Rincon Hill development project cases, the San Francisco Planning Department did not consider residential displacement or increased residential segregation, "environmental impacts" that fell within the purview of their review process. However, the Health Department made the case that *preventing* both direct and indirect residential displacement and increased segregation were not only significant health promotion issues but also required regulatory considerations in the environmental impact assessment process. By taking a precautionary and preventative approach, the SFDPH reoriented environmental health practice.

Another example of how a prevention frame alters the content of planning practice is the Healthy Development Measurement Tool, generated through the Eastern Neighborhoods Community Health Impact Assessment. A crucial aspect of the HDMT is that it offers both a set of indicators to measure the likely health impacts of a land use project and a suite of development alternatives that can mitigate potential adverse impacts. The HDMT offers both evaluative criteria and alternative interventions for a range of issues, from adequate and healthy housing to sustainable transportation to social cohesion. A central feature of the precautionary and preventative healthy city planning framework is a process for proposing and considering development and/or plan alternatives.

Alternatives assessment is one of the defining features of the precautionary principle (Tickner and Geiser 2004). Alternative assessments ask "how can likely impacts be reduced or avoided" and "what safer or health promoting alternatives are available," thereby shifting the planning process from characterizing problems to exploring solutions. The precautionary approach also alters the standards of evidence on which decisions about alternatives are based. While current environmental health processes aim for definitive proof of harm (which in regulatory decisions is almost an impossible standard), preventative planning takes action in the face of scientific uncertainty and includes ongoing monitoring to evaluate progress and adjust interventions as conditions change. Informed by health impacts, the Planning Department required the Trinity Plaza developer to propose and analyze a non-displacement alternative in the environmental review of the project. The SoMa Community Stabilization Fund and Advisory Council, the HDMT and the West Oakland Environmental Indicators Project are all examples of how to combine precautionary action with built-in ongoing monitoring.

In order to institutionalize the precautionary and preventative frame into healthy city planning, practitioners might look to experiments in adaptive management and collaborative ecosystem management (Weber 2003). These processes have been used to manage complex resources, such as watersheds and sensitive habitats, and involve local users, managers, scientists, and other public stakeholders in collaborative processes for making timely interventions. Instead of one-size-fits-all rules, adaptive management regimes aim for contingent interventions that are regularly adjusted over time as the group explores the efficacy of new technologies and reviews ongoing monitoring of, for instance, water quality.

Another lesson from these cases for adopting a precautionary approach and consistent with the "adaptive environmental management" idea is that organizations must commit to becoming what Chris Argyris and Donald Schön (1996) called "double-loop" learners. According to Argyris and Schön, "single-loop" learning occurs when organizations acquire new ways to correct identified errors, implement, refine, or improve everyday existing routines but do not question the routine itself. In contrast, "double-loop" learning involves questioning core organizational routines and tends to open up and restructure the meanings and underlying fundamental assumptions of an organization's norms, goals, and mission. The organizational change demanded by the precautionary paradigm will require planning and public agencies, as well as urban planning and policy organizations not currently focused on health equity, to fundamentally re-examine their operating assumptions in order to move practice toward healthy city planning.

## Co-producing Science through New Measurement and Monitoring Networks

Healthy city planning will need to engage with and draw from a number of scientific tools and techniques, from epidemiologic investigation to forecasting models to measures and indicators of community well-being. Yet the cases examined here highlight that the "modern" view of science as rational, objective, universal, placeless, and efficient is often confronted and possibly yielding to a "new" science of pluralism, localism, and recurrent ambiguity. The science of healthy city planning is post-normal, since it (1) relies on emergent analytic methods, (2) is increasingly produced in contexts of application, (3) is transdisciplinary, or draws on and integrates empirical and theoretical elements from a variety of fields, and (4) demands timely responses to politically contentious issues. The co-production idea offers a way to conceptualize how the scientific and social objectives can emerge together for healthy city planning. Co-production is especially important in the practice of healthy city planning where the participants in science have grown more aware of the social implications of their work just as publics have become more conscious of the ways in which science and technology affect their interests and values.

The Eastern Neighborhoods Community Health Impact Assessment (ENCHIA) process was an example of how the notion of co-production can be applied in practice. Scientists and community members not only gathered, interpreted and applied a range of new data in the ENCHIA process, but the evidence gathering process itself re-shaped political arrangements and social relations. The human health and land use evidence gathered within the ENCHIA highlighted to many participants, but especially the SFDPH, that they needed to forge new and closer ties with the city's Planning Department. While this relationship took time to develop, scientific evidence acted as an important means to justify and legitimate this institutional alliance. Similarly, advocacy groups working on single issues, such as affordable housing or economic development, began to see their work in a different light through the data-gathering process in the ENCHIA, and subsequently re-framed their political organizing as including human health promotion.

The development and publication of indicators, from the HDMT to the West Oakland Environmental Indicators Project, also highlight the co-production of science, society, and political order. These public indicator processes allowed participants to discuss, question, and formulate responses to the links among the social, economic, and environmental qualities of urban places. The indicator development process also highlighted to citizens that they have important expertise for understanding and analyzing the contextual meanings of material and social characteristics of places, and that this expertise is crucial for healthy and equitable city planning. Community involvement in measuring and monitoring health equity indicators can disrupt, what Nancy Scheper-Hughes (1992) has called, the state's "averted gaze," or the government's failure to see issues and problems that should be right before their eyes. As the examples presented here highlighted, measurement and indicator processes revealed that community members not only made claims as qualified "experts" that could weigh in on questions about planning, place, and health, but that their participation was crucial for ensuring that government processes re-negotiated, or at least re-considered, what the salient questions were in the first place. In these ways the co-production frame recasts the role of science and expertise for healthy city planning.

## A Relational View of Place

Just as the co-production framework emphasizes the overlapping spheres of science, society, and politics, the relational view of places emphasizes that healthy city planning cannot promote well-being using a limited, physically deterministic framework. The notion of designing healthy communities is one such approach that runs the risk of being physically deterministic. Much of the design and built environment and public health work today overemphasizes change to the physical landscape for producing health-promoting social and behavioral changes, such as increased physical activity (Ewing et al. 2003; Frank et al. 2006). As the cases in this book have highlighted, such work grossly oversimplifies how places—composed of complex relations among physical features, social forces, and processes of meaning-making—influence human health.

The reframing of environmental health that stimulated much of the healthy city planning work in San Francisco first emerged out of environmental justice narratives over what might make the Bayview–Hunters Point community a more healthy place. These narratives emphasized, for example, the relationships for community members between crime and safety and access to healthy food. These were insights that surprised the Health Department but also contributed to the agency developing new intervention programs and research projects to engage with the multiple and overlapping influences of place on human health, such as the food security program. In a similar way the ENCHIA process was a public forum where participants could deliberate over the vision of the healthy city and the meanings of indicators to measure this vision. The narratives were not simply metaphorical but reflected existing material and social conditions and possibilities for action. In both cases quantitative measures were complemented by and often tempered by the personal stories and community narratives that give life and meaning to physical measures of places.

In these ways the relational view of place acts as a key catalyst for healthy urban governance, since it helps mobilize populations typically excluded from public decision making to care enough to re-engage with the politics of their place. The abstractions of epidemiology and statistics is often brought "close to home" when participants debate what uniquely promotes health in their place and how this might be typical of other similarly situated places. Yet valuing place-based meanings of local people does not necessarily lead to parochial practices and outcomes. As the ENCHIA process revealed, a focus on the complexities of what makes a place healthy can contribute to plans and evaluative tools that have universal appeal, and the narratives of place can combine with quantitative indicators to offer new ways of measuring and monitoring community well-being.

The relational view of place as incorporated into healthy city planning demands new practices of public participation. Public hearings, comment periods, and even community-professional research partnerships are not enough. Democratic forums where open deliberation can occur among a range of governmental, community-based, and private sector participants are crucial for capturing the relational aspects of place. The ENCHIA process provides one example of such a process. The ENCHIA was organized using participatory and democratic principles used for consensus conferences and science shops, and these models may provide the best forums for deliberating over the relational aspects of place while also moving toward concrete actions.

The relational view of place will also demand new orientations to urban health research, particularly epidemiology. As noted throughout this book, epidemiologists, and to some extent urban planners, regularly document the problems and social inequities in cities. Yet the relational view of place requires that researchers and practitioners spend more time investigating and evaluating the strengths and assets of a place, not just its problems. This is not a call for documenting "best practices" but rather a desire for research and evaluation that offers rich descriptions of what is working along with critical inquiry into how and why. These insights into how places currently promote health are crucial, since they can act as the basis for processes that aim to expand on success, encourage further innovation within a system's strengths and help skeptical practitioners and publics visualize the path toward a desired future.

## Merging the Laboratory and Field Site Views for Urban Health

The laboratory view, as this book has shown, reflects the biomedical model of health and related urban health interventions that focus on changing individual lifestyles. Behavioral change strategies in the biomedical model tend to treat all places and individuals the same, at least viewing their contexts as merely the background for lifestyle choices. The laboratory view of the city also emphasizes urban health policies that aim to improve the health of everyone with nonspecific interventions, such as the chlorination of drinking water. Moving toward the healthy city will require merging insights from the laboratory view with those of the field site view of cities, where the complex qualities of places and their interactions are considered crucial determinants of health.

The health impact assessment work of the SFDPH, particularly the ENCHIA and the HDMT, reflects an attempt to merge the laboratory and field site views of urban health. These processes started with the goal of addressing health inequities through participatory research and action. The health impact assessment process also reflected the social justice mission of the Program on Health, Equity, and Sustainability. While these processes employed tools of environment health science, they did not seek one single intervention to improve well-being. They recognized that cities are complex and variable systems that cannot be easily dissected or meliorated with permanent solutions. Instead, these processes emphasized the multiple, overlapping burdens of unhealthy development, the specific ways that particular development can adversely impact some communities and population groups, and offered a range of "healthy development" alternatives. In other words, the experiments in healthy city planning reviewed here were not exercises aiming at decontextualized interventions nor general health improvements, but were explicitly focused on how to change the qualities and processes in cities that adversely impact the health of the poor and people of color.

## New Institutions and Regional Coalition-Building

Finally, healthy city planning will not come about by either government or civil society working alone. All the cases emphasize that both new government and governance strategies are necessary. Yet the institution building by and knowledge of community-based organizations and regional coalitions across the Bay Area should not be overlooked. Regional coalitions are building new alliances and networks outside their traditional allies to engage in the difficult work of health impact assessment and policy making. The SoMa Community Stabilization Fund created a new institution that is aiming to shift the ways the benefits of development are distributed and to act as a potential model for other places across the region. Organizations participating in the ENCHIA process have formed new alliances across the region and state to extend their involvement in healthy urban planning. The new institutions that are necessary for supporting healthy city planning must engage with procedures for collecting, aggregating, validating, and wielding claims to knowledge about health and society in public policy settings.

As the cases suggest, regional and statewide institutions are also essential for healthy city planning. Community-based organizations can only carry healthy planning so far; regional networks of groups and government agencies will be necessary for healthy city planning. These networks are beginning to take shape in the Bay Area and even weigh in on state policy. Private investment, in the form of the California Endowment, is helping these emerging networks build their capacity and membership.

## Toward the Healthy City: An Unfinished Symphony

Moving toward the healthy city is a continual struggle for social, political economic, and institutional change; it is not a static endpoint. The histories of American urban planning and public health suggest that change will likely be incremental and difficult, since each field has entrenched practices that do not currently promote or place a high priority on health equity in cities. Yet change is occurring. Beyond the work described here in the San Francisco Bay Area, cities from Atlanta to Chicago to Boston are experimenting with health impact assessment that takes the social determinants of health seriously (Dannenberg et al. 2008). The National Association of County and City Health Officials and the American Planning Association have developed a joint project aimed at restoring the bridge between land use planning and public health and are conducting trainings and workshops around the country with practitioners from both fields (www.planning.org/research/healthycommunities.htm). As these and other efforts increase, so too does the importance of articulating a historically grounded political framework, not just a set of physical design or spatial analytic tools, for planning more healthy and equitable cities.

As this book has emphasized, the forces that make cities healthy include features of the physical, economic, and social environments and, most important, the political institutions and governance processes that shape place-based outcomes and opportunities. Yet I've also stressed the contingent and contested character of places, the science of the city and urban governance. The health of a city cannot be tallied on a simple morbidity or mortality graph but has to be understood within the complex social, economic, and cultural milieu in which it is negotiated. This way, moving toward the healthy city is an unfinished symphony; an extended piece of music with more than one movement, played by groups with different expertise, but all aiming to harmoniously construct a sound that is greater than the sum of its parts. The symphony must simultaneously be descriptive and analytic, invoke science and emotion, focused yet broad enough to include all sounds, and inspire participants and listeners to strive for something that may seem, at present, beyond the realm of the possible. There is much work yet to be done to contribute to the unfinished symphonies that are healthy and equitable cities.

# Notes

## Chapter 1

1. Health inequities are differences in which disadvantaged social groups—such as the poor, racial/ethnic minorities, women, and other groups who have persistently experienced social disadvantage or discrimination—systematically experience worse health or greater health risks than more advantaged social groups. Social advantage refers to one's relative position in a social hierarchy determined by wealth, power, and/or prestige (Braveman 2006).

2. The United Nations Center for Human Settlements (UN-HABITAT), as part of its "Inclusive City" declaration and Global Campaign on Urban Governance, emphasizes the continual struggle and conflicts inherent in urban governance. UN-HABITAT defines urban governance as:

[T]he sum of the many ways individuals and institutions, public and private, plan and manage the common affairs of the city. It is a continuing process through which conflicting or diverse interests may be accommodated and cooperative action can be taken. It includes formal institutions as well as informal arrangements and the social capital of citizens. . . . Good urban governance must enable women and men to access the benefits of urban citizenship. Good urban governance, based on the principle of urban citizenship, affirms that no man, woman or child can be denied access to the necessities of urban life, including adequate shelter, security of tenure, safe water, sanitation, a clean environment, health, education and nutrition, employment and public safety and mobility. Through good urban governance, citizens are provided with the platform which will allow them to use their talents to the full to improve their social and economic conditions. (UNCHS 2007)

3. "Normal" science is paradigmatic in the sense described by philosopher of science Thomas Kuhn.

4. "Upstream" refers to the story of the hero who saves one drowning person after another from the river but never looks to see that someone upstream is pushing people into the water.

5. While the concept of relationships may seem abstract as presented here, the idea is a foundation for most sociological thinking. For example, Karl Marx (1978:247) noted that "society does not consist of individuals, but expresses the sum of inter-relations, the relations within which these individuals stand."

6. Structural racism differs from interpersonal and institutional racism. Individual racism is the kind of blatant discrimination by one person toward another, and can be done with malice or it may be unintended. Institutional racism is often the result of formal rules and laws, like school segregation and Jim Crow laws. Structural racism emphasizes that analysis and actions recognize and address: (1) that racism is a societal, not purely an individual, outcome; (2) the effects of racism; (3) the significance of both overt and covert racism; and (4) that contemporary racial disparities are partly derivative from historic norms and conditions, some of which were established without racial intent.

7. The San Francisco Bay Area consists of over seven million people across the nine counties of San Francisco, Marin, Napa, Sonoma, Solano, Contra Costa, Alameda, Santa Clara, and San Mateo.

### Chapter 2

8. By "truth spot," I mean a delimited geographical location that lends credibility to claims by referencing the particular natural and human-built environments and cultural interpretations and narrations that together give meaning to places (Hayden 1998).

9. An important exception was in Milwaukee, where Socialists were elected in 1910 and built widespread community support, including business people, clergy, women's groups, populists, and trade unionists, for public health reforms (Leavitt 1986).

10. This era also acted as the stage for grand utopian ideas for the healthy city. British physician Benjamin W. Richardson proposed *Hygeia—A City of Health*, in 1876, where 100,000 people would live on 4,000 acres, tobacco and alcohol would be prohibited, technology would remove air pollution and purify drinking water, and a public health system would serve the entire population. Richardson also proposed specific housing, street layout, and park system design guidelines that together would reduce mortality and improve the moral health of the community, especially children (Richardson 1875).

11. Importantly, as Lasch-Quinn (1993) notes, while the Settlement House movement embraced immigrants, it often refused to serve impoverished African-Americans.

12. Reflecting on this era, Lewis Mumford (1955:36–37) would write: "In nineteenth-century city planning, the engineer was the willing servant of the land monopolist; and he provided a frame for the architect . . . where site-value counted

for everything, and sight-value was not even an afterthought.... That a city had any other purpose than to attract trade, to increase land values, and to grow is something, if it uneasily entered the mind of an occasional Whitman, never exercised any hold upon the minds of the majority of our countrymen."

13. Burnham also had a role in planning San Francisco, starting in 1904, and he issued a report for the comprehensive plan of the city in 1906, only days before the great earthquake and fire of the same year leveled the city.

14. Their model, known as concentric zone theory and first published in *The City* (1925), predicted that cities would take the form of five concentric rings with areas of social and physical deterioration concentrated near the city center and more prosperous areas located near the city's edge. Concentric zone theory was one of the earliest models developed to explain the spatial organization of urban areas, including the existence of social problems such as unemployment and crime in certain districts of Chicago.

15. "Benign neglect" was proposed by Daniel Patrick Moynihan, Nixon's advisor on urban and social policy, in his 1970 memo reprinted in the *New York Times* on January 30 entitled, *Text of the Moynihan memorandum on the status of negroes*.

## Chapter 3

16. See, for example, http://www.dec.ny.gov/public/333.html and California Government Code Section 65040.2 (requiring the Office of Policy and Research to develop EJ guidelines for local General Plans), and California Environmental Protection Agency's EJ program, http://www.calepa.ca.gov/EnvJustice.

17. Other decisions within the environmental planning process also limit the scope of human health analyses. For example, the number of project, plan, or policy alternatives that are examined in the review process impacts whether key questions such as "is this necessary and what other alternatives are possible?" In most planning review processes three options are typically considered; "no-build"; the proposed project, plan, or policy; and an extreme version of the project or policy. Similarly decisions about the timing of and participants in planning processes also shape the content and outcomes of planning processes.

18. Of course, private developers and "growth coalitions" have an enormous influence over what gets built in a city. The point here is to highlight that a range of planning processes also have a role in shaping land use decisions and their potential impacts on human well-being.

19. Title III of the US Clean Air Act Amendments of 1990 required that the US Environmental Protection Agency (EPA) begin to regulate 189 HAPs considered most likely to have the greatest impact on ambient air quality and human health. The list of HAPs regulated by EPA is published in Section 112 of the 1990 Clean Air Act Amendments. Thirty-three HAPs, plus diesel particulate matter, were

deemed the most hazardous to urban health and were included in the EPA's National-Scale Air Toxics Assessment (NATA), www.epa.gov/ttn/atw/nata/34poll .html.

20. An important exception is the work of Howell Baum (2004), who argues that community planners ought to make disparities in educational quality and outcomes a central focus of their work.

21. Of the various conceptual dimensions of segregation, evenness as measured by the dissimilarity index has most often been employed in health studies. Evenness measures the degree to which the proportion of a particular racial or ethnic group living in residential areas (e.g., census tracts) approximates that group's relative percentage of an entire metropolitan area. It is measured using the dissimilarity index, which is interpreted as the proportion of the racial group of interest that would need to relocate to another census tract to achieve an even distribution throughout a metropolitan area. Although most health studies involving measurement of segregation are limited to dyadic comparisons, such as black/white segregation, a multi-group dissimilarity index has been developed to characterize segregation in the more typically multiethnic contemporary metropolis (Iceland 2004).

### Chapter 4

22. In 2005 the European Union passed a directive changing the way it regulates toxics with the aim of better protecting public health, and used the precautionary principle as the basis of this new environmental health strategy.

23. I discuss San Francisco's adoption of the precautionary principle and its effect on environmental health across the entire Bay Area in chapter 6.

24. See the mission statements of these movements at the following websites: http://www.cnu.org/, http://www.smartgrowth.org, and http://www .activelivingbydesign.org.

25. James Baldwin highlighted place-based meanings and identities, both explicit and implicit, in his 1963 essay, A Talk for Teachers: "I still remember my first sight of New York. . . . It was Park Avenue, but I didn't know what Park Avenue meant downtown. The Park Avenue I grew up on, which is still standing, is dark and dirty. No one would dream of opening up a Tiffany's on that Park Avenue, and when you go downtown you discover that you are literally in the white world. It is rich—or at least it looks rich. It is clean—because they collect the garbage. There are doormen. People walk about as though they owned where they are—and indeed they do. . . . You know—you know instinctively—that none of this is for you. You know before you are told."

26. An example of how social and economic circumstances get expressed in the human body, or "biologically imprinted," is low birth weight. Low birth weight is

the result of a host of social inequalities leading to exposures (during and prior to the pregnancy) to such factors as maternal malnutrition, toxic substances (e.g., lead), smoking, infections, domestic violence, racial discrimination, economic adversity in neighborhoods, and inadequate medical and dental care (Adler and Newman 2002).

27. The Ditching Dirty Diesel Collaborative is a Bay Area collaborative of over a dozen environmental justice and health organizations who have been working together since October 2004 to reduce diesel pollution and improve health in environmental justice communities throughout the Bay Area. The Ditching Dirty Diesel Collaborative has three active areas of work: diesel idling, goods movement, and capacity building. The steering committee of the Ditching Dirty Diesel Collaborative includes Bayview Hunters Point Community Advocates, BVHP Health and Environmental Task Force of SFDPH, Contra Costa Health Services/ Contra Costa Asthma Coalition, Ethnic Health Institute, Healthy San Leandro Collaborative, Natural Resources Defense Council, Neighborhood House of North Richmond, Pacific Institute, Regional Asthma Management and Prevention Initiative, and West Oakland Environmental Indicators Project (Pacific Institute 2006).

28. Currently most truckers that haul goods from ports are independent contractors and barred from unions by US antitrust laws.

## Chapter 5

29. Interview quote courtesy of Fernando Ona, former director of food policy for San Francisco Department of Health.

30. Examples of work groups include District 10 working group (access to healthy food), Organizational working group (structure, identity, media), Policy working group (developing and influencing policy locally and statewide), Education working group (nutrition, food assistance, sustainable agriculture, global issues), and Food System Assessment and Report Card working group.

31. According to the IOM and reinterpreted by the SFDPH in their 2004 Prevention Strategic Plan, the core functions of public health are to assess and improve the health of the entire population; to focus on prevention of disease spread and occurrence of injury by promoting conditions and behaviors that support and enhance health; to emphasize social justice; and to employ a systematic approach toward achieving these aims.

## Chapter 6

32. See chapter 3 for more detail on the origins, mission, and goals of the Program on Health Equity and Sustainability within the San Francisco Department of Public Health.

33. The International Association of Impact Assessment notes that "development planning without adequate consideration of human health may pass hidden "costs" on to affected communities, in the form of an increased burden of disease and reduced well-being. From an equity point of view, it is often marginalized and disadvantaged groups who experience most of these adverse health effects. From an institutional point of view, it is the health sector that must cope with development-induced health problems and to which the costs are incurred of dealing with an increased disease burden. HIA provides a systematic process through which health hazards, risks, and opportunities can be identified and addressed upstream in the development planning process, to avoid the transfer of these hidden costs and to promote multi-sectoral responsibility for health and well-being (Quigley et al. 2006:1).

34. Today, the SoMa is one of San Francisco's most eclectic neighborhoods and with some of its least-well-off population groups. The neighborhood has the highest concentration of homeless or formerly homeless in the city. SoMa is also populated by formerly incarcerated men, since inmates released from jails are given a voucher to stay in a single room occupancy (SRO) hotel and most of San Francisco's remaining SROs are concentrated in SoMa.

35. The I-Hotel was one of the few remaining buildings in San Francisco's Manilatown, once a thriving community of Filipino immigrants in SoMa. The community was mostly male because Asian women were largely excluded from entering the United States until 1965 and California's anti-miscegenation laws prevented Filipinos and other Asians from marrying outside the race.

36. Members of the advisory committee in March 2008, included: Angelica Cabande; Ada Chan; Jazzie L. Collins, chair; Rudy Corpuz Jr.; Conny Ford, vice-chair; Steven Sarver; and Kelly Wilkinson.

### Chapter 7

37. This chapter is the result of a collaborative process involving Rajiv Bhatia, Lili Farhang, and other members of the PHES team at the SFDPH.

38. This process was very similar to a conflict assessment process used in designing consensus-building processes (Susskind et al. 1999). In a conflict assessment a mediator often conducts interviews with interested parties and those outside the conflict in an effort to understand the substantive issues at stake, historical relationships among stakeholders, and to recruit participants to attend the dispute resolution process.

39. The list of ENCHIA participants and their organization affiliation included Beth Altshuler, San Francisco Food Alliance; Gretchen Ames, Low Income Investment Fund; Larry Bain, Jardiniere/Nextcourse; Judith Baker, South of Market Family Resource Center; Joe Boss, Potrero Boosters Neighborhood Association;

Jerin Browne, People Organized to Win Employment Rights; Angelica Cabande, South of Market Community Action Network; Emily Claassen, Mission Community Council; Peter Cohen, Asian Neighborhood Design; Jazzie Collins, Mission SRO Collaborative; Jeff Condit, Neighborhood Parks Council; Erin Coppin, Low Income Investment Fund; Emily Drennen, Walk San Francisco; Tim Dunn, Tenants and Owners Development Corporation; Scott Falcone, Citizens Housing Corporation; Kyle Fiore, Mission Community Council; Aumijo S. Gomes, San Francisco Youth Works; Luis Granados, Mission Economic Development Agency; Oscar Grande, People Organizing to Demand Environmental and Economic Rights; Bob Hernandez, SEIU Local 790; Lila Hussein, Urban Habitat; Wesley Kirkman, Walk San Francisco; Ezra Mersey, Jackson Pacific Ventures; Fernando Marti, Asian Neighborhood Design; Cindy Mendoza, South of Market Employment Center; Elyse Miller, San Francisco General Hospital; Steven Moss, San Francisco Community Power; Charlie O'Hanlon, Charlie's Place; Paul Okamoto, Okamoto Saijo Architecture; Tom Radulovich, Transportation for a Livable City; Stephanie Rosenfeld, SEIU Local 790; Leah Shahum, San Francisco Bicycle Coalition; Andrea Spagat, Center for Human Development; Debra Stein, GCA Strategies; Andy Thornley, San Francisco Bicycle Coalition; April Veneracion, South of Market Community Action Network; Steven Vettel, law firm of Morrison and Foerster; Linda Weiner, American Lung Association; Bruce Wolfe, San Francisco Community Land Trust; Greg Asay, Board of Supervisors, Maxwell; Angela Calvillo, Board of Supervisors, Ammiano; Christina Carpenter and Maria X. Martinez, San Francisco Department of Public Health; Miriam Chion, Sue Exline, and Teresa Ojeda, San Francisco Department of Planning; Officer Glen Ghiselli and Captain Albert Pardini, San Francisco Police Department; David Habert, San Francisco Redevelopment Agency; Rachel Redondiez, Assistant to Supervisor Chris Daly; Eileen Ross, San Francisco Department of Parking and Traffic; Joe Speaks, Municipal Transportation Agency; Lydia Zaverukha, San Francisco Recreation and Parks Department.

40. The vision was later revised and expanded into seven elements by adding transportation and community participation and combining infrastructure with goods and services into one category.

41. Much of the data used for this section of the chapter comes from three rounds of confidential interviews with ENCHIA participants and related city agency personnel, observations at most meetings and content analysis of meeting transcripts. ENCHIA participant interviewees included members of nongovernmental organizations such as Asian Neighborhood Design, Mission Economic Development Association, Mission SRO Collaborative/Mission Agenda, Neighborhood Parks Council, People Organizing to Demand Environmental and Economic Rights (PODER), People Organized to Win Employment Rights (POWER), SF Land Trust, SF Food Alliance, Urban Habitat, and Urban Solutions. In order to preserve confidentiality in what was, at the time of most interviews, an ongoing public process, names of individuals and their organization affiliations are not included here.

42. One organization that participated in both the ENCHIA and the Richmond Health Element drafting process was Urban Habitat. There were additional technical advisors that also participated in both processes.

## Chapter 8

43. American universities that offer joint professional degrees in city planning and public health include the University of California at Berkeley, Columbia University, and the University of North Carolina at Chapel Hill.

# References

Abrams, C. 1955. *Forbidden Neighbors: A Study of Prejudice in Housing*. New York: Harper.

Abramson, M., and the Young Lords Party. 1971. *Palante: Young Lords Party*. New York: McGraw-Hill.

Acevedo-Garcia, D., and Lochner, K. 2003. Residential segregation and health. In Kawachi, I., and Berkman, L., eds., *Neighborhoods and Health*. Oxford: Oxford University Press, pp. 265–87.

Acheson, D., Barker, D., Chambers, J., Graham, H., Marmot, M., and Whitehead, M. 1998. *The Report of the Independent Inquiry into Health Inequalities*. London: Stationary Office. http://www.archive.official-documents.co.uk/document/doh/ih/contents.htm.

Addy, C., Wilson, D., Kirtland, K. A., Ainsworth, B. E., Sharp, P., and Kimsey, D. 2004. Associations of perceived social and physical environmental supports with physical activity and walking behavior. *American Journal of Public Health* 94(3): 440–43.

Adler, N. E., and Newman, K. 2002. Socioeconomic disparities in health: Pathways and policies. *Health Affairs* 21(2): 60–76.

Agency for Healthcare Research and Quality (AHRQ). 2005. *National Healthcare Disparities Report*. AHRQ Publication 05-0014. http://www.ahrq.gov/QUAL/nhdr04/nhdr04.htm.

Agnew, J. A., and Duncan, J. S. 1989. *The Power of Place: Bringing Together Geographical and Sociological Imaginations*. Boston: Unwin Hyman.

Aicher, J. 1998. *Designing Healthy Cities: Prescriptions, Principles and Practice*. Malabar, FL: Krieger.

Alameda County. 2005. Department of Public Health, *Community Information Book Update*, October. http://www.acphd.org/User/data/datareports.asp.

Alejandrino, S. V. 2000. *Gentrification in San Francisco's Mission District: Indicators and Policy Recommendations*. A report prepared for the Mission Economic Development Association, San Francisco. http://www.medasf.org.

Altschuler, A., Somkin, C. P., and Adler, N. E. 2004. Local services and amenities, neighborhood social capital, and health. *Social Science and Medicine* 59, 1219–29.

American Public Health Association (APHA). 1938. *Basic Principles of Healthful Housing*. Committee on the Hygiene of Housing. Chicago: Public Administration Service.

American Public Health Association (APHA). 1948. *Planning the Neighborhood: Standards for Healthful Housing*. Committee on the Hygiene of Housing. Chicago: Public Administration Service.

Anderson, M., and Cook, J. 1999. Community food security: Practice in need of theory? *Agriculture and Human Values* 16: 141–50.

Appadurai, A. 2001. Deep democracy: Urban governmentality and the horizon of politics. *Environment and Urbanization* 13: 23–43.

Aragón, T. J., Lichtensztajn, D. Y., Katcher, B. S., Reiter, R., and Katz, M. H. 2007. *Calculating Expected Years of Life Lost to Rank the Leading Causes of Premature Death in San Francisco*. San Francisco Department of Public Health. www.sfdph.org.

Aranda, D. 2008. Personal communication.

Argyris, C., and Schön, D. 1996. *Organizational Learning II: Theory, Method and Practice*. Reading, MA: Addison Wesley.

Ashton, J., ed. 1992. *Healthy Cities*. Milton Keynes, UK: Open University Press.

Aspen Institute. 2004. *Structural Racism and Community Building*. Washington, DC: Aspen Institute.

Babcock, R. F. 1966. *The Zoning Game: Municipal Practices and Policies*. Madison: University of Wisconsin Press.

Baer, N. 2007. Manager of injury prevention and physical activity promotion projects, Contra Costa Health Services. Personal communication.

Bajaj, V., and Story, L. 2008. Mortgage crisis spreads past subprime loans. *New York Times*. February 12. http://www.nytimes.com/2008/02/12/business/12credit.html.

Bamberger, L. 1966. Health care and poverty: What are the dimensions of the problem from the community's point of view? *Bulletin of the New York Academy of Medicine* 42: 1140–49.

Banerjee, T., and Baer, W. C. 1984. *Beyond the Neighborhood Unit: Residential Environments and Public Policy*. New York: Plenum.

Banfield, E. 1961. *Political Influence*. New York: Free Press.

Barnes, R., and Scott-Samuel, A. 2002. Health impact assessment and inequalities. Pan *American Journal of Public Health* 11(5–6): 449–53.

Bartlett, R. V. 1997. The rationality and logic of NEPA revisited. In Clark, R., and Canter, L., eds., *Environmental Policy and NEPA: Past, Present and Future*. Boca Raton, FL: St. Lucie Press, pp. 51–60.

Barton, H., and Tsourou, C. 2000. *Healthy Urban Planning*. London: Spon Press.

Bashir, S. A. 2002. Home is where the harm is: Inadequate housing as a public health crisis. *American Journal of Public Health* 92(5): 733–38.

Bauer, C. 1945. Good neighborhoods. *Annals of the American Academy of Political and Social Science* 242: 104–15.

Baum, H. 2004. Smart growth and school reform: What if we talked about race and took community seriously? *Journal of the American Planning Association* 70(1): 14–26.

Bay Area Alliance. 2004. State of the Bay. *A Regional Report. Bay Area Indicators. Bay Area Alliance for Sustainable Communities and Northern California Council for the Community*. http://www.bayareaalliance.org/publications.html.

Bay Area Economics. 2006. *Presentation, The Richmond Economy*. www.cityofrichmondgeneralplan.org/docManager/1000000297/BAE%20Ec%20Background%20Report%20EDC%209-13-06.pdf.

Bay Area Regional Health Inequalities Initiative (BARHII). 2007. www.barhii.org.

Bay Area Working Group on the Precautionary Principle (BAWG). 2006. www.takingprecaution.org/index.html.

Bayview Hunters Point, Health and Environmental Assessment Task Force (BVHP HEAP). 2001. *Community Survey*. http://www.dph.sf.ca.us/Reports/BayviewHlthRpto9192006.pdf.

Belussi, F. 1996. Local systems, industrial districts and institutional networks: Towards a new evolutionary paradigm of industrial economics? *European Planning Studies* 4(3): 5–26.

Benveniste, G. 1989. *Mastering the Politics of Planning*. San Francisco: Jossey-Bass.

Berkman, L., and Kawachi, I., eds. 2000. *Social Epidemiology*. New York: Oxford University Press.

Berry, F. S., and Berry, W. D. 1999. Innovation and diffusion models in policy research. In Sabatier, P., ed., *Theories of the Policy Process*. Boulder, CO: Westview Press, pp. 169–200.

Besser, L., and Dannenberg, A. 2005. Walking to public transit: Steps to help meet physical activity recommendations. *American Journal of Preventative Medicine* 29(4): 273–80.

Bhatia, R., and Katz, M. 2001. Estimation of health benefits from a local living wage ordinance. *American Journal of Public Health* 91(9): 1398–1402.

Bhatia, R. 2003. Swimming upstream in a swift current: Public health institutions and inequality. In Hofricter, R., ed., *Health and Social Justice: Politics, Ideology, and Inequity in the Distribution and Disease.* San Francisco: Jossy-Bass, pp. 557–78.

Bhatia, R. 2005, 2006, 2007. Director, Environmental Health, San Francisco Department of Public Health. Personal communication.

Birley, M. H. 1995. *The Health Impact Assessment of Development Projects.* London: HMSO.

Black, K., and Cho, R. 2004. *New Beginnings: The Need for Supportive Housing for Previously Incarcerated People.* New York: Coalition for Supportive Housing and Common Ground.

Bloomberg, M. 2003. *Mayor's Management Report, Fiscal Year 2003.* New York: Office of the Mayor.

Blumenfeld, J. 2003. New approaches to safeguarding the Earth: An environmental version of the Hippocratic Oath. San Francisco Chronicle Open Forum. August 4.

Bobo, K., Kendall, J., and Max, S. 1996. *Organizing for Social Change: A Manual for Activists in the 1990s.* Santa Ana, CA: Seven Locks.

Bolen, E. 2003. *Neighborhood Groceries: New Access to Healthy Food in Low-Income Communities.* San Francisco: California Food Policy Advocates.

Bolton, R. 1992. "Place prosperity vs prosperity" revisited: An old issue with a new angle. *Urban Studies* 29: 185–203.

Bonilla-Silva, E. 1997. Rethinking racism: Toward a structural interpretation. *American Sociological Review* 62: 465–80.

Booth, C. 1902. *Life and Labour of the People in London.* New York: Macmillan.

Borsook, P. 1999. How the Internet ruined San Francisco. *Salon Magazine.* www.salon.com/news/feature/1999/10/28/internet/print.html.

Bourdieu, P. 1990. *The Logic of Practice.* Cambridge: Polity Press.

Boyer, C. 1983. *Dreaming the Rational City: The Myth of American City Planning.* Cambridge: MIT Press.

Brahinsky, R. 2005. Housing for whom? Looming plans to reshape the eastern half of the city could alter the city's socioeconomic balance. *San Francisco Bay Guardian* 39: 32.

Brandt, A. 1987. *No Magic Bullet: A Social History of Venereal Disease in the United States since 1880.* New York: Oxford University Press.

Brazil, E. 1998. S.F. housing a story of endless shortage. *San Francisco Examiner* July, 28.

Brenner, N. 2004. *New State Spaces: Urban Governance and the Rescaling of Statehood.* Oxford: Oxford University Press.

British Medical Association (BMA). 1998. *Health and Environmental Impact Assessment: An Integrated Approach.* www.bma.org.uk/ap.nsf/Content/ Healthenvironmentalimpact~Recommendations.

Broussard, A. S. 1993. Black San Francisco: The Struggle for Racial Equality in the West, 1900–1954. Lawrence: University Press of Kansas.

Brown, B., and Campell, R. 2005. *Smoothing the Path from Prison to Home.* New York: Vera Institute of Justice. www.vera.org/publication_pdf/319_590.pdf.

Building a Healthier San Francisco (BHSF). 2004. *Community Health Assessment, San Francisco.* Northern California Council for the Community. www.hcncc.org/ Upload/2004_Building_Healthier_SF_Needs_Assessment.pdf.

Building a Healthier San Francisco (BHSF). 2007. *Community Health Assessment, San Francisco.* http://www.healthmattersinsf.org/index.php?module=htmlpages &func=display&pid=29.

Bullard, R., ed. 2007. *Achieving Livable Communities, Environmental Justice, and Regional Equity.* Cambridge: MIT Press.

Bullard, R. 1994. *Unequal Protection: Environmental Justice and Communities of Color.* San Francisco: Sierra Club Books.

Bullard, R. D., and Johnson, G. S. 2000. Environmental justice: Grassroots activism and its impact on public policy decision making. *Journal of Social Issues* 56: 555–78.

Burris, S., Hancock, T., Lin, V., and Herzog, A. 2007. Emerging strategies for healthy urban governance. *Journal of Urban Health: Bulletin of the New York Academy of Medicine* 84(1): 154–63.

Burrows, E. G., and Wallace, M. 1999. *Gotham: A History of New York City to 1898.* New York: Oxford University Press.

California Environmental Health Tracking Program (CEHTP). 2006. *Community Perspective on Environmental Health Tracking.* West Oakland Environmental Indicators Project-Indicators Study. www.neip.org.

California Environmental Protection Agency (CalEPA). 2004. *Intra-agency Environmental Justice Strategy.* August. Sacramento: CALEPA.

California Environmental Protection Agency (CalEPA). 2005. *Air Quality and Land Use Handbook: A Community Health Perspective.* Sacramento: California Air Resources Board.

California Environmental Protection Agency (CalEPA). 2007. *Precautionary Approaches Guidance Development Update.* Draft Work Plan. April 16.

California Environmental Quality Act (CEQA). 1998. *Appendix G, Checklist.* http://ceres.ca.gov/topic/env_law/ceqa/guidelines/Appendix_G.html.

California, State of. 2006. *General Plan Guidance.* Office of Planning and Research. http://www.opr.ca.gov/index.php?a=planning/gpg.html.

California, State of. 2007. *School Physical Fitness Test Report, 2006–07.* Sacramento.

Carroll, M. 2006. City set to end wrangling over Trinity Plaza with OK on deal. *San Francisco Examiner,* August 3. www.examiner.com/a-203469~City_set _to_end_wrangling_over_Trinity_Plaza_with_OK_on_deal.html?cid=rss-San _Francisco.

Cars, G., Healey, P., Madanipour, A., and De Magalhaes, C. 2002. *Urban Governance, Institutional Capacity and Social Milieux.* Aldershot: Ashgate.

Carson, M. 1990. *Settlement Folk: Social Thought and the American Settlement Movement, 1885–1930.* Chicago: University of Chicago Press.

Carson, R. 1962. *Silent Spring.* New York: Houghton Mifflin.

Case, A., Fertig, A., and Paxson, C. 2005. The lasting impact of childhood health and circumstance. *Journal of Health Economics* 24(2): 365–89.

Cash, D. W., Clark, W. C., Alcock, F., Dickson, N. M., Eckley, N., Guston, D. H., Jager, J., and Mitchell, R. B. 2003. Knowledge systems for sustainable development. *Proceedings of the National Academy of Science USA* 100: 8086–91.

Castells, M. 1983. The city and the grassroots: A cross-cultural theory of urban social movements. Berkeley: University of California Press, 1983.

Centers for Disease Control and Prevention (CDC). 2004. *Designing and Building Healthy Places.* http://www.cdc.gov/healthyplaces.

Chadwick, E. 1842. *Report on the Sanitary Condition of the Labouring Population of Great Britain.* Edinburgh, Edinburgh University Press.

Chion, M. 2005. Former director of Community and Environmental Planning, San Francisco Department of City Planning. Personal communication.

Chu, A., Thorne, A., and Guite, H. 2004. The impact of mental well-being of the urban and physical environment: An assessment of the evidence. *Journal of Mental Health Promotion* 3(2): 17–32.

Clancy, K. 2004. Potential contributions of planning to community food systems. *Journal of Planning Education and Research* 22: 435–38.

Clark, K. 1965. *Dark Ghetto: Dilemmas of Social Power*. New York: Harper.

Clark, W. C., Crutzen, P. J., and Schellnhuber, H. J. 2005. Science for global sustainability: Toward a new paradigm. Working paper 120. Center for International Development, Harvard University, Cambridge.

Clarke, A. 2005. *Situational Analysis: Grounded Theory after the Postmodern Turn*. Thousand Oaks, CA: Sage.

Cleary, S. 2007. Project manager, Urban Habitat. Personal communication.

Cohen, S. 1972. *Folk Devils and Moral Panics*. London: MacGibbon and Kee.

Cole, B. L., Willhelm, M., Long, P. V., Fielding, J. E., Kominski, G., and Morgenstern, H. 2004. Prospects for health impact assessment in the United States: New and improved environmental impact assessment or something different? *Journal of Health Politics, Policy and Law* 29(6): 1153–86.

Cole, B. L., Shimkhada, R., Fielding, J. E., Kominski, G., and Morgernstern, H. 2005. Methodologies for realizing the potential of health impact assessment. *American Journal of Preventative Medicine* 28: 382–89.

Cole, L. 1994. The struggle of Kettleman City: Lessons for the movement. *Maryland Journal of Contemporary Legal Issues* 5: 67–80.

Collins, J. 2006, 2007. SOMCAN organizer. Personal communication.

Collins, J. W. Jr., David, R. J., Handler, A., Wall, S., and Andes, S. 2004. Very low birthweight in African American infants: The role of maternal exposure to interpersonal racial discrimination. *American Journal of Public Health* 94(12): 2132–38.

Commission of the European Communities. 2000. *Communication from the Commission on the Precautionary Principle*. COM(2000) 1. Brussels. http://europa.eu.int/comm/dgs/health_consumer/library/pub/pub07_en.pdf.

Cone, M. 2005. Europe's rules forcing U.S. firms to clean up; unwilling to surrender sales, companies struggle to meet the EU's tough stand on toxics. *Los Angeles Times*, May 16, p. A1.

Conklin, T. J., Lincoln, T., and Flanigan, T. P. 1998. A public health model to connect correctional health care with communities. *American Journal of Public Health* 88(8): 1249–50.

Conley, D., and Bennett, N. G. 2000. Is biology destiny? Birth weight and life chances. *American Sociological Review* 65: 458–67.

Contra Costa County. 2005. *Community Health Indicators for Selected Cities and Places in Contra Costa County*. Hospital Council Report, March 3.

Cooper, R., and David, R. 1986. The biologic concept of race and its application to public health and epidemiology. *Journal of Health Politics, Policy and Law* 11: 97–116.

Cooper, R. S., Kaufman, J. S., and Ward, R. 2003. Race and genomics. *New England Journal of Medicine* 348(12): 1166–70.

Corburn, J. 2003. Bringing local knowledge into environmental decision-making: Improving urban planning for communities at risk. *Journal of Planning Education and Research* 22: 420–33.

Corburn, J. 2004. Confronting the Challenges in reconnecting urban planning and public health. *American Journal of Public Health* 94(4): 541–46.

Corburn, J. 2005. *Street Science: Community Knowledge and Environmental Health Justice*. Cambridge: MIT Press.

Council on Environmental Quality (CEQ). 1997a. *The National Environmental Policy Act: A Study of Its Effectiveness after Twenty-five Years*. Washington, DC: CEQ.

Council on Environmental Quality (CEQ). 1997b. *Environmental Justice Guidance under the National Environmental Policy Act*. www.epa.gov/compliance/resources/policies/ej/ej_guidance_nepa_ceq1297.pdf.

Cronon, W. 1992. *Nature's Metropolis: Chicago and the Great West*. New York: Norton.

Cummins, S., Curtis, S., Diez-Roux, A. V., and Macintyre, S. 2007. Understanding and representing "place" in health research: A relational approach. *Social Science and Medicine* 65: 1825–38.

Cummins, S., and Macintyre, S. 2005. Food environments and obesity—Neighborhood or nation? *International Journal of Epidemiology* 35: 100–104.

Cummins, S., Stafford, M., Macintyre, S., Marmot, M., and Ellaway, A. 2005. Neighborhood environment and its association with self-rated health: Evidence from Scotland and England. *Journal of Epidemiology and Community Health* 59: 207–31.

Cunningham, G., and Michael, Y. 2004. Concepts guiding the study of the impact of the built environment on physical activity for older adults: A review of the literature. *American Journal of Health Promotion* 18(6): 435–43.

Curtis, S. E. 1990. Use of survey data and small area statistics to assess the link between individual morbidity and neighborhood deprivation. *Journal of Epidemiology and Community Health* 44: 62–68.

Dafoe, J. 2007. Green collar jobs in New York City. *Urban Agenda*. http://www.urbanagenda.org/projects.htm#growing.

Dahl, R. 1961. *Who Governs?* New Haven: Yale University Press.

Daily, G. C., Alexander, S., Ehrlich, P. R., Goulder, L., Lubchenco, J., Matson, P. A., Mooney, H. A., Postel, S., Schneider, S. H., Tilman, D., and Woodwell, G. M. 1997. Ecosystem services: Benefits supplied to human societies by natural ecosystems. *Issues in Ecology* 1(2): 1–18.

Daniels, R. 1997. No lamps were lit for them: Angel Island and the historiography of Asian American immigration. *Journal of American Ethnic History* 17: 2–18.

Dannenberg, A., Bhatia, R., Cole, B., Heaton, S., Feldman, J., and Rutt, C. 2008. Use of health impact assessment in the United States: 27 Case studies, 1999–2007. *American Journal of Preventive Medicine* 34: 241–56.

Dannenberg, A. L., Bhatia, R., Cole, B. L., Dora, C., Fielding, J. E., Kraft, K., McClymont-Peace, D., Mindell, J., Onyekere, C., Roberts, J. A., Ross, C. L., Rutt, C. D., Scott-Samuel, A., and Tilson, H. H. 2006. Growing the field of health impact assessment in the United States: An agenda for research and practice. *American Journal of Public Health* 96: 262–70.

Dannenberg, A. L., Jackson, R. J., Frumkin, H., Schieber, R. A., Pratt, M., Kochtitzky, C., and Tilson, H. H. 2003. The impact of community design and land-use choices on public health: A scientific research agenda. *American Journal of Public Health* 93: 1500–1508.

Davenport, C., Mathers, J., and Parry, J. 2005. Use of health impact assessment in incorporating health considerations in decision making. *Journal of Epidemiology and Community Health* 60: 196–201.

Davey-Smith, G. 2000. Learning to live with complexity: Ethnicity, socioeconomic position, and health in Britain and the United States. *American Journal of Public Health* 90: 1694–98.

De Leeuw, E., and Skovgaard, T. 2005. Utility-driven evidence for healthy cities: Problems with evidence generation and application. *Social Science and Medicine* 61: 1331–41.

De Leeuw, E. 1999. Healthy Cities: Urban social entrepreneurship for health. *Health Promotion International* 14: 261–69.

De Leeuw, E. 2001. Global and local (glocal) health the WHO healthy cities program. *Global Change and Human Health* 2: 34–45.

De Vries, S., Verheij, R., Groenewegen, P., and Spreeuwenberg, P. 2002. Natural environments–healthy environments? An exploratory analysis of the relationship between greenspace and health. *Environment and Planning* A35: 1717–31.

Deegan, M. J. 2002. *Race, Hull House, and the University of Chicago: A New Conscience against Ancients Evils*. Westport, CT: Praeger.

DeLeon, R. E. 1992. *Left Coast City: Progressive Politics in San Francisco, 1975–1991*. Lawrence: University Press of Kansas.

Department of Housing and Urban Development (HUD). 1996. *Expanding Housing Choices for HUD-Assisted Families*. First Biennial Report to Congress: Moving to Opportunity Fair Housing Demonstration. Washington, DC: Office of Policy Development and Research. April.

Di Chiro, G. 1996. Nature as community: The convergence of environment and social justice. In Cronon, W., ed., *Uncommon Ground: Rethinking the Human Place in Nature*. New York: Norton, pp. 298–320.

Diez-Roux, A. V., Merkin, S. S., Arnett, D., Chambless, L., Massing, M., Nieto, F. J., Sorlie, P., Szklo, M., Tyroler, H. A., and Watson, R. L. 2001. Neighborhood of residence and incidence of coronary heart disease. *New England Journal of Medicine* 345: 99–106.

Diez-Roux, A. 2000. Multilevel analysis in public health research. *Annual Review of Public Health* 21: 171–92.

Diez-Roux, A. V., Nieto, J., Muntaner, C., Tyroler, H. A., Comstock, G. W., Shahar, E., Cooper, L. S., Watson, R. L., and Szklo, M. 1997. Neighborhood environments and coronary heart disease. *American Journal of Epidemiology* 146: 48–63.

Diez-Roux, A. V. 1998. Bringing context back into epidemiology: Variables and fallacies in multilevel analysis. *American Journal of Public Health* 88: 287–93.

Diez-Roux, A. V. 2001. Investigating neighborhood and area effects on health. *American Journal of Public Health* 91: 1808–14.

Diez-Roux, A. V. 2002. Places, people, and health. *American Journal of Epidemiology* 155: 516–19.

Domhoff, G. W. 1986. The growth machine and the power elite: A challenge to pluralists and Marxists alike. In Waste, R., ed., *Community Power: Directions for Future Research*. Beverly Hills, CA: Sage, pp. 53–75.

Dora, C., and Phillips, M. 1999. *Transport, Environment, and Health: Reviews of Evidence for Relationships between Transport and Health*. Geneva: World Health Organization.

Dreier, P., Mollenkopf, J., and Swanstrom, T. 2004. *Place Matters: Metropolitics for the Twenty-first Century*, 2nd ed. Lawrence: University Press of Kansas.

DuBois, W. E. B., ed. 1906. *The Health and Physique of the Negro American*. Atlanta: Atlanta University Press. Reprinted 2003 in the *American Journal of Public Health* 93: 272–76.

Duchon, L. M., Andrulis, D. P., and Reid, H. M. 2004. Measuring progress in meeting healthy people goals for low birth weight and infant mortality among the 100 largest cities and their suburbs. *Journal of Urban Health* 81: 323–39.

Duffy, J. 1990. *The Sanitarians: A History of American Public Health*. Chicago: University of Illinois Press.

Duggan, T. 2004. Bringing healthy produce to poor neighborhoods. *San Francisco Chronicle*, July 16. http://temp.sfgov.org/sfenvironment/articles_pr/2004/article/071604.htm.

Duhl, L., ed. 1963. *The Urban Condition: People and Policy in the Metropolis*. New York: Simon and Schuster.

Duhl, L. J., and Sanchez, A. K. 1999. *Healthy Cities and the City Planning Process*. http://www.who.dk/document/e67843.pdf.

Duncan, C., and Jones, K. 1993. Do places matter? A multi-level analysis of regional variation in health related behaviour in Britain. *Social Science and Medicine* 37: 725–33.

Durazo, C. 2005. South of Market Community Action Network (SOMCAN). Personal communication.

Ecob, R., and Macintyre, S. 2000. Small area variations in health-related behaviors: Do these depend on the behavior itself, its measurement, or on personal characteristics? *Health and Place* 6: 261–74.

Edquist, C. 2001. Innovation policy—A systemic approach. In Archibugi, D., and Lundvall, B.-Å., eds., *The Globalizing Learning Economy*. New York: Oxford University Press, pp. 219–38.

Edsall, T. B., and Edsall, M. D. 1991. *Chain Reaction: The Impact of Race, Rights, and Taxes on American Politics*. New York: Norton.

Ellen, I. G., Dillman, K., and Mijanovich, T. 2001. Neighborhood effects on health: Exploring the links and assessing the evidence. *Journal of Urban Affairs* 23: 391–408.

Ellen, I. G., and Turner, M. A. 1997. Does neighborhood matter? Assessing recent evidence. *Housing Policy Debate* 8: 833–66.

Emirbayer, M. 1997. Manifesto for a relational sociology. *American Journal of Sociology* 103: 281–317.

Engels, F. [1844] 1968. *The Condition of the Working Class in England*. Henderson, W. O., and Chaloner, W. H., trans./eds. Stanford: Stanford University Press.

Epstein, E. 1999. Money changing everything in the Mission. *San Francisco Chronicle*, September 18, p. A17.

Escobar, A. 2001. Culture sits in places: Reflections on globalism and subaltern strategies of localization. *Political Geography* 20: 139–74.

Eslinger, B. 2006. SF plans green community. *The Examiner*, August 12.

Etzkowitz, H., and Leydesdorff, L. 2000. The dynamics of innovation: From national system and "mode 2" to a triple helix of university–industry–government relations. *Research Policy* 29: 109–23.

Evans, P. B., ed. 2002. *Livable Cities? Urban Struggles for Livelihood and Sustainability*. Berkeley: University of California Press.

Evans, R. G., and Stoddart, G. L. 1990. Producing health, consuming health care. *Social Science and Medicine* 31: 1347–63.

Evans, R., Barer, M., and Marmor, T. 1994. *The Determinants of Health of Populations*. New York: Aldine de Gruyter.

Ewing, R., Schmid, T., Killingsworth, R., Zlot, A., and Raudenbush, S. 2003. Relationship between urban sprawl and physical activity, obesity, and morbidity. *American Journal of Health Promotion* 18: 47–57.

Exline, S. 2006. San Francisco Department of City Planning. Personal Communication.

Fagan, J., and Davies, G. 2004. The natural history of neighborhood violence. *Journal of Contemporary Criminal Justice* 20(2): 127–47.

Fainstein, S. 2005. Planning theory and the city. *Journal of Planning Education and Research* 25: 121–30.

Fairfield, J. D. 1994. The scientific management of urban space: Professional city planning and the legacy of progressive reform. *Journal of Urban History* 20: 179–204.

Farhang, L. 2006, 2007. Personal communication.

Farhang, L., Bhatia, R., Comerford Scully, C., Corburn, J., Gaydos, M., and Malekafzali, S. 2008. Creating tools for healthy development: Case study of San Francisco's Eastern Neighborhoods Community Health Impact Assessment. *Journal of Public Health Management and Practice* 14(3): 255–65.

Farmer, P. 1999. *Infections and Inequalities: The Modern Plagues*. Berkeley: University of California Press.

Feagin, J. R. 2000. *Racist America: Roots, Current Realities, and Future Reparations*. New York: Routledge Press.

Federal Housing Authority (FHA). 1936. *Planning Neighborhoods for Small Houses*. Technical Bulletin 5. July 1. Washington, DC: FHA.

Feenstra, G. 1997. Local food systems and sustainable communities. *American Journal of Alternative Agriculture* 12(1): 28–36.

Feldman, C. 2000. MAC Attack. Anti-displacement group puts planning commission on the defensive. *San Francisco Bay Guardian*, September 13.

Fischer, C., Leydesdorff, L., and Schophaus, M. 2004. Science shops in Europe: The public as stakeholder. *Science and Public Policy* 31(3): 199–211.

Fischler, R. 1998. For a genealogy of planning. *Planning Perspectives* 13(4): 389–410.

Fisher, I. D. 1986. *Frederick Law Olmsted and the City Planning Movement in the United States*. Ann Arbor: UMI Research Press.

Fishman, R., ed. 2000. *The American Planning Tradition: Culture and Policy*. Washington, DC: Woodrow Wilson Center Press.

Fitzpatrick, K., and LaGory, M. 2000. *Unhealthy Places: The Ecology of Risk in the Urban Landscape*. London: Routledge.

Flournoy, R., and Treuhaft, S. 2005. *Healthy Food, HealthyCommunities: Improving Access and Opportunities through Food Retailing. Policylink and The California Endowment*. www.policylink.org/pdfs/HealthyFoodHealthyCommunities.pdf.

Fone, D., and Dunstan, F. 2006. Mental health, places and people: A multilevel analysis of economic inactivity and social deprivation. *Health and Place* 12(3): 332–44.

Food Trust, The. 2004. *Farmer's Market Program Evaluation*. www.thefoodtrust.org/catalog/resource.detail.php?product_id=68.

Ford, G. B. 1915. The city scientific. *Proceedings of the Fifth National Conference in City Planning*, Boston: National Conference on City Planning, pp. 31–39.

Ford, R. T. 1994. The boundaries of race: Political geography in legal analysis. *Harvard Law Review* 107: 1844–1921.

Forester, J. 1999. *The Deliberative Practitioner*. Cambridge: MIT Press.

Foster, S. 1999. Impact assessment. In Gerrard, M., ed., *The Law of Environmental Justice*. Chicago: American Bar Association, pp. 256–306.

Foucault, M. 1995. *Discipline and Punish: The Birth of the Prison*. New York: Vintage Books.

Fox, D. M., Jackson, R. J., and Jeremiah, A. B. 2003. Health and the built environment. *Journal of Urban Health* 80(4): 534–35.

Frank, L. D., Sallis, J. F., Conway, T. L., Chapman, J. E., Saelens, B. E., and Bachman, W. 2006. Many pathways from land use to health: Associations between neighborhood walkability and active transportation, body mass index, and air quality. *Journal of the American Planning Association* 72(1): 75–87.

Freudenberg, N. 2001. Jails, prisons and the health of urban populations: A review of the impact of the correctional system on community health. *Journal of Urban Health* 78: 214–35.

Freudenberg, N., Galea, S., and Vlahov, D., eds. 2006. *Cities and the Health of the Public*. Nashville: Vanderbilt University Press.

Fried, J. P. 1976. City's housing administrator proposes "planned shrinkage" of some slums. *New York Times*, February 3, p. A1.

Frieden, B. 1979. *The Environmental Protection Hustle*. Cambridge: MIT Press.

Friedman, D. J., Hunter, E. L., and Parrish, R. G. 2002. *Shaping a Vision of Health Statistics for the 21st Century*. National Committee on Vital and Health Statistics. http://www.ncvhs.hhs.gov/hsvision/visiondocuments.html.

Friedmann, J. 1987. *Planning in the Public Domain: From Knowledge to Action*. Princeton: Princeton University Press.

Frug, G. E. 1999. *City Making: Building Communities without Building Walls*. Princeton: Princeton University Press.

Frumkin, H. 2001. Beyond toxicity: The greening of environmental health. *American Journal of Preventative Medicine* 20: 234–40.

Frumkin, H. 2002. Urban sprawl and public health. *Public Health Reports* 117: 201–17.

Frumkin, H. 2003. Healthy places: Exploring the evidence. *American Journal of Public Health* 93: 1451–56.

Frumkin, H. 2005. Health, equity, and the built environment. *Environmental Health Perspectives* 113: A290–91.

Frumkin, H., Frank, L., and Jackson, R. J. 2004. *Urban Sprawl and Public Health*. Washington, DC: Island Press.

Fulbright, L. 2006. Big victory for Hunters Point activists: As PG&E closes its old, smoky power plant, the neighborhood breathes a sigh of relief. *San Francisco Chronicle*, May 15, p. A1.

Fullilove, M. 2006. Personal communication.

Fullilove, M. T. 2003. Neighborhoods and infectious disease. In Kawachi, I., and Berkman, L. F., eds., *Neighborhoods and Health*. New York: Oxford University Press, pp. 211–23.

Fullilove, M. T. 2004. *Root Shock: How Tearing up City Neighborhoods Hurts America and What We Can Do about It*. New York: Ballantine.

Fullilove, M. T., and Fullilove, R. E. 2000. What's housing got to do with it? *American Journal of Public Health* 90: 183–84.

Fung, A. 2006. *Empowered Participation: Reinventing Urban Democracy*. Princeton: Princeton University Press.

Funtowitcz, S., and Ravetz, J. R. 1993. Science for the post-normal age. *Futures* 25(7): 739–59.

Gagen, E. A. 2000. Playing the part: Performing gender in America's playgrounds. In Holloway, S. L., and Valentine, G., eds., *Children's Geographies: Playing, Living, Learning*. London: Routledge, pp. 213–29.

Galea, S., and Vlahov, D. 2005. *Handbook of Urban Health: Populations, Methods, and Practice*. New York: Springer.

Galea, S., Freudenberg, N., and Vlahov, D. 2005. Cities and population health. *Social Science and Medicine* 60: 1017–33.

Galobardes, B., Lynch, J. W., and Davey Smith, G. 2004. Childhood socioeconomic circumstances and cause-specific mortality in adulthood: Systematic review and interpretation. *Epidemiologic Reviews* 26: 7–21.

Gans, H. 1967. *The Levittowners*. New York: Pantheon.

Garrett, L. 2000. *Betrayal of Trust: The Collapse of Global Public Health*. New York: Hyperion.

Gaventa, J. 1980. *Power and Powerlessness: Quiescence and Rebellion in an Appalachian Valley*. Urbana: University of Illinois Press.

Gee, G., and Takeuchi, D. 2004. Traffic stress, vehicular burden and well-being: A multilevel analysis. *Social Science and Medicine* 59: 405–14.

Gee, G. C., and Payne-Sturges, D. C. 2004. Environmental health disparities: A framework integrating psychosocial and environmental concepts. *Environmental Health Perspectives* 112: 1645–53.

Gelobter, M. 2006. Personal communication.

Geronimus, A. T., and Thompson, J. P. 2004. To denigrate, ignore, or disrupt: The health impact of policy-induced breakdown of urban African American communities of support. *Du Bois Review* 1(2): 247–79.

Geronimus, A. T. 1994. The weathering hypothesis and the health of African American women and infants: Implications for reproductive strategies and policy analysis. In Sen, G., and Snow, R. C., eds., *Power and Decision: The Social Control of Reproduction*. Cambridge: Harvard University Press.

Geronimus, A. T. 2000. To mitigate, resist, or undo: Addressing structural influences on the health of urban populations. *American Journal of Public Health* 90: 867–72.

Ghosh, A. 2005. San Francisco Department of City Planning. Personal communication.

Giddens, A. 1984. *The Constitution of Society*. Cambridge, UK: Polity Press.

Gieryn, T. F. 1999. *Cultural Boundaries of Science: Credibility on the Line*. Chicago: University of Chicago Press.

Gieryn, T. 2000. A place for space in sociology. *Annual Review of Sociology* 26: 463–96.

Gieryn, T. 2006. City as truth-spot: Laboratories and field-sites in urban studies. *Social Studies of Science* 36(1): 5–38.

Gilens, M. 1999. *Why Americans Hate Welfare*. Chicago: University of Chicago Press.

Gillette Jr., H. 1983. The evolution of neighborhood planning: From the Progressive Era to the 1949 Housing Act. *Journal of Urban History* 9(4): 421–44.

Glaser, E., Davis, M. M., and Aragón, T. 1998. *Cancer Incidence among Residents of the Bayview–Hunters Point Neighborhood, San Francisco, California, 1993–1995*. Sacramento: California Department of Health Services.

Goodman, A. H. 2000. Why genes don't count (for racial differences in health). *American Journal of Public Health*, 90, pp. 1699–1702.

Goodman, R. 1971. *After the Planners*. New York: Simon and Schuster.

Goodno, J. B. 2004. Feet to the fire. *Planning* 70(4): 14–19.

Goodyear, C. 2005a. Deal protests tenants of Trinity Plaza apartments. *San Francisco Chronicle*, June 15, p. B4.

Goodyear, C. 2005b. Rincon Hill's huge towers put on hold. *San Francisco Chronicle*, December 8, p. A1.

Gordon, M. 2007. West Oakland Environmental Indicators Project. Personal communication.

Gottlieb, R. 1993. *Forcing the Spring. The Transformation of the American Environmental Movement*. Washington, DC: Island Press.

Graham, S., and Marvin, S. 2001. *Splintering Urbanism*. New York: Routledge.

Graham, S., and Healey, P. 1999. Relational concepts of space and place: Issues for planning theory and practice. *European Planning Studies* 7: 623–46.

Grande, O. 2005. People Organized for the Defense of Economic and Environmental Rights (PODER). Personal Communication.

Granovetter, M. 1973. The Strength of Weak Ties. *American Journal of Sociology* 81: 1287–1303.

Greenberg, M., and Schneider, D. 1994. Violence in American cities: Young black males is the answer, but what was the question? *Social Science and Medicine* 39(2): 179–87.

Greenberg, M. 1991. American Cities: Good and bad news about public health. *Bulletin of the New York Academy of Medicine* 67: 17–21.

Greenhouse, S. 2001. Hispanic workers die at higher rates. *New York Times*, July 16, p. A11.

Grey, M. 1999. *New Deal Medicine: The Rural Health Programs of the Farm Security Administration*. Baltimore: Johns Hopkins University Press.

Gross, J., LeRoy, G., and Janis-Aparicio, M. 2002. Community benefit agreements: Making development projects accountable. California: Good Jobs First and the California Public Subsidies Project.

Gunder, M. 2006. Sustainability: Planning's saving grace or road to perdition? *Journal of Planning Education and Research* 26: 208–21.

Haar, C. M., and Kayden, J. S., eds. 1989. *Zoning and the American Dream: Promises Still to Keep*. Chicago: Planners Press.

Haber, S. 1964. *Efficiency and Uplift: Scientific Management in the Progressive Era, 1890–1920*. Chicago: University of Chicago Press.

Habermas, J. 1975. *Legitimation Crisis*. Boston: Beacon Press.

Hacking, I. 1999. *The Social Construction of What?* Cambridge: Harvard University Press.

Haines, M. R. 2001. The urban mortality transition in the United States, 1800–1940. NBER Historical Paper 134. http://www.nber.org/papers/h0134.pdf.

Hajer, M. 2001. The need to zoom out: Understanding planning processes in a post-corporatist society. In Madanipour, A., Hull, A., and Healey, P., eds., *The Governance of Place: Space and Planning Processes*. Aldershot: Ashgate, pp. 178–202.

Hall, P. 1996. *Cities of Tomorrow: An Intellectual History of Urban Planning and Design in the Twentieth Century*, rev. ed. Oxford: Blackwell.

Hall, T., and Hubbard, P. 1998. *The Entrepreneurial City*. Chichester: Wiley.

Hamilton, A. 1943. *Exploring the Dangerous Trades: The Autobiography of Alice Hamilton*. Boston: Northeastern University Press.

Hamilton, D. C., and Hamilton, C. V. 1997. *The Dual Agenda: The African American Struggle for Civil and Economic Equality*. New York: Columbia University Press.

Hancock, T. 1993. The evolution, impact, and significance of the healthy cities/communities movement. *Journal of Public Health Policy* (spring): 5–18.

Hancock, T., and Duhl, L. 1988. *Promoting Health in the Urban Context*. World Health Organization, Healthy Cities Papers. Copenhagen: FADL Publishers.

Handy, S. L., Boarnet, M. G., Ewing, R., and Killingsworth, R. E. 2002. How the built environment affects physical activity: Views from urban planning. *American Journal of Preventative Medicine* 23(suppl 2): 64–73.

Harloe, M., Pickvance, C. G., and Urry, J., eds. 1990. *Place, Policy, and Politics: Do Localities Matter?* Boston: Unwin Hyman.

Harrington, M. 1962. *The Other America: Poverty in the United States.* New York: Macmillan.

Harrison, P. M., and Karberg, J. C. 2004. Prison and jail inmates at midyear 2003. US Department of Justice, Office of Justice Programs, Washington, DC. *Bureau of Justice Statistics Bulletin* NCJ 203947: 1–14.

Hartig, T., and Lawrence, R. J. 2003. The residential environment and health. *Journal of Social Issues* 59(3): 455–73.

Hartman, C. 2002. *City for Sale: The Transformation of San Francisco.* Berkeley: University of California Press.

Harvey, D. 1989. *The Urban Experience.* Baltimore: Johns Hopkins University Press.

Harvey, D. 1996. *Justice, Nature and the Geography of Difference.* Oxford: Blackwell.

Harvey, P. 1989. From managerialism to entrepreneurialism: the transformation of urban politics in late capitalism. *Geografiska Annaler* B71(1): 3–18.

Hayden, D. 1997. *Power of Place: Urban Landscapes as Public History.* Cambridge: MIT Press.

Healey, P. 1998. Building institutional capacity through collaborative approaches to urban planning. *Environment and Planning* A30(5): 1531–56.

Healey, P. 1999. Institutionalist analysis, communicative planning and shaping places. *Journal of Planning and Environment Research* 19(2): 111–22.

Healey, P. 2003. Collaborative planning in perspective. *Planning Theory* 2(2): 101–23.

Healey, P. 2007. *Urban Complexity and Spatial Strategies: Towards a Relational Planning for Our Times.* London: Routledge.

Health Canada. 1986. *Achieving Health for All: A Framework for Health Promotion.* http://www.hc-sc.gc.ca/hcs-sss/pubs/care-soins/1986-frame-plan-promotion/index_e.html.

Hinkle, L. E., and Loring, W. C., eds. 1977. *The Effect of the Manmade Environment on Health and Behavior.* CDC 77-8318. Atlanta, GA: US Public Health Service.

Hirsh, A. R. 1983. *Making the Second Ghetto: Race and Housing in Chicago, 1940–1960*. Cambridge: Cambridge University Press.

Hoch, C. 1994. *What Planners Do: Power, Politics and Persuasion*. Chicago: Planners Press.

Hochschild, J. L. 1995. *Facing up to the American Dream: Race, Class, and the Soul of the Nation*. Princeton: Princeton University Press.

Holton, S. S. 2001. Segregation, racism and white women reformers: A transnational analysis, 1840–1912. *Women's History Review* 10(1): 5–25.

Hood, E. 2005. Dwelling disparities: How poor housing leads to poor health. *Environmental Health Perspectives* 113: A310–19.

Horowitz, C. R., Colson, K. A., Hebert, P. L., and Lancaster, K. 2004. Barriers to buying healthy foods for people with diabetes: Evidence of environmental disparities. *American Journal of Public Health* 94(9): 1549–54.

Howard, E. 1965. *Garden Cities of Tomorrow*. Cambridge: MIT Press.

Hull-House, Residents of. 1895. *Hull House Maps and Papers: A Presentation of Nationalities and Wages in a Congested District of Chicago, Together with Comments and Essays on Problems Growing out of the Social Conditions*. New York: Crowell.

Huntersview Tenants Association and Green Action for Health and Environmental Justice. 2004. *Pollution, Health, Environmental Racism and Injustice: A Toxic Inventory of Bayview Hunters Point, San Francisco*. www.partnerships.ucsf.edu/pdfs/pdf_commdata_02.pdf.

Hurley, A. 1995. *Environmental inequalities: Class, Race, and Industrial Pollution in Gary, Indiana, 1945–1980*. Chapel Hill: University of North Carolina Press.

Iacofano, D. 2007. Principal, MIG planning firm. Personal communication.

Iceland, J. 2004. Beyond black and white: Metropolitan residential segregation in multi-ethnic America. *Social Science Research* 33: 248–71.

Iglesias, T. 2003. Housing impact assessments: Opening new doors for state housing regulation while localism persists. *Oregon Law Review* 82: 433–516.

Initiative for a Competitive Inner City. 2002. *The Changing Models of Inner City Grocery Retailing*. Boston: Initiative for a Competitive Inner City.

Innes, J. E. 1995. Planning theory's emerging paradigm: Communicative action and interactive practice. *Journal of Planning Education and Research* 14(4): 183–89.

Innes, J. E. 1996. Planning through consensus building: A new view of the comprehensive planning ideal. *Journal of the American Planning Association* 62: 460–72.

Institute of Medicine (IOM). 1988. *The Future of Public Health.* Washington, DC: National Academy Press.

Institute of Medicine (IOM). 2001. *Rebuilding the Unity of Health and the Environment: A New Vision of Environmental Health for the 21st Century.* Washington, DC: National Academy Press.

Institute of Medicine (IOM). 2000a. Neighborhood and community. In Shonkoff, J., and Phillips, D. A., eds., *From Neurons to Neighborhoods: The Science of Early Childhood Development.* Washington, DC: National Academy Press, pp. 328–36.

Institute of Medicine (IOM). 2000b. *Promoting Health: Intervention Strategies from Social and Behavioral Research.* Washington, DC: National Academy Press.

Institute of Medicine (IOM). 2003. *Unequal Treatment: Confronting Racial and Ethnic Disparities in Health Care.* Washington, DC: National Academies Press.

International Association of Impact Assessment (IAIA). 2006. *Health Impact Assessment: International Best Practice Principles.* http://www.iaia.org/Non_Members/Pubs_Ref_Material/SP5.pdf.

Isaacs, R. 1948. The neighborhood unit is an instrument of segregation. *Journal of Housing* 5: 215–19.

Ison, E. 2000. *Resource for Health Impact Assessment: The Main Resource,* vols. 1–2. London: NHS Executive.

Iton, T. 2007. Director of Alameda County Public Health Department. Presentation to the Port of Oakland Maritime Air Quality Improvement Plan, Task Force Meeting. August 14.

Jackson, S. A., and Anderson, R. T. 2000. The relation of residential segregation to all-cause mortality: A study in black and white. *American Journal of Public Health* 90: 615–17.

Jackson, J. B. 1984. *Discovering the Vernacular Landscape.* New Haven: Yale University Press.

Jacobs, J. 1961. *The Death and Life of Great American Cities.* New York: Random House.

James, S. 1993. Racial and ethnic differences in infant mortality and low birth weight: A psychosocial critique. *Annals of Epidemiology* 3: 130–36.

James, S., Schultz, A. J., and van Olphen, J. 2001. Social capital, poverty, and community health: An exploration of linkage. In Saegert, S., Thompson, J. P., and Warren, M. R., eds., *Social Capital and Poor Communities.* New York: Russell Sage Foundation, pp. 165–88.

Jamison, A. 2002. *The Making of Green Knowledge: Environmental Politics and Cultural Transformation.* Cambridge: Cambridge University Press.

Jasanoff, S. 2004. The idiom of co-production. In Jasanoff, S., ed., *States of Knowledge: The Co-production of Science and Social Order*. London: Routledge, pp. 1–45.

Jasanoff, S. 2005. *Designs on Nature: Science and Democracy in Europe and the United States*. Princeton: Princeton University Press.

Jasanoff, S. 2006. Transparency in public science: Purposes, reasons, limits. *Law and Contemporary Problems* 69: 21–45.

Jencks, C., and Petersen, P. E., eds. 1991. *The Urban Underclass*. Washington, DC: Brookings Institution.

Johnson, C. 2007. Chevron looks to profits, Richmond looks to health. *San Francisco Chronicle*, June 8, p. B1.

Jones, K., and Duncan, C. 1995. Individuals and their ecologies: Analyzing the geography of chronic illness within a multilevel modeling framework. *Health and Place* 1: 27–30.

Jones, C. P. 2000. Levels of racism: A theoretic framework and a gardener's tale. *American Journal of Public Health* 90;8: 1212–15.

Jones, P. 2006. Personal communication.

Jones, V. 2008. *The Green Collar Economy*. New York: HarperOne.

Judd, D. R., and Swanstrom, T. 1998. *City Politics: Private Power and Public Policy*. New York: Longman.

Kaplan, G. A. 1999. What is the role of the social environment in understanding inequalities in health? *Annals of the New York Academy of Sciences* 896: 116–20.

Kaplan, G. A., Pamuk, E. R., Lynch, J. M., Cohen, R. D., and Balfour, J. L. 1996. Inequality in income and mortality in the United States: Analysis of mortality and potential pathways. *British Medical Journal* 312: 999–1003.

Karkkainen, B. C. 2002. Toward a smarter NEPA: Monitoring and managing government's environmental performance. *Columbia Law Review* 102: 903–72.

Karpati, A. 2004. Assistant Commissioner, Brooklyn District Public Health Office. *Testimony before New York State Assembly Committee on Health and the Black, Puerto Rican and Hispanic Legislative Caucus*. April 22. Division of Health Promotion and Disease Prevention, New York City Department of Health and Mental Hygiene. Assembly Hearing Room, New York, New York. http://www.nyc.gov/html/doh/html/public/testi/testi20040422.html.

Karpati, A., Kerker, B., Mostashari, F., Singh, T., Hajat, A., Thorpe, L., Bassett, M., Henning, K., and Frieden, T. 2004. *Health Disparities in New York City*. New York City Department of Health and Mental Hygiene. www.nyc.gov/html/doh/pdf/epi/disparities-2004.pdf.

Kates, R., Clark, W., Corell, R., Hall, J. M., Jaeger, C. C., Lowe, I., McCarthy, J. J., Schellnhuber, H. J., Bolin, B., Dickson, N. M., Faucheux, S., Gallopin, G. C., Grübler, A., Huntley, B., Jäger, J., Jodha, N. S., Kasperson, R. E., Mabogunje, A., Matson, P., Mooney, H., Moore III, B., O'Riordan, T., and Svedin, U. 2001. Sustainability science. *Science* 292(5517): 641–42.

Katz, B. 2007. *Blueprint for American Prosperity: Metronation.* Washington, DC: Brookings Institute. http://www.brookings.edu/projects/blueprint.aspx.

Katz, M. 2006. Health programs in Bayview Hunter's Point and recommendations for improving the health of Bayview Hunter's Point residents. San Francisco Department of Public Health, Office of Policy and Planning. September 19.

Katz, M. 2006b. Personal communication.

Kaufman, J. 2004. Introduction. Special issue: Planning for community food systems. *Journal of Planning Education and Research* 23: 335–40.

Kawachi, I., and Berkman, L. 2003. *Neighborhoods and Health.* New York: Oxford University Press.

Kawachi, I., and Kennedy, B. 1999. Income inequality and health: Pathways and mechanisms. *Health Services Research* 34(1): 215–27.

Kearns, R. 1993. Place and health: towards a reformed medical geography. *Professional Geographer* 45: 139–47.

Kegler, M. C., Norton, B. L., and Aronson, R. E. 2003. *Evaluation of the Five-Year Expansion Program of California Healthy Cities and Communities (1998–2003).* http://www.civicpartnerships.org/docs/publications/TCEFinalReport9-2003.pdf.

Keller, E. F. 1985. *Reflections on Gender and Science.* New Haven: Yale University Press.

Keller, E. F. 2000. *The Century of the Gene.* Cambridge: Harvard University Press.

Kelly, M. P., Morgan, A., Bonnefoy, J., Butt, J., and Bergman, V. 2007. The social determinants of health: Developing an evidence base for political action. World Health Organization, Commission on the Social Determinants of Health. International Institute for Health and Clinical Excellence, Geneva.

Kemm, J. 1999. Developing health impact assessment in Wales. Cardiff: Health Promotion Division, National Assembly for Wales.

Kemm, J. 2005. The future challenges for HIA. *Environmental Impact Assessment Review* 25: 799–807.

Kemm, J., Parry, J., and Palmer, S., eds. 2004. *Health Impact Assessment.* New York: Oxford University Press.

Kevles, D. J. 1985. *In the Name of Eugenics: Genetics and the Uses of Human Heredity.* New York: Knopf.

Killingsworth, R., Earp, J., and Moore, R. 2003. Supporting health through design: Challenges and opportunities. *American Journal of Health Promotion* 18(1): 1–2.

Kingdon, J. W. 1995. *Agendas, Alternatives and Public Policies,* 2nd ed. NewYork: Harper-Collins.

Kjellstrom, T., Mercado, S., Sattherthwaite, D., McGranahan, G., Friel, S., and Havemann, K. 2007. Our cities, our health, our future: Acting on social determinants for health equity in urban settings. World Health Organization, Centre for Health Development, Kobe City, Japan.

Klinenberg, E. 2002. *Heat Wave: A Social Autopsy of a Disaster.* Chicago: University of Chicago Press.

Kling, J. R., Liebman, J. B., Katz, L. F., and Sanbonmatsu, L. 2004. *Moving to Opportunity and Tranquility: Neighborhood Effects on Adult Economic Self-sufficiency and Health from a Randomized Housing Voucher Experiment.* http://nber.org/~kling/mto/481.pdf.

Kling, J. R., and Del Conte, A. 2001. Synthesis of MTO research on self-sufficiency, safety and health, and behavior and delinquency. *Poverty Research News* 5(1): 3–6.

Knight, H. 2008. San Francisco officials on legislative binge to make the city healthier. *San Francisco Chronicle,* August 4, p. A1.

Kraut, A. 1988. Silent travelers: Germs, genes, and American efficiency, 1890–1924. *Social Science History* 12: 377–93.

Kreidler, A. G. 1919. A community self organized for preventive health work. *Modern Medicine* 1: 26–31.

Krieger, J., and Higgins, D. L. 2002. Housing and health: Time again for public health action. *American Journal of Public Health* 92(5): 758–68.

Krieger, N. 1999. Sticky webs, hungry spiders, buzzing flies, and fractal metaphors: On the misleading juxtaposition of "risk factor" vs "social" epidemiology. *Journal of Epidemiology and Community Health* 53: 678–80.

Krieger, N. 2001. Theories of social epidemiology for the 21st century: An ecosocial perspective. *International Journal of Epidemiology* 30: 668–77.

Krieger, N., ed. 2004. *Embodying Inequality: Epidemiologic Perspectives.* Amityville, NY: Baywood.

Krieger, N., and Davey Smith, G. 2004. "Bodies count," and body counts: Social epidemiology and embodying inequality. *Epidemiolgic Reviews* 26: 92–103.

Krieger, N. 2000. Epidemiology and social sciences: Toward a critical reengagement in the 21st century. *Epidemiologic Reviews* 22: 155–63.

Krieger, N. 2005. Embodiment: A conceptual glossary for epidemiology. *Journal of Epidemiology and Community Health* 59: 350–55.

Krieger, N. 2006. A century of census tracts: Health and the body politic (1906–2006). *Journal of Urban Health* 83: 355–61.

Krieger, N. 2008. Proximal, distal, and the politics of causation: What's level got to do with it? *American Journal of Public Health* 98: 221–30.

Krugman, P. 1998. Space: The final frontier. *Journal of Economic Perspectives* (spring): 161–74.

Kuehn, R. R. 1996. The environmental justice implications of quantitative risk assessment. *University of Illinois Law Review* 38: 103–72.

Kuehn, R. R. 2000. A taxonomy of environmental justice. *Environmental Law Reporter* 30: 10681–703.

Kuznets, S. 1965. *Economic Growth and Structure.* New York: Norton.

Lane, S. 2007. Urban Habitat. Personal communication.

Lasch-Quinn, E. 1993. *Black Neighbors: Race and the Limits of Reform in the American Settlement House Movement, 1890–1945.* Chapel Hill: University of North Carolina Press.

Lashley, K. 2008. Health-care provision meets microcredit finance in Argentina. *Bulletin of the World Health Organization* 86(1): 9–10.

Latour, B. 1987. *Science in Action: How to Follow Engineers and Scientists through Society.* Cambridge: Harvard University Press.

Latour, B. 1993. *We Have Never Been Modern.* Cambridge: Harvard University Press.

LaVeist, T. A., and Wallace, J. M. Jr. 2000. Health risk and inequitable distribution of liquor stores in African American neighborhood. *Social Science and Medicine* 51: 613–17.

Lawrence, D. P. 2003. *Environmental Impact Assessment: Practical Solutions to Recurrent Problems.* New York: Wiley-Interscience.

Leal, S. 2006. San Francisco's clean energy revolution is here. *San Francisco Chronicle,* August 14, p. B7.

Lear, L. 1997. *Rachel Carson: Witness for Nature.* New York: Henry Holt.

Leavitt, J. W. 1992. Typhoid Mary strikes back: Bacteriological theory and practice in early twentieth-century public health. *Isis* 83: 608–29.

Leavitt, J. W. 1996. *The Healthiest City: Milwaukee and the Politics of Health Reform.* Madison, WI: University of Wisconsin Press.

Leavitt, J. W. 1996b. *Typhoid Mary: Captive to the People's Health.* Boston: Beacon Press.

LeClere, F. B., Rogers, R. G., and Peters, K. D. 1997. Ethnicity and mortality in the United States: Individual and community correlates. *Social Forces* 76: 169–98.

Lee, M., and Rubin, V. 2007. The impact of the built environment on community health: The state of current practice and next steps for a growing movement. *Policy Link and The California Endowment.* http://www.calendow.org/Collection_Publications.aspx?coll_id=44&ItemID=310.

Lefebvre, H. 1991. *The Production of Space.* Oxford: Basil Blackwell.

Lefkowitz, B. 2007. *Community Health Centers: A Movement and the People Who Made It Happen.* New Brunswick: Rutgers University Press.

Lehto, J., and Ritsatakis, A. 1999. Health impact assessment as a tool for intersectoral health policy. Discussion paper for the Conference on Health Impact Assessment: From Theory to Practice. Gothenburg: European Center for Health Policy.

Lemann, N. 1991. *The Promised Land: The Great Black Migration and How It Changed America.* New York: Knopf.

Lempinen, E. W. 1998. Loft-war raging in SoMa live-work spaces provide housing but displace businesses, artists. *San Francisco Chronicle,* March 30, p. A1.

Lewis, N. P. 1916. *The Planning of the Modern City: A Review of the Principles Governing City Planning.* New York: Wiley.

Link, B., and Phelan, J. 2000. Evaluating the fundamental cause explanation for social disparities in health. In Bird, C., Conrad, P., and Freemont, A., eds., *The Handbook of Medical Sociology,* 5th ed. Upper Saddle River, NJ: Prentice-Hall, pp. 33–46.

Logan, J. 2003. Life and death in the city: Neighborhoods in context. *Contexts* 2: 33–40.

Logan, J. R., and Molotch, H. 1987. *Urban Fortunes: The Political Economy of Place.* Los Angeles: University of California Press.

Logan, T. 1976. The Americanization of German zoning. *Journal of the American Institute of Planning* 42(4): 377–85.

*London Health Observatory.* 2002. A guide to health and health services for town planners in London. Regeneration and Planning Task Group of the Health of Londoners Project (London). www.lho.org.uk/Publications/Attachments/PDF_Files/ghhstpl_text.pdf.

Lubchenco, J. 1998. Entering the century of the environment: A new social contract for science. *Science* 279: 491–97.

Lubove, R. 1974. *The Progressives and the Slums: Tenement House Reform in New York City, 1870–1917.* Westport: Greenwood.

Luks, S. 2005. *Power: A Radical View,* 2nd ed. Basingstoke: Palgrave Macmillan.

Lynch, S. M. 2003. Cohort and life-course patterns in the relationship between education and health: A hierarchical approach. *Demography* 40: 309–31.

Maantay, J. 2001. Zoning, equity and public health. *American Journal of Public Health* 91: 1033–41.

MacArthur, I. D. 2002. *Local Environmental Health Planning: Guidance for Local and National Authorities.* Copenhagen: World Health Organization.

Macintyre, S., Ellaway, A., and Cubbins, S. 2002. Place effects on health: How can we conceptualize, operationalize, and measure them? *Social Science and Medicine* 55: 125–39.

Macintyre, S., Maciver, S., and Sooma, A. 1993. Area, class, and health: Should we be focusing on places or people? *Journal of Social Policy* 22: 213–34.

Macris, D. 2006. Interim planning director, City of San Francisco. Personal communication, October 14.

Majone, G. 1989. *Evidence, Argument and Persuasion in the Policy Process.* New Haven: Yale University Press.

Marcuse, P. 1980. Housing policy and city planning: The puzzling split in the United States, 1893–1931. In Cherry, G. E., ed., *Shaping an Urban World.* London: Mansell, pp. 23–58.

Markel, H. 2004. *When Germs Travel: Six Major Epidemics That Have Invaded America Since 1900 and the Fears They Have Unleashed.* New York: Pantheon.

Markel, H. 1997. *Quarantine! East European Jewish Immigrants and the New York City Epidemics of 1892.* Baltimore: Johns Hopkins University Press.

Markel, H., and Stern, A. M. 2002. The foreignness of germs: The persistent association of immigrants and disease in American society. *Milbank Quarterly* 80(4): 757–88.

Marmot, M., Siegrist, J., Theorell, T., and Feeney, A. 2005. Health and the psychosocial environment at work. In Marmot, M., and Wilkinson, R. G., eds., *Social Determinants of Health.* Oxford: Oxford University Press.

Marris, P. 1996. *The Politics of Uncertainty: Attachment in Private and Public Life.* New York: Routledge.

Marsh, B. 1908. City planning in justice to the working man. *Charities and the Commons* 19 (February): 1514.

Marsh, B. 1909. *An Introduction to City Planning: Democracy's Challenge to the American City.* New York: Committee on Congestion of Population in New York.

Martin, G. 2005. San Francisco sits at the vanguard of urban areas trying to keep the future a deep shade of green. *San Francisco Chronicle,* May 29, p. D1.

Marx, K. 1978. *The Marx-Engels Reader,* 2nd ed. Robert C. Tucker, ed. New York: Norton.

Massey, D. S., and Denton, N. A. 1993. *American Apartheid: Segregation and the Making of the Underclass.* Cambridge: Harvard University Press.

McClain, C. 1988. Of medicine, race, and American law: The bubonic plague outbreak of 1900. *Law and Social Inquiry* 13(3): 447–513.

McCord, C., and Freeman, H. P. 1990. Excess mortality in Harlem. *New England Journal of Medicine* 322: 173–77.

McCormick, E., and Holding, R. 2004. Too young to die. A Special Report. *San Francisco Chronicle.* October 7. http://www.sfgate.com/cgi-bin/article.cgi?file=/c/a/2004/10/07/MNGII94D931.DTL.

McEwen, B. 1998. Protective and damaging effects of stress mediators. *New England Journal of Medicine* 338(3): 171–79.

McEwen, B. S., and Seeman, T. 1999. Protective and damaging effects of mediators of stress: Elaborating and testing the concepts of allostasis and allostatic load. In Adler, N., Marmot, M., McEwen, B., and Stewart, J., eds., Socioeconomic status and health in industrial nations: Social, psychological and biological pathways. *Annals of the New York Academy of Sciences* 896: 30–47.

McGrath, J. J., Matthews, K. A., and Brady, S. S. 2006. Individual versus neighborhood socioeconomic status and race as predictors of adolescent ambulatory blood pressure and heart rate. *Social Science and Medicine* 63(6): 1442–53.

McKeown, T. 1976. *The Modern Rise of Population.* New York: Academic Press.

Meeker, E. 1972. The improving health of the United States, 1850–1915. *Explorations in Economic History* 9(4): 353–73.

Melendez, M. 2003. *We Took the Streets: Fighting for Latino Rights with the Young Lords.* New York: St. Martin's Press.

Melosi, M. V. 1973. "Out of sight, out of mind:" The environment and disposal of municipal refuse, 1860–1920. *Historian* 35: 629–40.

Melosi, M. V. 1980. *Pollution and Reform in American Cities, 1870–1930.* Austin: University of Texas Press.

Melosi, M. V. 2000. *The Sanitary City: Urban Infrastructure in America from Colonial Times to the Present*. Baltimore: Johns Hopkins University Press.

Merchant, C. 1985. The Women of the Progressive Conservation Crusade: 1900–1915. In Bailes, K. E., ed., *Environmental History: Critical Issues in Comparative Perspective*. New York: New York University Press, pp. 153–75.

Merchant, C. 1993. *Major Problems in American Environmental History: Documents and Essays*. Lexington, MA: Heath.

Meyerson, M., and Banfield, E. C. 1955. *Politics, Planning, and the Public Interest; the Case of Public Housing in Chicago*. Glencoe, IL: Free Press.

Milio, N. 1986. *Promoting Health through Public Policy*. Ottawa: Canadian Public Health Association.

Miller, Z. L., and Melvin, P. M. 1987. *The Urbanization of Modern America: A Brief History*, 2nd ed. New York: Harcourt Brace Jovanovich.

Mindell, J., and Joffe, M. 2003. Health impact assessment in relation to other forms of impact assessment. *Journal of Public Health Medicine* 25: 107–13.

Mindell, J., Boaz, A., Joffe, M., Curtis, S., and Birley, M. 2004. Enhancing the evidence base for health impact assessment. *Journal of Epidemiology and Community Health* 58: 546–51.

Mindell, J., Ison, E., and Joffe, M. 2003. A glossary for health impact assessment. *Journal of Epidemiology and Community Health* 57(9): 647–51.

Mishel, L., Bernstein, J., and Allegretto, S. 2007. *The State of Working America 2006/2007*. Ithaca: ILR Press.

Mishler, E. G. 1981. Viewpoint: Critical perspectives on the biomedical model. In Mishler, E. G., Amara Singham, L. R., Hauser, S. T., Liem, R., Osherson, S. D., and Waxler, N. E., eds., *Social Contexts of Health, Illness, and Patient Care*. New York: Cambridge University Press, pp. 1–24.

Mission Anti-displacement Coalition (MAC). 2004. *The Hidden Costs of the New Economy: A Study of the Northeast Mission Industrial Zone*. www.uncanny.net/~wetzel/nemizreport.htm.

Mission Anti-displacement Coalition (MAC). 2005. *People's Plan*. http://podersf.org/docs/PeoplesPlan.pdf.

Mitchell, R. 2007. Director of city planning, City of Richmond, California. Personal communication. July.

Mohl, R. A. 2000. Planned destruction: The interstates and central city housing. In Bauman, J. F., Biles, R., and Szylvian, K. M., eds., *From Tenements to the Taylor Homes: In Search of an Urban Housing Policy in 20th Century America*. University Park: Pennsylvania State University Press, pp. 226–45.

Mollenkopf, J. 1983. *The Contested City.* Princeton: Princeton University Press.

Molotoch, H. 1976. The city as growth machine: Toward a political economy of place. *American Journal of Sociology* 82(2): 309–32.

Morello-Frosch, R., and Jesdale, B. M. 2006. Separate and unequal: Residential segregation and estimated cancer risks associated with ambient air toxics in U.S. metropolitan areas. *Environmental Health Perspective* 114: 386–93.

Morland, K., Wing, S., Diez Roux, A., and Poole, C. 2002. Neighborhood characteristics associated with the location of food stores and food service places. *American Journal of Preventive Medicine* 22: 23–29.

Moses, R. 1945. Slums and city planning. *Atlantic Monthly* 175(1): 63–68.

Mullan, F. 1989. *Plagues and Politics: The Story of the United States Public Health Service.* New York: Basic Books.

Mumford, L. 1955. *Sticks and Stones: A Study of American Architecture and Civilization.* 2nd rev. ed. New York: Dover.

National Association of County and City Health Officials (NACCHO). 2004. *Integrating Public Health into Land Use Decision-Making.* http://www.naccho.org/project84.cfm.

National Conference on City Planning. 1909. *Proceedings of the First National Conference on City Planning, Washington, DC, May 21–22, 1909.* Reprint 1967: Chicago: American Society of Planning Officials.

National Institutes of Health (NIH). 2004. What Are Health Disparities? http://healthdisparities.nih.gov/whatare.html.

National Oceanic and Atmospheric Administration (NOAA). 1994. Interorganizational Committee on Guidelines and Principles for Social Impact Assessment. National Marine Fisheries Service. Washington, DC: United States Department of Commerce. http://www.nmfs.noaa.gov/sfa/social_impact_guide.htm.

National Research Council. 2002. *Equality of Opportunity and the Importance of Place: Summary of a Workshop.* Washington, DC: National Academy Press.

National Science Foundation (NSF). 2007. Top scientists promote innovative, multidisciplinary global problem-solving strategies. http://www.nsf.gov:80/discoveries/disc_summ.jsp?cntn_id=110848.

Nelson, N. A. 1919. Neighborhood organizing vs. tuberculosis. *Modern Medicine* 1: 515–21.

New York City Department of Correction (DOC). 2003. *Annual Report. New York.* http://www.nyc.gov/html/doc/html/stats/doc_stats.shtml.

New York City Department of Health and Mental Hygiene (NYCDOHMH). 2004. *Take Care New York.* http://nyc.gov/html/doh/html/tcny/index.shtml.

Nolen, J. 1924. *Importance of Citizens' Committees in Securing Public Support for a City Planning Program.* Cambridge, MA: National Conference on City Planning.

Norberg-Hodge, H., Merrifield, T., and Gorelick, S. 2002. *Bringing the Food Economy Home: Local Alternatives to Global Agribusiness.* London: Zed.

Norris, T., and Pittman, M. 2000. The healthy communities movement and the coalition for healthier cities and communities. *Public Health Reports* 115: 118–23.

Nowotny, H., Scott, P., and Gibbons, M. 2001. *Re-thinking Science: Knowledge and the Public in an Age of Uncertainty.* Cambridge: Polity Press.

Nussbaum, M. 2000. *Women and Human Development.* Cambridge: Cambridge University Press.

Oberlander, P. H., and Newbrun, E. 1999. *Houser: The Life and Work of Catherine Bauer.* Vancouver: UBC Press.

O'Connor, A. 2002. *Poverty Knowledge: Social Science, Social Policy, and the Poor in Twentieth-Century U.S. History.* Princeton: Princeton University Press.

Office of Inspector General (OIG). 2006. *United States Environmental Protection Agency (EPA) Needs to Conduct Environmental Justice Reviews of Its Programs, Policies, and Activities.* www.epa.gov/oig/reports/2006/20060918-2006-P-00034.pdf.

Olmsted, F. L. Jr. 1910. City planning: An introductory address at the second national conference on city planning and congestion of population, Rochester, NY, May 2. American Civic Association, Department of City Making, series 2, no. 4.

Ona, F. 2005. Personal communication.

Orfield, M. 1997. *Metropolitics: A Regional Agenda for Community and Stability.* Washington, DC: Brookings Institution.

Pacific Institute. 2002. *Neighborhood Knowledge for Change: The West Oakland Environmental Indicators Project.* www.pacinst.org.

Pacific Institute. 2003. *Clearing the Air: Reducing Diesel Pollution in West Oakland. Issued in conjunction with the Coalition for West Oakland Revitalization.* www.pacinst.org/diesel.

Pacific Institute. 2006. *Paying with Our Health: The Real Cost of Freight Transport in California.* www.pacinst.org/reports/freight_transport.

Parfitt, J. 1987. *The Health of a City: Oxford, 1770–1974.* Oxford: Amate Press.

Park, R. E. 1929. The city as social laboratory. In Smith, T. V., and White, L. D., eds., *Chicago: An Experiment in Social Science Research.* Chicago: University of Chicago Press, pp. 1–19.

Parry, J. M., and Kemm, J. 2005. Criteria for use in evaluation of health impact assessments. *Public Health* 119: 1122–29.

Passchier-Vermeer, W., and Passchier, W. F. 2000. Noise exposure and public health. *Environmental Health Perspectives* 108: 123–31.

Pastor, M., Benner, C., and Rosner, R. 2006. *Edging toward Equity: Creating Shared Opportunity in America's Regions.* cjtc.ucsc.edu/docs/r_CORE_Edging_Toward_Equity_summary.pdf.

Pastor, M. J., Saad, J., and Morello-Frosh, R. 2007. *Still Toxic after All These Years: Air Quality and Environmental Justice in the San Francisco Bay Area.* Center for Justice, Tolerance and Community, University of California, Santa Cruz. http://cjtc.ucsc.edu.

Payne-Sturges, D. C., Burke, T. A., Breysse, P., Diener-West, M., and Buckley, T. J. 2004. Personal exposure meets risk assessment: A comparison of measured and modeled exposures and risks in an urban community. *Environmental Health Perspectives* 112: 589–98.

Pearce, N., Foliaki, S., Sporle, A., and Cunningham, C. 2004. Genetics, race, ethnicity, and health. *British Medical Journal* 328: 1070–72.

Pellow, D. 2002. *Garbage Wars: The Struggle for Environmental Justice in Chicago.* Cambridge: MIT Press.

Peoples Grocery. 2008. http://www.peoplesgrocery.org/index.php?topic=programs.

Perera, F. P., Rauh, V., Whyatt, R. M., Tsai, W. Y., Tang, D., Diaz, D., Hoepner, L., Barr, D., Tu, Y. H., Camann, D., and Kinney, P. 2006. Effect of prenatal exposure to airborne polycyclic aromatic hydrocarbons on neurodevelopment in the first 3 years of life among inner-city children. *Environmental Health Perspectives* 114(8): 1287–92.

Perry, C. A. 1929. City planning for neighborhood life. *Social Forces* 8(1): 98–100.

Petersen, P. E., ed. 1985. *The New Urban Reality.* Washington: Brookings Institution.

Peterson, J. 1979. The impact of sanitary reform upon American urban planning, 1840–1890. *Journal of Social History* 13: 83–103.

Peterson, J. 2003. *The Birth of City Planning in the United States, 1840–1917.* Baltimore: Johns Hopkins University Press.

Petts, J. 1999. Public participation in environmental impact assessment. In Petts, J., ed., *Handbook of Environmental Impact Assessment: Process, Methods and Potential,* vol. 1. Oxford: Blackwell, pp. 145–77.

Philpott, T. L. 1991. *The Slum and the Ghetto: Immigrants, Blacks, and Reformers in Chicago, 1880–1930.* Belmont, CA: Wadsworth.

Pluntz, R. 1990. *A History of Modern Housing in New York City: Dwelling Type and Social Change in the American Metropolis*. New York: Columbia University Press.

Polednak, A. P. 1996. Trends in U.S. urban black infant mortality, by degree of residential segregation. *American Journal of Public Health* 86: 723–26.

PolicyLink. 2002. *Reducing Health Disparities through a Focus on Communities*. Oakland: PolicyLink. www.policylink.org/Research/HealthDisparities.

Port of Oakland. 2007. *Maritime Air Quality Improvement Plan*. Task Force Meeting, August 14. http://www.portofoakland.com/environm/prog_04c_info.asp.

Porter, D. 2001. *Health, Civilization and the State: A History of Public Health from Ancient to Modern Times*. London: Routledge.

Porter, T. 1995. *Trust in Numbers: The Pursuit of Objectivity in Science and Public Life*. Princeton: Princeton University Press.

Portney, K. 2004. *Taking Sustainable Cities Seriously*. Cambridge: MIT Press.

Pothukuchi, K., and Kaufman, J. 1999. Placing the food system on the urban agenda: The role of municipal institutions in food systems planning. *Agriculture and Human Values* 16: 213–24.

Pothukuchi, K., and Kaufman, J. 2000. The food system: A stranger to the planning field. *American Planning Association Journal* 66(2): 113–24.

Powell, J. A. 2000. *The Racial Justice and Regional Equity Project*. http://www1.umn.edu/irp/rjreindex.html.

Prakash, S. 2007. Pacific Institute project director, Ditching Dirty Diesel Collaborative, Personal communication.

Prentice, B. 2007. BARHII. Personal communication.

Puentes, R., and Warren, D. 2006. *One Fifth of America: A Comprehensive Guide to America's First Suburbs*. Washington, DC: Brookings Institution.

Quigley, R., den Broeder, L., Furu, P., Bond, A., Cave, B., and Bos, R. 2006. *Health Impact Assessment International Best Practice Principles*. Special Publication series no. 5. Fargo, ND: International Association for Impact Assessment. http://www.iaia.org/modx/assets/files/SP5.pdf.

Raphael, D. 2006. Social determinants of health: Present status, unresolved questions, and future directions. *International Journal of Health Services* 36: 651–77.

Ratner, B. 2004. "Sustainability" as a dialogue of values: Challenges to the sociology of development. *Sociological Inquiry* 74(1): 50–69.

Reiss, J. R. 2006. *Making History: Precautionary Principle Law in the San Francisco Bay Area*. The Bay Area Working Group on the Precautionary Principle. Public presentation. www.takingprecation.org.

Reps, J. W. 1965. *The Making of Urban America: A History of City Planning in the United States.* Princeton: Princeton University Press.

Richardson, B. W. 1875. *Hygeia: A City of Health.* London: Macmillan.

Richmond, City of. 2007a. Richmond General Plan Update. *Issues and Opportunities Paper 8: Community Health and Wellness.* http://www.cityofrichmondgeneralplan.org/docs.php?view=topics.

Richmond, City of. 2007b. *Health Policy Element Added to General Plan.* http://www.cityofrichmondgeneralplan.org/news.php?display=1&oid=1000000375.

Riis, J. 1890. *How the Other Half Lives: Studies among the Tenements of New York.* New York: Penguin.

Robert Wood Johnson Foundation (RWJF). 2004. *Active Living by Design Program.* http://www.activelivingbydesign.org.

Roberts, D. 2003. *Shattered Bonds: The Color of Child Welfare.* New York: Basic Books.

Roberts, S. 1991. A critical evaluation of the city life cycle idea. *Urban Geography* 12: 431–43.

Rodgers, V. 2006. Land-use and health project director, National Association of City and County Health Officials (NACCHO). Personal communication.

Rodwin, V. 1984. *The Health Planning Predicament: France, Quebec, England, and the United States.* Berkeley: University of California Press.

Rojas, A. 1997. High rates of disease in Bayview: Study lends weight to pollution fears. *San Francisco Chronicle,* June 9, p. A1.

Rosen, G. 1971. The first neighborhood health center movement—Its rise and fall. *American Journal of Public Health* 61: 1620–37.

Rosen, G. 1993. *A History of Public Health,* exp.ed. Baltimore: Johns Hopkins University Press.

Rosenbaum, J., and Rubinowitz, L. S. 2000. *Crossing the Class and Color Lines: From Public Housing to White Suburbia.* Chicago: University of Chicago Press.

Rosenkrantz, B. 1972. *Public Health and the State: Changing Views in Massachusetts, 1842–1936.* Cambridge: Harvard University Press.

Rosenzweig, R., and Blackmar, E. 1992. *The Park and the People: A History of Central Park.* Ithaca: Cornell University Press.

Rosner, D., and Markowitz, G. 1985. The early movement for occupational safety and health. In Leavitt, J. W., and Numbers, R. L., eds., *Sickness and Health in America: Readings in the History of Medicine and Public Health.* Madison: University of Wisconsin Press, pp. 507–21.

Rubin, V. 2007. Personal communication.

Sabatier, P. A., and Jenkins-Smith, H. C., eds. 1993. *Policy Change and Learning: An Advocacy Coalition Approach.* Boulder, CO: Westview Press.

*San Francisco Chronicle.* 2005. Shakedown at City Hall. editorial. http://sfgate.com/cgi-bin/article.cgi?f=/c/a/2005/08/10/EDG9OE4U9U1.DTL.

San Francisco Department of Public Health (SFDPH). 1992. Hospitalizations for Bayview Hunters Point, 1991–1992.

San Francisco Department of Public Health (SFDPH). 1994. Comparison of incidence of cancer in selected sites between Bayview Hunters Point and the Bay Area.

San Francisco Department of Public Health (SFDPH). 2000. Overview of Health. Community Programs Division. www.dph.sf.ca.us.

San Francisco Department of Public Health (SFDPH). 2001. Overview of Health. Community Programs Division. www.dph.sf.ca.us.

San Francisco Department of Public Health (SFDPH). 2003a. Comment letter on Trinity Plaza Project. September 8. http://www.sfdph.org/phes/publications/comments/Comment_on_Trinity_DEIR_scope.pdf.

San Francisco Department of Public Health (SFDPH). 2003b. Comment letter on Spear and Folsom Towers. http://www.sfdph.org/phes/publications/comments/Comment_on_Spear_Folsom_DEIR.pdf.

San Francisco Department of Public Health (SFDPH). 2004a. Trinity Plaza EIR comment letter. http://www.sfdph.org/phes/publications/reports/HIAR-May2004.pdf.

San Francisco Department of Public Health (SFDPH). 2004b. Rincon Hill EIR comments. www.dph.sf.ca.us/phes/publications/comments/RinconAreaPlanDEIRcomment.pdf.

San Francisco Department of Public Health (SFDPH). 2004c. The case for housing impacts assessment: The human health and social impacts of inadequate housing and their consideration in CEQA policy and practice. http://www.sfdph.org/phes/publications/reports/HIAR-May2004.pdf.

San Francisco Department of Public Health (SFDPH). 2004d. Demographic, economic, and housing data: A lens into the Mission District, San Francisco, California. http://www.dph.sf.ca.us/ehs/phesmain.htm.

San Francisco Department of Public Health (SFDPH). 2004e. Prevention Strategic Plan, 2004 2008, Five-Year Plan. http://www.sfdph.org/Reports/PPRpts.htm.

San Francisco Department of Public Health (SFDPH). 2005. *Program on Health, Equity and Sustainability, 2005 Annual Report.* http://www.sfdph.org/phes/publications/PHES_2005_Annual_Report.pdf.

San Francisco Department of Public Health (SFDPH). 2007a. *Eastern Neighborhoods Community Health Impact Assessment*. Final report. Program on Health, Equity and Sustainability. http://www.sfphes.org/enchia/2007_09_05_ENCHIA_FinalReport.pdf.

San Francisco Department of Public Health (SFDPH). 2007b. Impacts on Community Health of Area Plans for the Mission, East SoMa, and Potrero Hill / Showplace Square: An Application of the Healthy Development Measurement Tool. December 25. www.thehdmt.org.

San Francisco Environment (SF Environment). 2005. *2004–2005, Annual Report. San Francisco Department of the Environment*. http://www.sfenvironment.org/index.html.

San Francisco Environment (SF Environment). 2006. *Precautionary Principle Ordinance*. http://www.sfenvironment.com/aboutus/policy/legislation/precaution_principle.htm.

San Francisco Fetal Infant Mortality Review Program. 1998. *Annual Report of Findings to the Community*. California Birth Defects Monitoring Program, 1999.

San Francisco Food Alliance. 2006. June 1 Meeting Minutes. http://www.sffoodsystems.org/pdf/SF%20Food%20Alliance%20Meeting%2006-01-06.pdf.

San Francisco Food Systems (SFFS). 2004. *Increasing Access of Low-Income San Franciscans to Farmers' Markets. December*. San Francisco Department of Public Health.

San Francisco Food Systems (SFFS). 2005. *Collaborative Food Systems Assessment*. A project of the San Francisco Foundation Community Initiative Funds and the San Francisco Department of Public Health. http://www.sffoodsystems.org/pdf/FSA-online.pdf.

San Francisco Mayor's Office of Community Development (SFMOCD). 2005. SoMa Community Stabilization Fund and Advisory Committee. http://www.sfgov.org/site/mocd_index.asp?id=44635.

San Francisco Planning Department (SFPD). 2003. *Community Planning in the Eastern Neighborhoods: Rezoning Options Workbook*. Department of Planning, City and County of San Francisco.

San Francisco Planning Department (SFPD). 2006. *Executive Park: Sub-area Plan of the Bayview Hunters Point Area Plan*. http://www.sfgov.org/site/planning_index.asp?id=42414.

San Francisco Planning Department (SFPD). 2007. Executive park subarea plan: Community workshop summary of comments. November 1. http://www.sfgov.org/site/planning_index.asp?id=42414.

Sassen, S. 1991. *The Global City; New York, London, Tokyo.* Princeton: Princeton University Press.

Satcher, D., Fryer, G. E., McCann, J., Troutman, A., Woolf, S. H., and Rust, G. 2005. What if we were equal? A comparison of the black-white mortality gap in 1960 and 2000. *Health Affairs* 24: 459–64.

Satterfield, D. 2002. The "in-between people": Participation of community health representatives in diabetes prevention and care in American Indian and Alaska Native communities. *Health Promotion Practice* 3(2): 166–75.

Saxenian, A. 1996. *The Regional Advantage: Culture and Competition in Silicon Valley and Route 128.* Cambridge: Harvard University Press.

Scheper-Hughes, N. 1992. *Death without Weeping: The Violence of Everyday Life in Brazil.* Berkeley: University of California Press.

Schultz, S., and McShane, C. 1978. To engineer the metropolis: Sewers, sanitation and city planning in late nineteenth century. *American Journal of American History* 65(2): 389–411.

Schulz, A. J., Williams, D. R., Israel, B. A., and Bex Lempert, L. 2002. Racial and spatial relations as fundamental determinants of health in Detroit. *Milbank Quarterly* 80: 677–707.

Schulz, A. J., Kannan, S., Dvonch, J. T., Israel, B. A., Allen, A. III., James, S. A., House, J. S., and Lepkowski, J. 2005. Social and physical environments and disparities in risk for cardiovascular disease: The Healthy Environments Partnership Conceptual Model. *Environmental Health Perspectives* 113: 1817–25.

Scott, J. 1998. *Seeing Like a State: How Certain Schemes to Improve the Human Condition Have Failed.* New Haven: Yale University Press.

Scott, M. 1971. *American City Planning Since 1890.* Berkeley: University of California Press.

Scott-Samuel, A. 1996. Health impact assessment: An idea whose time has come. *British Medical Journal* 313(1): 183–84.

Scott-Samuel, A. 1998. Health impact assessment: Theory into practice. *Journal of Epidemiology and Community Health* 52: 704–705.

Scott-Samuel, A., Birley, M., and Ardern, K. 1998. *The Merseyside guidelines for Health Impact Assessment.* Liverpool: Merseyside Health Impact Assessment Steering Group. http://www.liv.ac.uk/~mhb/publicat/merseygui/index.htm.

Seligman, K. 1998. Everyone wants a piece of the Mission. *San Francisco Examiner,* October 26, p. A1.

Sellers, C. 1994. Factory as environment: Industrial hygiene, professional collaboration and the modern sciences of pollution. *Environmental History Review* 18: 55–84.

Selna, R. 2007. Trinity deal hits a snag; some supervisors want more units at a rate below market. *San Francisco Chronicle*, January 4, p. B1.

Selznick, P. 1992. *The Moral Commonwealth: Social Theory and the Promise of Community*. Berkeley: University of California Press.

Semenza, J. C., McCullough, J. E., Flanders, W. D., McGeehin, M. A., and Lumpkin, J. R. 1999. Excess hospital admissions during the July 1995 heat wave in Chicago. *American Journal of Preventative Medicine* 16(4): 269–77.

Shah, N. 2001. *Contagious Divides: Epidemics and Race in San Francisco's Chinatown*. Berkeley: University of California Press.

Sharfstein, J., Sandel, M., Kahn, R., and Bauchner, H. 2001. Is child health at risk while families wait for housing vouchers? *American Journal of Public Health* 91: 1191–92.

Sharfstein, J., and Sandel, M., eds. 1998. *Not Safe at Home: How America's Housing Crisis Threatens the Health of Its Children*. Boston: Boston University Medical Center.

Shaw, M., David, G., Danny, D., Richard, M., and Davey Smith, G. 2000. Increasing mortality differentials by residential area level of poverty: Britain 1981–1997. *Social Science Medicine* 51: 151–53.

Shaw, R. 1996. *The Activist's Handbook: A Premier for the 1990s and Beyond*. Berkeley: University of California Press.

Shaw, R. 2007. The future of San Francisco's Mission District. *Beyond Chronicle*, January 22. www.beyondchron.org/news/index.php?itemid=4110.

Shon, D., and Rein, M. 1994. *Frame Reflection: Toward the Resolution of Intractable Policy Controversies*. New York: Basic Books.

Silicon Valley Network, Joint Venture. 2000. *Index of Silicon Valley: Measuring Progress toward the Goals of Silicon Valley 2010*. www.Jointventure.org.

Smith, M. P. 2001. *Transnational Urbanism: Locating Globalization*. Malden, MA: Blackwell.

Smith, S. 1995. *Sick and Tired of Being Sick and Tired: Black Women's Health Activism in America, 1890–1950*. Philadelphia: University of Pennsylvania Press.

Snow, C. P. 1962. *The Two Cultures and the Scientific Revolution*. New York: Cambridge University Press.

Soja, E. W. 1989. *Postmodern Geographies: The Reassertion of Space in Critical Social Theory*. London: Verso.

Solnit, R. 2000. *Hollow City*. New York: Verso.

Solomon, L. R. 1998. *Roots of Justice: Stories of Organizing in Communities of Color*. San Francisco: Jossey-Bass.

Sood, V. 2007. Project director, MIG planning. Personal communication. July.

South of Market Community Action Network (SOMCAN). 2004. Comment letter to the Department of City Planning on the Rincon Hill Draft Environmental Impact Report. December 8.

South of Market Community Action Network (SOMCAN). 2006. State of SoMa presentation.

Sparer, G., and Johnson, J. 1971. Evaluation of OEO neighborhood health centers. *American Journal of Public Health* 61(5): 931–42.

Stansfeld, S., Haines, M., and Brown, B. 2000. Noise and health in the urban environment. *Review of Environmental Health* 15(1–2): 43–82.

Steinemann, A. 2000. Rethinking human health impact assessment. *Environmental Impact Assessment Review* 20: 627–45.

Steinhauer, J. 2004. Drug and sex offenders face restrictions on public housing. *New York Times*, June 25, p. B1.

Stoll, M. A. 2005. *Job Sprawl and the Spatial Mismatch between Blacks and Jobs*. Washington, DC: Brookings Institution. www.brookings.edu/metro/pubs/20050214_jobsprawl.htm.

Stone, C. 2004. It's more than the economy after all: Continuing the debate about urban regimes. *Journal of Urban Affairs* 26: 1–19.

Stradling, D. 1999. *Smokestacks and Progressives: Environmentalists, Engineers, and Air Quality in America, 1881–1951*. Baltimore: Johns Hopkins University Press.

Suggs, E. 2005. Evictions from public housing near: Tenants told last October to get jobs or else. *Atlanta Journal-Constitution*, June 29.

Sugrue, T. J. 1996. *The Origins of the Urban Crisis: Race and Inequality in Postwar Detroit*. Princeton: Princeton University Press.

Susser, M., and Susser, E. 1996. Choosing a future for epidemiology: I. Eras and paradigms. *American Journal of Public Health* 86: 668–73.

Susskind, L., and Thomas-Larmer, J. 1999. Conducting a conflict assessment. In Susskind, L., McKearnan, S., and Thomas-Learner, J., eds., *The Consensus Building Handbook*. Thousand Oaks, CA: Sage.

Sydenstricker, E. 1934. Health and the depression. *Milbank Memorial Fund Quarterly* 12: 273–80.

Takano, T. 2003. *Healthy Cities and Urban Policy Research*. London: Taylor and Francis.

Tarr, J. A. 1996. *The Search for the Ultimate Sink: Urban Pollution in Historical Perspective*. Akron: University of Akron Press.

Tarr, J. A., and Lamperes, B. 1981. Changing fuel use behavior and energy transitions: The Pittsburgh smoke control movement, 1940–1950. A case study in historical analogy. *Journal of Social History* 14: 561–88.

Temple, J. 2003. Can rezoning satisfy housing advocates? *San Francisco Business Times*, June 20. www.sanfrancisco.bizjournals.com/sanfrancisco/stories/2003/06/23/focus2.html.

Tesh, S. 1988. *Hidden Arguments: Political Ideology and Disease Prevention Policy.* New Brunswick: Rutgers University Press.

Tesh, S. 1995. Miasma and "social factors" in disease causality: Lessons from the nineteenth century. *Journal of Health Politics Policy and Law* 20: 1001–24.

*The Health of Boston.* 2007. Boston Public Health Commission. Research Office. Boston.

Thomas, N. 2007. Personal communication.

Thomson, H., Petticrew, M., and Morrison, D. 2001. Health effects of housing improvement: Systematic review of intervention studies. *British Medical Journal* 323: 187–90.

Tickner, J. A., and Geiser, K. 2004. The precautionary principle stimulus for solutions- and alternatives-based environmental policy. *Environmental Impact Assessment Review* 24: 810–24.

Tickner, J. A. 2002. The precautionary principle and public health trade-offs: Case study of west Nile virus. *ANNALS, AAPSS* 584: 69–79.

Townsend, P., and Davidson, N., eds. 1982. *Inequalities in Health: The Black Report.* Harmondsworth: Penguin.

Trauner, J. B. 1978. The Chinese as medical scapegoats in San Francisco, 1870–1905. *California History* 57: 70–87.

Travis, J., Soloman, A. L., and Waul, M. 2001. *From Prison to Home: The Dimensions and Consequences of Prisoner Reentry.* Washington, DC: The Urban Institute.

Tritsch, S. 2007. The deadly difference. *Chicago Magazine.* October. http://www.chicagomag.com/Chicago-Magazine/October-2007/The-Deadly-Difference.

Tsouros, A., and Draper, R. A. 1993. The Healthy Cities project: New developments and research needs. In Davies, J. K., and Kelly, M. P., eds., *Healthy Cities—Research and Practice.* New York: Routledge, pp. 25–33.

United Nations Centre on Human Settlements (UNCHS). 2001. *The State of The World's Cities Report, 2001.* http://ww2.unhabitat.org/Istanbul+5/statereport.htm.

United Nations Centre on Human Settlements (UNCHS). 2007. *Global Campaign on Urban Governance: Principles.* http://www.unhabitat.org/content.asp?typeid=19&catid=25&cid=2097.

United States Department of Labor (DOL). 2001. *Census of Fatal Occupational Injuries. Bureau of Labor Statistics.* www.bls.gov/oshcfoi1.html?H6.

Urban Habitat. 1999. *There Goes the Neighborhood: A Regional Analysis of Gentrification and Community Stability in the San Francisco Bay Area.* Oakland, CA: Urban Habitat.

US Conference of Mayors. 2006. *Climate Action Plan.* http://usmayors.org/climateprotection/agreement.htm.

US EPA. 1997. *Environmental Justice Guidance under the National Environmental Protection Act (NEPA).* www.epa.gov/oeca/ofa/ejepa.html.

US EPA. 2006. *CARE Facilitation Case Study.* West Oakland Collaborative. www.epa.gov/adr.

Vega, C. 2005. SoMa developer fee gets signed into law. *San Francisco Chronicle,* August 20, p. B2.

Veneracion, A. 2005. Executive director, South of Market Community Action Network. Personal communication.

Villermé, L. R. 1829. Mémoire sure la taille de l'homme en France. *Annales d'hygiène publique et de médicine légale* 1: 351–99.

Villerme, L. R. 1830. De la mortalite dans divers quarters de la ville de Paris. *Annales d'hygiene publique* 3: 294–341.

Vlahov, D., Freudenberg, N., Proietti, F., Ompad, D., Quinn, A., Nandi, V., and Galea, S. 2007. Urban as a determinant of health. *Journal of Urban Health* 84: 16–26.

Von Hoffman, A. 2000. A study in contradictions: The origins and legacy of the housing act of 1949. *Housing Policy Debate* 11(2): 299–326.

Von Zielbauer, P. 2003. City creates post-jail plan for inmates. *New York Times,* September 20, p. B1.

Wachelder, J. 2003. Democratizing science: Various routes and visions of Dutch science shops. *Science, Technology and Human Values* 28(2): 244–73.

Wacquant, L. 1993. Urban outcasts: Stigma and division in the black American ghetto and the French urban periphery. *International Journal of Urban and Regional Research* 17: 366–83.

Wacquant, L. 2002. Deadly symbiosis: Rethinking race and imprisonment in 21st Century America. *Boston Review.* www.bostonreview.net/BR27.2/wacquant.html.

Walker, R. 2007. *The Country in the City: The Greening of the San Francisco Bay Area.* Seattle: University of Washington Press.

Wallace, D., and Wallace, R. 1998. *A Plague on Your Houses: How New York Was Burned Down and National Public Health Crumbled*. New York: Verso.

Wallace, R., and Wallace, D. 1990. Origins of public health collapse in New York City: The dynamics of planned shrinkage, contagious urban decay, and social disintegration. *Bulletin of the New York Academy of Medicine* 66: 391–437.

Walter, N., Bourgois, P., and Loinaz, H. M. 2002. Social context of work injury among undocumented day laborers in San Francisco. *Journal of General Internal Medicine* 17(6): 221–29.

Waters, A. 2004. Slow food, slow schools: Transforming education through a school lunch curriculum. www.edibleschoolyard.org/alice_message.html.

Weatherell, C., Tregear, A., and Allinson, J. 2003. In search of the concerned consumer: UK public perceptions of food, farming and buying local. *Journal of Rural Studies* 19: 233–44.

Weber, E. 2003. *Bringing Society Back In: Grassroots Ecosystem Management, Accountability, and Sustainable Communities*. Cambridge: MIT Press.

Weir, M. 1994. Urban poverty and defensive localism. *Dissent* 41: 337–42.

Weir, M. 2000. Planning, environmentalism and urban poverty. In Fishman, R., ed., *The American Planning Tradition: Culture and Policy*. Washington, DC: Woodrow Wilson Center Press, pp. 193–215.

Weiss, M. A. 1980. The origins and legacy of urban renewal. In Clavel, P., Forester, J., and Goldsmith, W. W., eds., *Urban and Regional Planning in an Age of Austerity*. New York: Pergamon Press, pp. 53–80.

Wekerle, G. 2004. Food justice movements: Policy, planning, and networks. *Journal of Planning Education and Research* 23: 378–86.

West County Toxics Coalition (WCTC). 2007. www.westcountytoxicscoalition.org.

West Oakland Project Area Committee (WOPAC). 2006. http://www.business2oakland.com/main/westoakland.htm.

Wetzel, T. 2000. *A Year in the Life of the Mission Anti-displacement Movement*. http://www.uncanny.net/~wetzel/macchron.htm.

Wetzel, T. 2001. San Francisco's space wars. *Processed World Magazine* (fall): 49–57.

White, R. D. 2008. Trucking firms line up for ports' clean-air programs. *Los Angeles Times*, September 6. www.latimes.com/business/la-fi-ports6-2008sep06,0,5629082.story.

Whitehead, M., and Dahlgren, G. 1991. What can we do about inequalities in health? *Lancet* 338: 1059–61.

Whitman, S., Silva, A., and Shah, A. M. 2006. Disproportionate impact of diabetes in a Puerto Rican community of Chicago. *Journal of Community Health* 31: 521–31.

Whyatt, R. W., Rauh, V., Barr, D. B., Camann, D. E., Andrews, H. F., Garfinkel, R., Hoepner, L. A., Diaz, D., Dietrich, J., Reyes, A., Tang, D., Kinney, P. L., and Perera, F. P. 2004. Prenatal insecticide exposures and birth weight and length among an urban minority cohort. *Environmental Health Perspective* 112: 1125–32.

Whyte, W. H. 1980. *The Social Life of Small Urban Spaces.* New York: Conservation Foundation.

Wiley, M. 2007. Smart growth and the legacy of segregation in Richland County, South Carolina. In Bullard, R., ed., *Growing Smarter.* Cambridge: MIT Press, pp. 149–70.

Wilkinson, R. G., and Marmot, M. 2003. *Social Determinants of Health: The Solid Facts*, 2nd ed. World Health Organization, Regional Office for Europe. www.euro .who.int/document/e81384.pdf.

Wilkinson, R. G. 1996. *Unhealthy Societies: The Afflictions of Inequality.* London: Routledge.

Williams, D., and Collins, C. 2001. Racial residential segregation: A fundamental cause of racial disparities in health. *Public Health Reports* 116: 404–16.

Williams, D. 1999. Race, socioeconomic status, and health: The added effects of racism and discrimination. *Annals of the New York Academy of Sciences* 896: 173–88.

Williams, G. 2007. Knowledge, politics and health improvement: The role of health impact assessment. Presentation at the South East Asian and Oceania Regional Health Impact Assessment Conference, Sydney, Australia, November.

Williams, M. T. 1991. *Washing "The Great Unwashed:" Public Baths in Urban America, 1840–1920.* Columbus: Ohio State University Press.

Willis, C. 1992. How the 1916 zoning law shaped Manhattan's central business districts. In New York City Department of City Planning and the City Planning Commission, *Planning and Zoning New York City: Yesterday, Today and Tomorrow.* DCP 92-03, pp. 1–19.

Wing, S. 2005. Environmental justice, science, and public health. *Environmental Health Perspectives.* http://www.ehponline.org/docs/2005/7900/7900.pdf.

Wirth, L. 1928. *The Ghetto.* Chicago: University of Chicago Press.

Wood, E. E. 1931. *Recent Trends in American Housing.* New York: Macmillan.

Woods, R. A., ed. 1898. *The City Wilderness: A Study of the South End.* Boston: Houghton Mifflin.

World Health Organization (WHO). 1948. *Preamble to the Constitution of the World Health Organization as adopted by the International Health Conference.* http://www.who.int/suggestions/faq/en.

World Health Organization (WHO). 1978. *Alma Ata Declaration.* http://www.who.int/hpr/NPH/docs/declaration_almaata.pdf.

World Health Organization (WHO). 1986. *Ottawa Charter for Health Promotion.* WHO, Geneva. http://www.who.int/hpr/NPH/docs/ottawa_charter_hp.pdf.

World Health Organization (WHO). 1988. *Healthy Cities Project: A Guide to Assessing Healthy Cities.* WHO Healthy Cities Papers 3. Copenhagen: FADL Publishers.

World Health Organization (WHO). 1989. *What Is Environmental Health Policy?* Frankfurt: The European Charter and Commentary. http://www.who.dk/eprise/main/who/Progs/HEP/20030612_1.

World Health Organization (WHO). 1995. *City Health Planning: The Framework.* Copenhagen: WHO Healthy Cities Project Office.

World Health Organization (WHO). 1997. *Twenty Steps for Developing a Healthy Cities Project,* 3rd ed. Copenhagen: WHO Regional Office for Europe.

World Health Organization (WHO). 1998. *Health Promotion Glossary.* Geneva: WHO.

World Health Organization (WHO). 1999. *Health Impact Assessment: Main Concepts and Suggested Approach.* Gothenburg Consensus Paper. European Centre for Health Policy. Copenhagen: WHO Regional Office for Europe.

World Health Organization (WHO). 2002. *Community Participation in Local Health and Sustainable Development: Approaches and Techniques.* University of Central Lancashire, European Sustainable Cities and Towns Campaign, European Commission, Healthy Cities Network. Copenhagen: WHO Regional Office for Europe. http://www.who.dk/healthy-cities/Links/20010907.

World Health Organization (WHO). 2007. *Achieving Health Equity: From Root Causes to Fair Outcomes.* Commission on Social Determinants of Health. www.who.int/social_determinants/resources/interim_statement/en/index.html.

World Health Organization (WHO). 2008. *Closing the Gap in a Generation: Health Equity through Action on the Social Determinants of Health.* Final report of the Commission on Social Determinants of Health. Geneva: WHO. www.who.int/social_determinants/final_report/en/index.html.

Wynne, B. 2003. Seasick on the third wave? Subverting the hegemony of propositionalism. *Social Studies of Science* 33: 401–17.

Yarne, M. 2000. Conformity as catalyst: Environmental Defense Fund *v.* Environmental Protection Agency. *Ecology Law Quarterly* 27: 841.

Yen, I. H., and Kaplan, G. A. 1999. Neighborhood social environment and risk of death: Multilevel evidence from the Alameda County Study. *American Journal of Epidemiology* 149: 898–907.

Yen, I. H., and Syme, S. L. 1999. The social environment and health: A discussion of the epidemiologic literature. *Annual Review of Public Health* 20: 287–308.

Yiftachel, O., and Huxley, M. 2000. Debating dominance and relevance: Notes on the "communicative turn" in planning theory. *International Journal of Urban and Regional Research* 24(4): 907–13.

Young, O. 1996. Rights, rules, and resources in international society. In Hanna, S., Folke, C., and Maler, K., eds., *Rights to Nature: Ecological, Economic, Cultural, and Political Principles of Institutions for the Environment.* Washington, DC: Island Press, pp. 245–64.

Young, T. K. 2006. *Population Health: Concepts and Methods.* New York: Oxford University Press.

Zima, B. T., Wells, K. B., and Freeman, H. E. 1999. Emotional and behavioral problems and severe academic delays among sheltered homeless children in Los Angeles County. *American Journal of Public Health* 84: 260–64.

# Index

Accountability, as WHO principle, 8
*Acheson Report* (Britain), 59
Active Living movement, 93
Activist city, 23, 56–57
Adaptive management, 201
Addams, Jane, 35. *See also* Settlement
  Houses movement
African-Americans
 in Bayview–Hunters Point
  neighborhood, 104
 and Chicago Exposition, 41
 community health centers for,
  39–40
 DuBois's study on, 31–32
 in foster care, 86
 infant mortality rate for, 56
 inordinate disease rates among, 3
 late 19th- and early 20th-century
  conditions for, 48
 and residential segregation, 55
 in San Francisco, 18
 and segregationist policies, 77
 and Settlement House movement,
  210n.11
 and split over jobs vs. environment,
  58
 and urban parks, 34
 and urban renewal, 53–54
 as removal, 85
Air quality. *See also* Pollution, urban
 and healthy urban governance, 70,
  71

San Francisco Bay Area campaign
 for, 101
West Oakland's fight for, 91
Alternative assessment, 201
Alternative issue framings, 23–24.
 *See also* New politics of healthy
 city planning
American Medical Association,
 neighborhood health centers
 opposed by, 40
American Planning Association,
 207
American Public Health
 Association
Committee on the Hygiene of
 Housing of, 50–52
public health adequacy questioned
 by, 55
American Sanitary era, 10, 96. *See*
 *also* Sanitary City era
Argyris, Chris, 201
Asian-Americans
 and barring of Asian women,
  214n.35
 and I-Hotel in San Francisco, 154,
  214n.35
Asian Pacific Environmental Network,
 Laotian Organizing Project of,
 194
Association for Improving the
 Condition of the Poor, New York
 (AICP), 34

Action Agenda for the Elimination of
  Health Disparities of, 59
Depression, the, health impact of, 50
Detroit, Sugrue on failures of, 56
Development. *See* Urban
  development; Urban renewal
Development impact fee, for Rincon
  Hill Area project, 155–58
Disease-specific death rates (selected
  cities), 49
Distribution, of disease and wellness,
  12–13, 59
Ditching Dirty Diesel Campaign,
  100–101, 102, 213n.27
Dotcom high-tech boom, and San
  Francisco gentrification, 132
Douglass, Frederick, 41
DuBois, W. E. B., 31
Duhl, Leonard, 6–7

East Bay Community Foundation, 194
Eastern Neighborhoods Community
  Health Impact Assessment
  (ENCHIA), 21, 165, 169–75, 196
community articulation of elements
  in, 174–79
and co-production of science, 202
criticisms of, 183
employment study, 179–80
evaluations of, 22
focus-group meetings, 179–80
formal authority lacking for, 199
goals and objectives of, 169
and HDMT, 21, 165, 185–87,
  200–201 (*see also* Healthy
  Development Measurement
  Tool)
healthy-city vision of, 165, 169–70,
  171, 188–90, 204
and experiences of community
  residents, 179
objectives in, 174–75, 177
positive consequences from,
  187–88
and merging of laboratory with
  field-site view, 205–206

metropolitan region and state
  influenced by, 193–96, 206
participants in, 214–15n.39
Planning Department shift as result
  of, 193
positive consequences of, 187–88
process map of, 168
professional relationships through,
  190–91
and public policy, 180
public trust built by, 191–92
and relational view of place, 204
"scorecard" developed by, 184–87
  (*see also* Healthy Development
  Measurement Tool)
East SoMa, 193
Economics, neoclassical, 54
Economy
in healthy city (ENCHIA vision), 174,
  177
and Rincon Hill Plan, 152
urban (assumptions about), 54–55
Ecosystem management, collaborative,
  201
Education
and healthy urban governance, 71,
  75–76
residential segregation adversely
  affects, 76
Elderly persons, concerns of
  (ENCHIA discussions), 180
Embodiment, of social condition, 12,
  16, 29, 97–99
Employment and economic
  opportunities, and healthy urban
  governance, 72, 78–70
and living wage (San Francisco),
  115–16, 122
residential segregation adversely
  affects, 76
Employment study (ENCHIA), 179,
  180
ENCHIA. *See* Eastern Neighborhoods
  Community Health Impact
  Assessment
Engels, Friedrich, 16, 29–30, 30

Health promotion, WHO on, 6, 8. *See also* Public health
Health research, and San Francisco community organizations, 160
Healthy cities movement, international, 6–9
Healthy Cities Project, 58–59
WHO principles for, 8, 58
Healthy city, 207
ENCHIA vision of, 165, 169, 171, 204
and experiences of community residents, 179
objectives in, 174–75, 177
positive consequences from, 187–88
and science, 9–11 (*see also* Science)
utopian ideas for, 210n.10
WHO characteristics of, 7
Healthy city planning, 1–2, 19, 197.
*See also* New politics of healthy city planning
in Bayview–Hunters Point neighborhood, 19–20 (*see also* Bayview–Hunters Point neighborhood)
challenges for, 198–99
"laboratory" and "field site" views to be avoided, 84
moral environmentalism and physical determinism to be avoided, 84
preventative strategies in, 83
and scientific rationality, 83–84
specialization and fragmentation to be avoided, 84
diffusion of, 193–96
for Eastern Neighborhoods of San Francisco, 21–22, 165–75 (*see also* Eastern Neighborhoods Community Health Impact Assessment)
governance issues crucial to, 197
and health impact analyses, 160 (*see also* Health impact assessment)
politics of, 199 (*see also* Politics of planning)

regional and statewide institutions in, 206
and relational view of place, 204 (*see also* Relational view of places)
and San Francisco Bay Area, 17–19
science of, 202 (*see also* Science)
and social movements, 159, 160
transformation of environmental health for, 127
for Trinity Plaza redevelopment, 20–21 (*see also* Trinity Plaza redevelopment project)
Healthy Development Measurement Tool (HDMT), 21, 165, 185–87, 191, 193, 195, 200–201, 201
certainty for developers through, 199
and co-production of science, 203
environmental stewardship example of, 186
and merging of laboratory with field-site view, 205–206
for Richmond, California, 194
Healthy Food Access Survey, 110
Healthy governance networks, from ENCHIA, 190
Healthy People 2010 (US document), 118
Healthy Places Coalition, 195
Healthy planning, politics of, 11–12, 68, 200
place in, 12, 13–15
population health in, 12, 12–13
power in, 12, 16–17
processes in, 12, 15–16
Healthy regional planning, 194–95
Healthy transit planning, 195
Healthy urban development, 159–61
and Trinity Plaza redevelopment, 20–21 (*see also* Trinity Plaza redevelopment project)
Healthy urban governance approach, 68–70, 81
air quality in, 70, 71
education and child care in, 71, 75–76
employment and economic opportunities in, 72, 78–80

Medical care, as limited contribution
    to health (SFDPH report), 118.
    *See also* Health care
Medical model, 49
Memphis, sanitary survey instituted
    in, 32–33
Merseyside Health Impact
    Assessment, 136, 167
Miasma
  environmental, 37
  in nineteenth-century theories, 3, 23,
    28–31, 38
MIG, Inc., 194
Milwaukee, Wisconsin, 210n.9
Minority communities
  medical care for, 95–96
  and NEPA reviews, 62, 63
Mission Agenda, 132
Mission Anti-displacement Coalition
    (MAC), 20, 132–33, 141–42, 159,
    165–66
  and health-impact assessment, 141,
    144, 167, 169
  and People's Plan, 134, 163
Mission District, San Francisco, 132
  activists from, 129
  Eastern Neighborhoods of, 193
  rezoning plan for, 164
Mission Economic Development
    Association (MEDA), 132–33, 191,
    196
Mission Housing Development
    Corporation (MHDC), 132
Mission Neighborhood Community
    Impact Assessment process, 163
Model Cities program, 57
Monitoring, Accountability,
    Reporting, and Impact
    assessment (MARI), 8–9
Monitoring and evaluation of health,
    as WHO requirement, 9
Monitoring networks, 90–93
Moral environmentalism, 10, 23,
    27–28
  avoidance of, 84
Morgenthau, Henry, 43

Mortgage insurance, 52–53
Mortgage subsidies, 77
Moses, Robert, 54
Muckrakers, 39
Mumford, Lewis, 210–211n.12
Municipal sanitary commissions, 28

National Association of County and
    City Health Officials (NACCHO),
    102, 207
National Conference on City Planning
    and the Problems of Congestion
    (first), 25, 43
National Conference on City Planning
    and the Problems of Congestion
    (second), 25–26, 43
National Conference on City Planning
    (third) 26
National Environmental Policy Act
    (NEPA)(1969), 61, 138
National Public Housing Conference,
    52
National Quarantine Act (1893), 33
Neighborhood health centers, 39–40,
    56, 96
Neighborhood Union, Atlanta, 39–40
Neighborhood unit concept, 45–46,
    47–48, 50–52
Neoclassical economics, 54
NEPA (National Environmental Policy
    Act)(1969), 61, 138
Networks, 190, 197
New Deal programs, 50
*New England Journal of Medicine, The*,
    on racial categories, 95
New politics of healthy city planning.
    *See also* Healthy city planning;
    Politics of planning
  challenges for, 83–85
  embodiment hypothesis, 97–99
  prevention and precaution in place
    of removal, 85–93
  regional coalitions in place of
    professionalization and
    specialization, 99–102
  relational view of place, 93–97

Newsom, Gavin, 157
New Urbanism, 93
New York Association for Improving
the Condition of the Poor
(AICP), 34
New York City
Central Park in, 34
neighborhoods of concentrated
incarceration in, 88
prevention approach in, 86, 87
Young Lords in, 56–57
New York City area, health disparities
in, 2
New York City Department of Health
and Mental Hygiene,
biomedically oriented program
of, 119–20, 121
Nixon administration, 57
Noise pollution, 68–69, 71
Nolen, John, 43–44
Nonprofit Housing Association of
Northern California, 194

Occupational councils, for
neighborhood health centers, 40
Occupational Health and Safety
Administration, 57
Olmsted, Frederick Law Jr., 25–26,
27, 43
Ona, Fernando, 113
Open space. *See also* Parks and
playgrounds
and ENCHIA discussions, 178
and healthy urban governance, 72, 78
*Origins of the Urban Crisis, The: Race
and Inequality in Postwar Detroit*
(Sugrue), 55–56
*Other America, The* (Harrington), 54
Ottawa Charter (1986), 6, 8
Oversight committees, and San
Francisco Department of Public
Health, 128

Pagoulatos, Nick, 133
Paris, health correlated with wealth
in, 28, 29

Park, Robert E., 46, 47
Parks and playgrounds, 34. *See also*
Open space
and ENCHIA discussions, 178
and healthy urban governance, 72,
78
potential drawbacks of, 176
Participation
and ENCHIA planning, 165
as PHES commitment, 125
Pathogenic city, 23, 49–55, 88
*Paying with Our Health: The Real Cost
of Freight Transport in California*,
101
Pedestrian injuries and activity, and
healthy urban governance, 71,
74
People of color, inordinate disease
rates in, 2
People Organizing to Demand
Environmental and Economic
Rights (PODER), 133, 141
People's Plan for Jobs Housing and
Community, 134, 141, 160, 163,
166
Perry, Clarence, 45, 47, 50
Petersen, Jon A., 26
PHES. *See* Program on Health, Equity
and Sustainability
Physical determinism, 93
avoidance of, 84
Physical removal and displacement,
27
Pittsburgh, California, 195
Places, in healthy city planning, 12
and city as field site, 10
relational view of, 13–15, 93–97, 98,
203–205
Baldwin on, 212n.25
vs. universal applicability, 46, 48
*Plan of Chicago*, 40–41
Planning. *See* City planning
Planning, healthy. *See* Healthy city
planning
Planning, politics of. *See* Politics of
planning

Planning for city health development, as WHO requirement, 9
Planning Department. *See* San Francisco Planning Department
*Planning of the Modern City, The* (Lewis), 43
*Planning the Neighborhood*, 50–52
*Planning Neighborhoods for Small Houses* (FHA), 53–53
Planning processes. *See also* Processes
 and alternative assessments, 201
 and city politics, 65–66
 community participation in, 158, 159, 165, 177, 192
 and ENCHIA, 183, 189, 190, 192
 regional organizations building on, 194
 and environmental impact assessment, 61
 health analyses obstructed in, 63, 198, 199, 211n.17
 and human health, 1, 68–70, 81
 air quality in, 70, 71
 education and child care in, 71, 75–76
 employment and economic opportunities in, 72, 78–80
 goods and services in, 73, 80
 health care in, 71, 80
 housing and residential environments in, 71, 76
 noise pollution in, 68–69, 71
 open space, parks and recreation in, 72, 78
 pedestrian activity in, 71, 74
 and racial residential segregation, 72, 76–77 (*see also* Segregation, residential)
 and residential environments, 77–78
 social cohesion in, 73, 80–81
 transit and land use sprawl in, 71 74–75
 Nolen on, 44
 and PHES, 131
 and politics of planning, 4–5, 83

and relational view of places, 14, 199
and social determinants of health, 23, 83 (*see also* Social determinants of health)
as urban governance, 66–68, 199
PODER (People Organizing to Demand Environmental and Economic Rights), 133, 141
PolicyLink, 195–196
Political coalition building, 38
Political frames, need to attend to, 197–98
Political governance practices, environmental health science linked with, 37
Political power, and healthy urban governance, 73
Politics of planning, 4–5, 65–66. *See also* New politics of healthy city planning
 of healthy planning, 11–12, 68, 200
 place in, 12, 13–15
 population health in, 12, 12–13
 power in, 12, 16–17
 processes in, 12, 15–16
Pollution, urban, 30
 air-quality pollutants, 70 (*see also* Air quality)
 in Bayview–Hunters Point neighborhood, 103
 and cancer findings, 107
 and green space, 78
 and sanitary engineering, 32–33
 West Oakland's fight against, 91
Population health
 determinants of, 1
 in healthy city planning, 12, 12–13
Population health perspective, 96–97
Pothukuchi, Kami, 114
Potrero Hill area, 164, 193
Poverty, urban, 2
 and health disparities, 59
 and NEPA reviews, 62, 63
 and Olmsted Jr.'s vision, 26
 "weathering" effect of, 98

in urban parks, 34
Seneca Village, 34
Sennett, Richard, 48
Settlement Houses movement, 10,
34–35, 96
and African-Americans, 210n.11
SFDPH. *See* San Francisco
Department of Public Health
*Shattered Bonds: The Color of Child
Welfare* (Roberts), 87
Shattuck, Lemuel, 30
Sheppard-Towner Act, 39, 40
Showplace Square-Potrero Hill area,
164, 193
*Silent Spring* (Carson), 57
Silicon Valley industries, and San
Francisco gentrification, 132
Simkhovitch, Mary, 25, 52
Sinclair, Upton, 39
Slum removal, 52, 53–54
"Slums and City Planning" (Moses),
54
Smart Growth, 93
Smoke control, 50
Social cohesion or exclusion
and healthy urban governance, 73,
80–81
and Rincon Hill Plan, 152
Social determinants of health
(SDOH), 4, 13, 63–64
and health-impact assessment across
country, 207
and new understanding of public
health, 118–19
and Planning Department
environmental review, 166
and planning processes, 23, 83
and San Francisco Department of
Public Health, 115, 116–20,
122
analysis of, 160–61
Social epidemiology, 23, 59, 96
and relational view of place, 204,
205
Social Statistics of Cities (Hull House
survey form), 36

Socioeconomic analysis, by Planning
Department, 173
*Solid Facts, The: The Social
Determinants of Health* (WHO),
119
SoMa Community Stabilization Fund,
156–58, 161, 201, 206
SoMa Community Stabilization Fund
Advisory Committee, 157, 157–58,
201
SOMCAN. *See* South of Market
Community Action Network
South Bronx
health disparities in, 2
incarceration in, 88
South of Market area (SoMa) of San
Francisco, 18, 20–21, 129, 132,
164, 214n.34
community land trust for, 157–58
division of, 153–55
East SoMa, 193
and Rincon Hill Plan, 148,154–55
South of Market Community Action
Network (SOMCAN)
ENCHIA continuation by, 191
in Rincon Hill controversy, 153–55,
159
and development impact fee, 155–58
and TCE, 196
in Trinity Plaza controversy, 141–42
"Spatial match," 151
*Special Investigation of the Slums of
Great Cities, A* (Congress-
sponsored study), 35
Specialization, 39
and BARHII, 102
as challenge, 84, 85, 99
vs. co-production of science, 92
in laboratory view of city, 95
Stakeholder Council, in health-impact
assessment, 173
Statistics
limitations of, 178–79
and relational views of place, 204
Social Statistics of Cities (Hull
House survey form), 36

Stress
  displacement-related, 142, 144
  as health-disparities cause, 59
  and housing affordability, 145–46
  PHES on strategies for, 123
  response to as moderating factor, 118
  as social determinant of health, 13,
    64, 72, 73
    and access to natural areas, 174
    and low birth weights, 75
    and noise pollution, 69, 74
    "weathering" effect from, 16, 98
  social support against, 81
  from unemployment, 78
  among workers, 180
  among young people, 180
Structural inequalities, and ENCHIA
  discussions, 175–76. See also
  Racism
Subprime lending, 77
Suburban sprawl, 53
  and healthy urban governance, 74
Sugrue, Thomas J., 55
Supermarkets, and HDMT, 185–87
Supportive environments, as WHO
  principle, 8
Supreme Court, in Euclid v. Ambler,
  44
Sustainability
  as PHES commitment, 124, 125
  in WHO principles for health impact
    assessment, 167
Sydenstricker, Edgar, 50

Take Care New York program, 120,
  121
TALC (Transportation and Land use
  Coalition), 194, 194–95, 196
Tales of the City's Workers: A Work and
  Health Survey of San Francisco's
  Workforce (SFDPH), 180
Tarr, Joel, 32
Taylorism, 43, 44
Technology, and healthy city,
  9–11

Training/capacity building activities,
  as WHO requirement, 9
Transportation (transit)
  and food access (BVHP), 111
  health disparities determined by
    (San Francisco work group), 119
  in healthy city (ENCHIA vision), 174,
    177
  and healthy urban governance, 71,
    74–75
  and racism (ENCHIA discussion),
    176
  as social determinant of health, 64
Transportation and Land use
  Coalition (TALC), 194, 194–95,
  196
Transportation for a Livable City,
  191
Triangle Shirtwaist fire, 39
Trinity Plaza redevelopment project,
  20, 21, 129–30, 133, 159, 161
  focus groups organized on (MAC
    and SOMCAN), 141–42
  health impacts of (SFDPH letter),
    144–46
  and Planning Department
    response, 146–49
  and nondisplacement alternative,
    201
"Truth spot," 27, 210n.8

UN Centre on Human Settlements
  (Habitat) (UNCHS), 11
Uncertainty
  and healthy city planning, 127
  and precautionary principle, 86
Unemployment. See also Employment
  and economic opportunities
  behavioral/educational explanation
    of, 54
  as BVHP concern, 105
United States. health-impact
  assessment in, 136
Universalism, vs. specifics of places
  and neighborhoods, 46, 48